BIRTHING JUSTICE

BLACK WOMEN, PREGNANCY, AND CHILDBIRTH

There is a global crisis in maternal health care for black women. In the United States, black women are over three times more likely to perish from pregnancy-related complications than white women; their babies are half as likely to survive the first year. Many black women experience policing, coercion, and disempowerment during pregnancy and childbirth and are disconnected from alternative birthing traditions. This book places black women's voices at the center of the debate on what should be done to fix the broken maternity system and foregrounds black women's agency in the emerging birth justice movement. Mixing scholarly, activist, and personal perspectives, the book shows readers how they too can change lives, one birth at a time.

Julia Chinyere Oparah is Professor and Chair of Ethnic Studies at Mills College and a founding member of Black Women Birthing Justice. She is co-editor of *Activist Scholarship: Antiracism, Feminism and Social Change* and *Outsiders Within: Writing on Transracial Adoption*.

Alicia D. Bonaparte is Associate Professor of Sociology at Pitzer College and a medical sociologist with a specialization in reproductive health and health disparities. She is currently working on a book on the lives of granny midwives in South Carolina.

"A truly original and innovative book—and an absolute necessity in the current field of research on reproduction."
—**Christa Craven**, College of Wooster, author of *Pushing for Midwives: Homebirth Mothers and the Reproductive Rights Movement*

"With its commitment to placing black women at the center of the conversation and scholarship about their own lives and the value it places on agency, activism, and putting scholarship to work for the purpose of social change, *Birthing Justice* makes an important and much-needed contribution to the small but growing number of books examining reproductive justice. This anthology of black women's experiences of pregnancy and childbirth is long overdue."
—**Jeanne Flavin**, Fordham University, author of *Our Bodies, Our Crimes: The Policing of Women's Reproduction in America*

BIRTHING JUSTICE

BLACK WOMEN, PREGNANCY, AND CHILDBIRTH

edited by

Julia Chinyere Oparah
and
Alicia D. Bonaparte

Routledge
Taylor & Francis Group

NEW YORK AND LONDON

First published in paperback 2016
by Routledge
711 Third Avenue, New York, NY 10017

and by Routledge
2 Park Square, Milton Park, Abingdon, Oxon, OX14 4RN

Routledge is an imprint of the Taylor & Francis Group, an informa business

First published in hardback by Paradigm 2015

Library of Congress Cataloging in Publication Data
Library of Congress Cataloging-in-Publication Data

Birthing justice : black women, pregnancy, and childbirth / edited by Julia Chinyere Oparah and Alicia D. Bonaparte.
    p. ; cm.
Includes bibliographical references and index.
    ISBN 978-1-61205-836-8 (hardcover : alk. paper) —
    ISBN 978-1-61205-837-5 (pbk. : alk. paper) —
    ISBN 978-1-61205-916-7 (library ebook) —
    ISBN 978-1-61205-838-2 (consumer ebook)
    I. Oparah, Julia Chinyere, editor. II. Bonaparte, Alicia D., editor.
    [DNLM: 1. Maternal Health Services—United States.   2. African Americans—ethnology—United States.   3. Civil Rights—United States.   4. Parturition—ethnology—United States.   5. Pregnant Women—ethnology—United States.   6. Social Justice—United States. WA 310 AA1]
    RG964.G72
    362.19820089'96073--dc23   2014049717

ISBN: 978-1-6120-5836-8 (hbk)
ISBN: 978-1-138-19145-7 (pbk)
ISBN: 978-1-315-64050-1 (ebk)

Typeset in Garamond
by Cenveo Publisher Services

Contents

Foreword, *Shafia Monroe*   *vii*
Foreword, *Jeanne Flavin*   *ix*
Acknowledgments   *xi*

Introduction Beyond Coercion and Malign Neglect: Black Women
and the Struggle for Birth Justice   1
    Julia Chinyere Oparah with Black Women Birthing Justice

I Birthing Histories

1 Queen Elizabeth Perry Turner: "Granny Midwife," 1931–1956   20
    Darline Turner
2 Regulating Childbirth: Physicians and Granny Midwives in
    South Carolina   24
    Alicia D. Bonaparte
3 Between Traditional Knowledge and Western Medicine:
    Women Birthing in Postcolonial Zimbabwe   34
    Christina Mudokwenyu-Rawdon, Peggy Dube, Nester T. Moyo,
    and Stephen Munjanja

II Beyond Medical versus Natural: Redefining Birth Injustice

4 An Abolitionist Mama Speaks: On Natural Birth and Miscarriage 46
    Viviane Saleh-Hanna
5 Mothering: A Post-C-Section Journey   55
    Jacinda Townsend
6 Confessions of a Black Pregnant Dad   63
    Syrus Marcus Ware
7 Birth Justice and Population Control   72
    Loretta J. Ross
8 Beyond Silence and Stigma: Pregnancy and HIV for Black
    Women in Canada   81
    Marvelous Muchenje and Victoria Logan Kennedy

 9 What I Carry: A Story of Love and Loss   90
     Iris Jacob
10 Images from the Safe Motherhood Quilt   96
     Ina May Gaskin and Laura Gilkey

III Changing Lives, One Birth at a Time

11 Birthing Sexual Freedom and Healing: A Survivor Mother's Birth
     Story   106
     Biany Pérez
12 Birth as Battle Cry: A Doula's Journey from Home to Hospital   112
     Gina Mariela Rodríguez
13 Sister Midwife: Nurturing and Reflecting Black Womanhood in an
     Urban Hospital   119
     Stephanie Etienne
14 A Love Letter to My Daughter: Love as a Political Act   126
     Haile Eshe Cole
15 New Visions in Birth, Intimacy, Kinship, and Sisterly Partnerships   131
     Shannon Gibney and Valerie Deus
16 I Am My *Hermana*'s Keeper: Reclaiming Afro-Indigenous Ancestral
     Wisdom as a Doula   137
     Griselda Rodriguez
17 The First Cut Is the Deepest: A Mother-Daughter Conversation
     about Birth, Justice, Healing, and Love   145
     Pauline Ann McKenzie-Day and Alexis Pauline Gumbs

IV Taking Back Our Power: Organizing for Birth Justice

18 Unexpected Allies: Obstetrician Activism, VBACs, and the Birth
     Justice Movement   156
     Christ-Ann Magloire and Julia Chinyere Oparah
19 Birthing Freedom: Black American Midwifery and Liberation
     Struggles   166
     Ruth Hays
20 Becoming an Outsider-Within: Jennie Joseph's Activism in Florida
     Midwifery   176
     Alicia D. Bonaparte and Jennie Joseph
21 Beyond Shackling: Prisons, Pregnancy, and the Struggle for
     Birth Justice   187
     Priscilla A. Ocen and Julia Chinyere Oparah

Notes   198
Index   220
About the Contributors   229

Foreword

Shafia Monroe

This anthology is a testimonial to the black women who have been leaders in the birth movement from the very beginning. Long before the term "birth justice" was coined, black women used traditional childbearing knowledge, oral histories, human rights organizing, and policy work in their efforts to end inequities in maternal, infant, and child health. Building on resistance to the abuse of pregnant black women during slavery and to the dismantling of our birth traditions and family structures, our foremothers paved the way for today's birth justice activism.

This work continues to be critical because African American women's maternal health is in a state of emergency: our cesarean section rate is disproportionately high, we experience the highest maternal mortality rate in the United States, we receive less medical support to continue breastfeeding past twelve weeks, and our infants are more than twice as likely to die before their first birthday than white infants. Only by giving women power to direct their birth experience, to access natural and home birth, and to breastfeed beyond one year will we be able to reduce intolerable rates of infant and maternal mortality.

Our present day birth justice movement honors its ancestors. We remember the Mississippi and Tuskegee nurse-midwifery schools, the Traditional Childbearing Group, Childbirth Providers of African Descent, and others, while lifting up sheroes, including Byllye Avery, Loretta Ross, Ayanna Ade, and Nonkululeko Tyehemba, as well as organizations such as the Harlem Birth Action Committee, the International Center for Traditional Childbearing, SisterSong, Ancient Song Doula Services, Mobile Midwife, Black Women Birthing Resistance, Black Women Birthing Justice, Commonsense Childbirth, and many others. This anthology is intimate and captivating, introducing the women and organizations who have paved the way, alongside current movements and future hopes for women to reclaim their birthing rights.

As we remember the ancestors and their struggles for safe and empowering childbirth, we must honor the traditional midwife. In black communities in the United States and other parts of the diaspora, the midwife was historically the protector of birth, teaching women how to birth and safeguarding childbearing and mothering traditions. As this anthology documents, the starkest birth injustice is the systemic eradication of the black midwife from her community by the Eurocentric patriarchal medical system. On the African continent, the demotion of midwives to traditional birth attendants mirrors the attack on traditional midwives in the United States. The after effect continues to this day. Fortunately, through the efforts of the birth justice movement, women of color are entering midwifery training and becoming midwives at record numbers; at the same time, the number of home births is rising in the black community.

Testifying to the resilience of black women is a critical part of a holistic approach to restoring our health. It is exciting that the hidden her-story of the battle waged by black women and trans/gender nonconforming birthing parents against birth injustice is finally in print. Here is an essential source for high schools and colleges, midwifery and medical schools, birth workers and birth activists. At last we have a blueprint for improving health equity and enabling black women—as well as other birthing parents of color—to believe in their bodies' sacred power and to direct their own birth experiences.

Birth justice is on the rise. Women and trans/gender nonconforming birthing parents are mobilizing internationally to reclaim birth as beautiful, spiritual, and normal and to demand their human right to birth and breastfeed their infants according to their own traditions. Women are returning to midwifery care as the norm, and many see midwives as guardians of normal birth. Black midwives are keeping it real and empowering families. It is up to all of us to ensure that this movement toward birth justice continues.

I am moved by this tribute to birth justice and relieved that it is authenticated through its origins in the birth justice movement. In chronicling the movement, Julia Chinyere Oparah, Alicia D. Bonaparte, and the women of Black Women Birthing Justice engender pride, build camaraderie, and inspire action. Thank you, sisters, for your work.

Foreword

Jeanne Flavin

It was a late August afternoon. I was riding a bike on the road that ran by our small family farm and got called into the house. I found Dad in the kitchen, doing dishes. Doing dishes? Though I was only ten years old, I grasped the situation immediately: Mom, pregnant with her fifth and last child, had started labor.

Dad left my little sister and me in the care of an older brother and drove Mom nineteen miles to the hospital in the next county. He came home just before dawn to tell us we had a brother, born at 3:03 a.m. Later that day, he packed us kids into the car and took us to the hospital. He stationed my little sister and me behind some bushes outside a window, and a few minutes later a nurse brought my little brother into the room. Mom carried him over to the window so we could meet him. We were completely smitten.

About a year later, Mom was diagnosed with cancer and hospitalized for treatment some 175 miles away. My dad moved to be with her, renting a room near the hospital while us five kids were looked after by a combination of siblings, neighbors, and other relatives. My little brother and I were briefly sent to stay with an aunt. I had only been separated from my parents on one other occasion—when my father was hospitalized in a neighboring state after a farm accident. I was heartsick both times. Years later, I asked Mom if she had been afraid she might not live. She replied in her matter-of-fact way, "I couldn't think about not surviving. I had five children and [the oldest] was still in high school."

Mom survived her first cancer diagnosis but recently passed away after a second fight with the disease. The editors invited me to write a foreword to *Birthing Justice* at a time when I still felt grief over my mother's death keenly. The timing reminded me how what Julia Chinyere Oparah refers to in the introduction as "mother-love as a radical praxis" has played out in my own life, even though I'm not a mother and have never birthed a baby. These life experiences—of welcoming a wanted (if not necessarily planned) child into a family, of being involuntarily separated from my parents, of feeling jackknifing grief as an adult—have shaped my scholarship on reproductive justice and kept it from being solely (or even mainly) an academic exercise.

Since 2006, I have worked with National Advocates for Pregnant Women (NAPW), an organization that defends the basic principle that, upon becoming pregnant, a person should not lose any civil or human rights. Along with executive director Lynn Paltrow and our NAPW colleagues, we have identified hundreds of cases where women were arrested or otherwise deprived of physical liberty because they were pregnant. Women have been locked up in mental hospitals after voluntarily seeking treatment for an opiate addiction, tied down with leather wrist and ankle restraints and forced to undergo cesarean sections, and charged with murder after surviving a suicide attempt but losing the pregnancy.

Like death and dying, pregnancy and childbirth can be powerful experiences, but they may also be a time of vulnerability—a time when we may have to depend on others to ensure that our wishes are carried out, our decisions are respected, and our rights and dignity are preserved. Increasingly, however, we find that surveillance, blame, and punishment characterize our government responses to basic human needs rather than respect, support, and compassion. Our criminal prosecution system en- forces ideas about who is "fit" to carry a pregnancy or mother a child and punishes those deemed to fall short. In this context, the rights of black women and trans/gender nonconforming individuals to privacy, to health care, and to birthing and parenting their children with dignity are brutally disregarded.

The contributors to this important volume write not only of the relationships between a parent and child and others in their lives but also about the racism and other structural forces that threaten these ties. Addressing these threats requires that we recognize the connections between birth justice and other forms of social justice, including racial and economic justice and the movement to end the war on drugs. Fittingly, *Birthing Justice* also speaks to resilience and the power of collective action forged out of struggle; it reminds us that black women and black trans/gender non- conforming individuals continue to resist the devaluation of their personhood and to mobilize for social change. This book and the advocacy and scholarship that inform and surround it promise to energize and advance our movements in important ways.

Birthing Justice accords experiences of pregnancy, birthing, and mothering respect, even reverence. Indeed, the creating and nurturing of new life and bringing it into the world—like the ways by which we take leave of it—deserve nothing less than this from all of us.

Acknowledgments

I give thanks and honor to the Iyami and the grandmother midwives who inspired and continue to guide my research in birthing work. Engaging and assisting the Sister Friends of the Nashville Village Birthing Project as a graduate student enabled me to better understand and be grateful for the examples of mothering and sisterhood I witnessed and experienced during the course of this work. Working on this anthology reaffirmed for me that recognizing and supporting the power and energy of the womb is life affirming. The deeply personal and riveting narratives within this book are testimony to the resilience of black women's birthing work, parental love, and social activism, and they remind me why the personal is political. Thank you to the team at Paradigm Publishers for seeing the significance of these voices and supporting the culmination of our vision. Thank you to Pitzer College for supporting this form of scholarship and providing me the time to engage in birthing scholarship domestically and abroad.

With heartfelt humility and grace, I am thankful to the following people for giving me supportive spaces to process the evolution of this work: my mother, Selena M. Bonaparte, France Winddance Twine, Alondra Nelson, David G. Leonard, Lucius and Freida Outlaw, Valorie Thomas, Angel Shannon, Kiera Lytle, Malaika Mose, Leisy Abrego, Linn Posey-Maddox, Olaomi Amoloku, and Myra Osunyoyin Foxworth. I give thanks to the Sister Goddess Circle women and to my many spiritually grounded families for reminding me of the purpose of my involvement in this work. Thank you, Chinyere, for inviting me to be a part of this important work.

—Alicia D. Bonaparte

This book was born from the collective love, passion, and labor of many mamas, and I am grateful to them all. I am immensely appreciative of my coeditor, Alicia D. Bonaparte, for her perseverance and courageous truth telling and to Shanelle Mat- thews for her vision of and contributions to this book. I would not have started on the journey toward birth justice were it not for Onyekachi Georgia Oparah, the baby girl whose hard little kicks from inside my womb softened my heart and prepared me for the struggle ahead. I am grateful beyond words to my beloved Shawn Nealy-Oparah for her encouragement, patience, and laughter. Throughout this project, I have been sustained, loved, and nurtured by the sisters of Black Women Birthing Justice; thank you for challenging me to grow and for being a solid oak to lean on when I felt weary.

The conceptualization of this volume is informed by the insights and courageous activism of doulas, midwives, and birth activists, some of whom are named in the following pages, as well as many involved in the racial and gender justice, antiviolence, and antiprison movements. I am grateful for every activist and scholar-activist who has shaped my analysis and politics. It takes time and resources to edit an anthology, and I thank Mills College for supporting for my birth justice scholarship and my wonderful student research assistants for their commitment and hard work. A big shout out to Helen Arega, Andrea Juarez, Graciela Morelo Olguin, and André Jones for designing our crowdfunding campaign and to all those who pledged. I am grateful to Jeanne Flavin, Kimala Price, Marlene Gerber Fried, Crista Craven, Zakiya Luna, Juli Grisgby, and Jade Sasser for their advocacy of this project and to all at Paradigm Publishers for sharing our vision and believing in this book. Thank you to my spiritual communities for providing me with the serenity and groundedness necessary to hold the powerful and sometimes painful stories gathered here. To my families of origin, from Winchester to Long Beach, I thank you for love, for roots, and for making me who I am. I acknowledge the wisdom and guidance of my ancestors who continue to sustain me across the oceans. And as always, I dedicate this work to Mami Wata, Great Mother, who governs the life-giving waters. May this work be a bearer of truth, healing, and wholeness.

—Julia Chinyere Oparah

Birthing Justice is a project of Black Women Birthing Justice. We acknowledge all members, past and present, for their leadership and dedication. Our current collective members are

Helen Arega
Aminah Barber
Lia Barrow
Jamilah Bradshaw
Ronnesha Cato
Jillian Faulks-Majuta
Linda Marie Jones
Shanelle Matthews
Julia Chinyere Oparah
Talita Oseguera
Traver Riggins
Ndeya Walker

Beyond Coercion and Malign Neglect

Black Women and the Struggle for Birth Justice

Julia Chinyere Oparah
with Black Women Birthing Justice

BIRTH STORIES: A BEGINNING

When I got pregnant with my first daughter, I was just nineteen. My mother was a doula, and I had listened to enough stories to know that I wanted a natural birth: I wanted to labor at home, I didn't want medicine, and I wanted her to coach me through it. But I had little idea how much stood in the way of my vision for my birth. At my thirty-eight-week prenatal visit, the doctor announced that my blood pressure was too high, and I needed to have the baby right then. I was rushed to delivery, hooked up to an IV, and strapped with wires to monitor my blood pressure and the baby's heartbeat. I felt like a patient, unable to resist the things they were doing to my body. By now I was scared, my blood pressure kept going up, and I felt completely powerless and unable to move. They gave me Pitocin, and the labor pains started to get really painful; the contractions were so harsh and artificial. My mother arrived and tried to coach me, but the pain was

1

too intense, so I told them to give me the epidural. I lay in the bed defeated and powerless until I was fully dilated and feeling the pressure to push. But there was no doctor around, and so the nurses told me to wait. Finally the doctor came, and I pushed until I was tired and I didn't want to do it any more, but Mom said, "If you don't push her out they're going to cut you."

When Zenaya came, she was only four pounds, fourteen ounces. They took her away from me, the doctor stitched me up, and the nurse put me in a wheelchair and took me to a postpartum room. They didn't clean me up: I remained covered in blood and afterbirth for about six hours until an African American nurse came and washed me. It was just horrible. It was hard for us to breastfeed because Zenaya wasn't latching on. One nurse put a tube on my nipple with formula to encourage her, but another nurse told me I should just give her a bottle. By the time we got home, the connection with my baby just wasn't there, the relationship was hard, and I was in pain. It took some time to get over the postpartum depression and gain my confidence as a new mother.

I started to believe that women should not feel this way after bringing life into this world. I read up about the medical industry, and started my journey to becoming a birth revolutionary. When I got pregnant again two years later, we decided to have a home birth so that I could be fully active and present for the birth. I pushed out Zwena, squatting in my bathroom, encouraged by the sweet voice of my midwife and surrounded by my community.

Ronnesha ends her story and breathes deeply as if to absorb fully what she has shared. There are tears, laughter, and murmurs of affirmation as the women sitting around her honor her testimony. This is a sharing circle, an intimate healing space where black women come together to share stories of pain, struggle, joy, and transformation in order to make sense of our experiences, heal birth trauma, and create an alternative vision of birth in black communities.

"Who would like to share next?" Chinyere begins her story.

A few days after I learned that I was finally pregnant, I found myself in the hospital. A reaction to a fertility drug I had taken led to a buildup of fluid in my abdomen, and my belly swelled as if I were six months pregnant. When the pressure on my lungs began to make me gasp for breath, I was rushed to the hospital. I began a ten-day fight for my daughter's life, and for my own. By the time I left the hospital, I was weak, anemic, ten pounds underweight, and drained of confidence in my body. My ob-gyn did nothing to rebuild my faith in my body's natural ability to birth. Instead, pointing to my "advanced maternal age" and fibroids, she was dismissive of my desire for a vaginal birth. I was so demoralized that I continued obediently to show up for the stressful and speedy checkups without thinking that perhaps it could be different.

In my final trimester, a prenatal yoga instructor asked me a question that began my journey to birth justice: Do the people who will be at your birth support your vision for your birth experience? At my next doctor's visit I asked her if she would support me in seeking a vaginal birth. It became clear that she might not even be at my birth, that I could be faced with a stranger in that most intimate and vulnerable moment, and that any birth plan I developed with her would be irrelevant. I asked Spirit for courage, and at eight months, I left my ob-gyn and hired one of only two midwives licensed to deliver babies at my local hospital. The few visits I had with my midwife were miraculous. She was part grandmother, part therapist, and part midwife.

I had found her just in time. In the final weeks of my pregnancy, I began to deal with painful feelings related to having been relinquished by my mother at birth. It started when a wave of grief hit me as I walked past the newborns in the neonatal care unit after attending a birthing class. In the days and nights that followed, I experienced body memories of that early separation. The thought of going to a hospital to give birth terrified me. My midwife listened attentively and gently but firmly talked with me about my fears. "This is your new birth story," she told me. "This time you get to make it turn out differently." By the time I went into labor, I was beginning to step into my power. I invited a circle of women to witness and guide the birth, including my midwife, doula, and close friends. We turned the hospital room into a sanctuary. With their support, pushing out my baby girl was a powerful, sacred, and healing experience.

These stories teach us a great deal about black women and the maternal-health-care system in the United States. It may be tempting to read them as cautionary tales about what happens when a patriarchal medical establishment seeks to control women's bodies or as uplifting affirmations of women's ability to take back their power and birth naturally. But this would ignore the complexity of black women's experiences of pregnancy and childbirth, which are shaped not simply by violence and coercion by patriarchal institutions but also by the multifaceted ways in which gender interacts with interlocking systems of race, class, age, ability, sexuality, and nation.

Ronnesha's desire to determine her own birth story was undermined by race-/class-/gender-based controlling images of irresponsible black pregnant teens and by dismal statistics regarding black infant and maternal mortality. Nearly half of black girls in the United States get pregnant at least once before they are twenty, and when they carry their pregnancies to term, their children are more likely to drop out of high school, experience incarceration, face unemployment, have health problems, and become teenage parents.[1] Since the early 1980s, conservatives and liberals alike have constructed teen pregnancy as a serious social problem and created programs to reduce it—the former by promoting chastity and parental control, the latter by improving teens' access to sex education and contraception.[2] Despite their different political agendas, these programs share in common a tendency to censure teen mothers, to assume that all teen pregnancies are the outcome of irresponsible sex, and to incorporate a heavy dose of paternalism and judgment of teens who are deemed in need of greater "personal responsibility" regarding sex. Viewed through the lens of this narrative of black teenage irresponsibility, Ronnesha was assumed to be incompetent to determine her own labor, delivery, and postpartum experience. Her desires to experience childbirth without medical interventions and to nurse her low-birth-weight baby were easily dismissed.

Ronnesha's interactions with medical staff were also impacted by the specter of high rates of black infant and maternal mortality. In the United States, these poor outcomes spark a fear of litigation in case of maternal or infant death. In California, where Ronnesha gave birth, black women are three times more likely to perish due to pregnancy-related causes than white women, and their babies are more than twice as likely to die within their first year.[3] Ob-gyns may be particularly fearful of litigation when they serve low-income women, partly because of higher risk factors and partly due to the belief that poor women sue more, leading to "defensive medicine" and more medical interventions.[4] This culture of fear is an ever-present undercurrent in labor and delivery wards and is evoked by medical staff who use the question "You do want a healthy baby, don't you?" to elicit compliance in unruly birthing women. Only when she removed herself from medical supervision was Ronnesha able to find a space for agency as a young black woman choosing to deliver and nurse her baby.

Whereas Ronnesha pushed out her second baby in her home in deep East Oakland, a neighborhood impacted by gun violence, drug dealing, and poverty, Chinyere lived in a solidly middle-class neighborhood in the East Oakland hills. Class matters—but not always in the way we might assume. The assumption that low-income black women have low-birth-weight babies solely because of poor nutrition and living conditions or that class, not race, determines poor maternal outcomes has been refuted by evidence that black professional women are not protected by their relative affluence.[5] In part, this may be due to the impact of stressors experienced by black women as "outsiders within" racially stratified workplace and public environments.[6] For Chinyere, this showed up as an internal sense of pressure to return to work before she was fully recovered from her hospitalization, due to her internalization of the "black superwoman" myth. This myth can be fatal: stress and overwork during pregnancy can result in premature birth and low birth weight, two key factors in black infant mortality.[7]

Class may not defend professional black women from poor maternal outcomes, but it does matter. In the context of a medical-industrial complex in which the ability to pay determines access, class matters a great deal to poor women who cannot afford birth alternatives.[8] It also matters to older women and queer women who may need assistance from reproductive technologies to get pregnant. But while economic privilege enabled Chinyere to overcome infertility, it did not protect her from a stressful pregnancy. She had to face the possibility of terminating her pregnancy when a blood test indicated a high probability of a fatal birth defect. The test was ultimately proven inaccurate, but only after it had caused immense stress during an already difficult pregnancy. Black women over thirty-five, like Chinyere, are subject to a double jeopardy. First, they are considered by medical professionals to be of "advanced maternal age" and are likely to be pressured to undergo invasive genetic testing. Second, they are considered to be an at-risk subset (older women) of an at-risk group (all black women). Thus, race, ageism, and disablism—in the form of societal devaluing of nonnormative pregnancies—place immense pressure on these women.

Separated by age and class, Ronnesha and Chinyere were united by a common determination to resist coercion and control and to lay claim to a birth experience that did not violate their bodies or their spirits. They and other women are organizing with Black Women Birthing Justice, a national organization that aims to create a space for black women and trans/gender nonconforming parents to tell their stories, to challenge medical violence, and to reclaim childbirth. This book is about the struggle for birth justice being waged by black women like Ronnesha and Chinyere in labor and delivery wards, birth centers, legislative chambers, and living rooms across the United States and internationally. It is about the birth revolutionaries who are working to change attitudes, practices, and legislation, to reclaim a legacy of traditional midwifery, to challenge the coercion and criminalization of pregnant black women and trans/gender nonconforming people, and to transform lives, one birth at a time.

REEXAMINING REPRODUCTIVE JUSTICE

Since the 1980s, black women and women of color seeking solidarity in resisting reproductive coercion and violence have been able to turn to the reproductive justice movement.[9] This movement is made up of national agencies such as the Black Women's Health Imperative and the National Latina Institute for Reproductive Health; faith-based and scholarly networks such as Seminarians for Reproductive Justice, ReproNet, and Law Students for Reproductive Justice; and community-based organizations such as Black Women for Reproductive Justice, Black Women for Wellness, Young Women United, and Forward Together. Perhaps the most visible face of the movement is SisterSong, a national coalition representing more than eighty organizations that for over a decade, under the leadership of veteran activist and contributor

Loretta Ross, has created a voice for women of color activists in the wider reproductive rights community. The term "reproductive justice" was coined by women of color as a radical, inclusive, and intersectional political analysis and praxis that challenged the narrow focus of the mainstream reproductive rights movement.[10] In advocating for reproductive rights—defined by Asian Communities for Reproductive Justice (now Forward Together) as "the right to have children, not have children, and to parent the children we have in safe and healthy environments"—the reproductive justice framework looks at the multiple ways in which women of color and poor women are denied reproductive freedom.[11] These include sterilization abuses, the exposure of immigrant women workers to pesticides and other chemicals that are hazardous to maternal health, and the promotion of dangerous contraceptives in communities of color. In addition, reproductive justice organizations have begun to explore the ways that race, economic status, and gender identity combine to generate lack of access to reproductive health care and passive eugenics directed at trans/gender nonconforming people of color.[12] In contrast to the "big four" reproductive rights organizations—NOW, NARAL Pro-Choice America, Planned Parenthood, and the Feminist Majority Foundation—which have tended to restrict their analysis to a pro-choice/pro-life binary, reproductive justice advocates push us to go beyond individualist and consumerist demands for choice and instead to work against the many systemic threats against the lives and autonomy of all those marginalized on the basis of gender.[13]

Reproductive justice proponents have made a significant contribution to the battle for reproductive freedom. They have popularized the concept of reproductive justice through conferences, workshops, and teaching materials for use in high schools, colleges, and universities. They have demonstrated that reproductive health cannot be separated from the many survival issues facing communities of color and that a multisector, intersectional approach is essential. They have modeled the use of an international human rights framework as a foundation for grassroots activism in the United States, refuting the myth that human rights abuses occur "somewhere else." They have shed light on the mainstream reproductive rights movement's complicity with racism and eugenics and challenged that movement to become accountable to women of color, poor women, young women, women with disabilities, and trans/gender nonconforming people. And they have countered the alienation of women of color and built a diverse and vibrant movement to challenge reproductive inequities.[14]

Despite their commitment to make visible and challenge reproductive oppression in all forms, reproductive justice organizations and advocates have been slow to confront the medical violence and coercion that women like Ronnesha and Chinyere experience during pregnancy, labor, and childbirth. In 2010, National Advocates for Pregnant Women (NAPW) issued a call to reproductive justice organizations to extend their advocacy to include women's treatment during labor and childbirth.[15] While immensely respect-ful of the work of the reproductive justice movement, NAPW made visible the inconsistencies that arise when the human right to a safe, respectful birth experience is not seen as a central part of the reproductive justice agenda. Reproductive justice advocates fight for access to safe contraception and abor-tion for low-income women and women of color, but they seldom defend the right of birthing women to out-of-hospital births, vaginal births after cesareans (VBACs), or midwifery care. Although they challenge the use of dangerous contraceptives such as Norplant and Depo-Provera on the grounds that they threaten women's health and autonomy, they have not made the connection between these practices and unnecessary medical interventions during childbirth. They put the racially targeted sterilization of women of color on the radar of those concerned with reproductive rights but say little about epidemic rates of C-sections, which are disproportionately performed on African American women. While vocal in opposing pro-life billboards that demonize black pregnant women, coalitions like Trust Black Women have failed to comment on media depictions of women who choose home births or refuse C-sections as spoiled or irresponsible. As a result, the misconcep-tion that natural and home births and doula and midwifery care are luxury concerns of white middle-class women goes unchallenged, and the potential activism of pregnant and parenting women of color who have been touched by birth injustice remains largely untapped.

At SisterSong's conference in 2011, thirty birth activists from around the United States came together to discuss the need for the reproductive justice movement to embrace birth oppression as a central concern for women of color. The activists present in that gathering called for a national movement led by women of color to challenge medical violence and coercion during pregnancy and childbirth, to reclaim midwifery traditions in communities of color, and to raise awareness among women of color about strategies to over-come birth inequities. These demands have much in common with the goals of the alternative or natural birth movement; yet this movement has failed to mobilize black women in large numbers. The next section explores why.

FROM PATRIARCHAL MEDICINE TO MEDICAL APARTHEID

Most accounts of the alternative or natural birth movement in the United States begin in the 1950s and 1960s, when mostly white, college-educated women discovered writings from Europe, including Grantley Dick-Read's *Childbirth without Fear* and Ferdinand Lamaze's *Painless Childbirth,* and began to claim their "right" to a joyful, empowered birth experience. These books claimed that a pain-free birth could be achieved not through numbing by anesthesia or powerful opiates but by retraining the mind to interpret the intense sensations associated with labor as normal rather than as a signal that something is wrong.[16] These women challenged the treatment of childbirth as a medical event, critiqued the dangers of the high-tech management of labor and delivery, and promoted out-of-hospital, midwife-attended birth as a means of self-determination for women. They also drew inspiration from the women's health, civil rights, and hippy movements, as well as from granny midwives, to build alternative, grassroots birthing communities across the country. Perhaps the best known is The Farm, a natural-living community established by Ina May Gaskin and a group of cultural dissidents who traveled in a caravan from San Francisco to rural Tennessee.[17] Gaskin's seminal manual *Spiritual Midwifery* challenged the hegemony of male physicians and medical technology and revived women's confidence in their ability to push out their babies with the simple philosophy that "nature mostly gets it right in birth."[18]

Although important, the story of Ina May Gaskin and the other white, middle-class birth activists who courageously took on "Big Medicine" is incomplete. As African American historians have demonstrated, our understanding of history depends on the social location of the storyteller and the limited perspective provided by that particular standpoint.[19] Starting from what Patricia Hill Collins calls the subjugated knowledge of black women, we might instead start our historical narrative from the standpoint of granny midwives—African American lay midwives who had served the black community in a tradition of spiritual calling and service since slavery. Or we might look to the seldom acknowledged immigrant midwives and *parteras* from Haiti, Jamaica, the Dominican Republic, and Puerto Rico, who attended home births and supported pregnant women and new mothers in Caribbean communities in Harlem, Brooklyn, New Jersey, Boston, and beyond. These women were the living archivists and keepers of traditional birth knowledge and the sacred understanding of birth not only as a natural event but as a ceremony.[20] They worked with all women in their communities, regardless of ability to pay, and can be seen as the earliest practitioners of the radical concept of health care as a universal human right.

Although early white natural birth activists saw themselves as reinvigorating the traditional knowledge of granny midwives, their claim to this legacy presents a false narrative of white midwives following in the footsteps of a vanishing class of black midwives. This narrative obscures both the continuing presence of black midwifery from the 1950s to the present day and the tensions that have existed between contemporary white and black midwives. While granny midwives were gradually being eliminated due to the turf wars fought by white physicians and the efforts of white women to modernize maternal health care,[21] young black women themselves were continuing the work of providing traditional birth support to poor and disenfranchised women. They formed organizations that mirrored those established by black women in the 1970s, such as the National Black Feminist Organization and the Combahee River Collective, as a result of middle-class women's refusal to tackle white privilege and racism within the women's liberation movement and in society at large. They had a dual agenda, reflecting the intersections of race, gender, and class and the duality of medical neglect and coercion in the lives of the women they served. In 1976, Shafia Monroe, motivated in part by the dominance of white women in the modern lay midwifery movement, founded the Traditional Childbearing Group in Boston. Its dual goals were to encourage African American women to consider midwife-assisted home birth and to address "the high rate of adverse reproductive outcomes within the black community and the medical system's difficulty in providing community-oriented care."[22] Similarly, the Harlem Birth Action Committee under the leadership of Nonkululeko Tyehemba offered midwifery care but also worked to valorize and support poor and homeless pregnant women and to challenge health inequalities and birth outcomes in the black community.

As a result of this bifurcated history, Crista Craven powerfully argues, the struggle against the management of childbirth by a predominantly male obstetrical profession should not be viewed as a tale of sisters transcending difference in order to claim reproductive freedom for all women. Instead, battles for alternative birth have been marked by conflictual and uneven relationships that reflect the race and class tensions and inequities of the time.[23] Despite assumptions that pregnancy and childbirth are the great equalizers, marking a time when women are defined by their gender more than any other identity, birthing women are in fact actors differentiated by race and class. The dichotomy at the center of understandings of natural birth is itself racialized. Natural birth advocates invoke women's right to natural, empowered, and joyful births, attended by women and free of medical interventions such as pain medications, epidurals, and cesareans. This natural experience is depicted as something that has been stolen from all women by a patriarchal medical establishment as a means to control and commodify women's bodies. Yet this story is only partially true, and what it leaves out is revealing.

When natural birth advocates portray medicalized birth as a patriarchal invention by male doctors, they gloss over the racial origins of the field of obstetrics. South Carolina physician J. Marion Sims, honored as the "father of American gynecology," developed instruments such as the speculum and medical techniques that laid the foundation for modern-day obstetrics. Sims's medical advances would not have been possible without unhindered access to the bodies of eleven enslaved black women at a time when physicians commonly dealt with white women's gynecological problems by touch only, to safeguard their honor.[24] The enslaved women had vesicovaginal fistulas, ruptures between the vagina and the bladder and rectum that caused constant leakage of urine and fecal matter. Harriet Washington tells the grueling story of the five years during which Sims performed numerous experimental surgeries, slicing open the vaginal tissues of the women he had addicted to morphine, as his assistants held them down by force. Rationalizing that black women were closer to livestock than humans and thus had a greater pain tolerance, Sims refused to use anesthesia on the women, even though a dose of ether could have spared them their agony. One of the women, Anarcha, subsequently became the first successful fistula patient, but only after thirty torturous surgeries. These soul-destroying experiments were carried out on Anarcha and her sisters not because of their gender alone. Instead, they suffered because, as chattel under a system of racial and economic oppression, they had no means to protect themselves from torture in the name of medical progress.

And they were not alone. As Washington documents, Louisiana surgeon François Marie Prévost, known for introducing the cesarean section to American obstetrics in the 1820s, first conducted the experimental procedure on an enslaved laboring woman. At the time, opening the abdomen was considered a death warrant, and physicians would typically rather destroy the infant's skull to save a mother with pelvic abnormalities.[25] Nearly all subsequent surgeries carried out by Louisiana surgeons to perfect the risky but profitable procedure were also conducted on enslaved black women, continuing the common practice of offering up black women's lives to the altar of medical science.[26] As coerced obstetric research subjects, black women have suffered intolerable pain, disability, and even death, as well as the loss of their infants, so that white physicians and their white female patients could benefit from the perfected medical procedures. Washington labels this process and its ongoing legacy of health inequities "medical apartheid." The development of medicalized childbirth owes much to this system of "medical apartheid" and can accurately be described as "obstetrical apartheid"—a convergence of patriarchal medical heroics, racialized medical violence, economic exploitation, and a cavalier disregard of black women's well-being.

The history of medicated pain relief during childbirth is another example of obstetrical apartheid. Medicated pain relief was promoted by male physicians in the early twentieth century in part to lure laboring women out of their homes into the hospitals and to present doctors as better equipped to attend birth than midwives. Twilight sleep, induced by a combination of morphine and the amnesiac drug scopolamine, allowed women to remain semiconscious but retain little memory of labor and delivery. US physicians introduced the German invention after a popular campaign by white feminists and suffragists determined to access pain-free birth as a means of women's emancipation.[27] However, segregated hospital facilities in the South, as well as economic inequalities nationwide, meant that "painless" childbirth was offered to middle-class and affluent white women alone. In fact, medicated birth was linked to the white supremacist eugenics movement, which advocated sterilization and contraception to limit African American, immigrant, and Indigenous women's reproduction while pressing white women to have more babies as a means to "improve the race." Physicians claimed that by making childbirth painless, they could encourage white women to have more children, thus ensuring that the "Anglo-Saxon race would not die out."[28] At the same time, they drew on biological racism and class ideologies to justify withholding pain relief from poor women and women of color who, being "closer to nature," were believed to have a greater natural ability to withstand pain and who, in any case, should not be encouraged to procreate. It would take another half century, the passage of the 1964 Civil Rights Act, and the introduction of Medicaid in 1965 for black birthing women to be ushered into the nation's hospital wards.

There is a danger of romanticizing the tradition of the granny midwife and the good fortune of the African American women they continued to serve for decades after the introduction of hospital births. It is true that many black women, along with poor, rural white women, Indigenous women, and immigrant women of color, continued to birth at home with the support of traditional community midwives for decades after most white birthing women came under medical management. However, midwifery was not a choice among numerous options; instead it resulted from hostility and neglect by white physicians and society at large. When Mildred Lee experienced difficulties during labor, her family rushed her to the closest hospital in search of a cesarean section. But it was 1946 in El Paso, Texas, and the hospital refused her entry. After several hours, she was finally admitted to the whites-only facility because her skin was light enough to "pass," and doctors delivered her daughter using forceps, tearing the skin on her forehead. That little girl became Congresswoman Barbara Lee, and the birth scar from that traumatic delivery became a warrior mark, reminding her "no matter how much black people have accomplished, it was less than forty years ago when we couldn't even share a bathroom, drinking fountain, or classroom with whites." Lee continues, "This history keeps me grounded and … it is why I try to fight injustice wherever I see it, no matter how uncomfortable it may be for me."[29]

The painful story of the laboring woman turned away from the whites-only hospital or giving birth in a car on the way to a distant facility that admitted blacks is engrained in the collective memory of African American women. In the early to mid-twentieth century, most black women in the rural South lived in conditions of extreme poverty and racial repression, scratching out a living through sharecropping or domestic service. For those who had pregnancy complications or whose newborns had health problems, "natural" birth meant exclusion from segregated hospitals or restriction to poorly resourced "colored-only" wards and delay or denial of potentially lifesaving medical treatment. Black women who migrated to Midwestern and northern cities from the southern states and from the Caribbean found themselves in overcrowded, overpriced tenements, where tuberculosis and other infectious diseases, as well as rodents, thrived. For these women, "natural" birth meant delivering in the unsanitary and unsafe conditions that resulted from the neglect of profiteering landlords and the state officials who failed to hold them accountable. For too many black women and their infants, denied adequate health care and nutrition for a lifetime, "natural" childbirth meant a preventable death.

As a result, black women had to develop a more complex politics of childbirth—one that resisted obstetrical apartheid with its double-edge sword of medical coercion and violence on the one hand and malign neglect on the other. While white, middle-class women in the 1960s and 1970s were building the natural birth movement, black women activists focused their energies on the civil rights and Black Power movements, which promised to transform the racist living conditions that shaped black women's vulnerability to pregnancy complications as well as the loss of their infants. In particular, civil rights activists focused on desegregating hospitals by fighting for their inclusion under the 1964 Civil Rights Act's Title VI, prohibiting allocation of government funds to any institution that engaged in racial segregation.[30] Reflecting that era's disillusionment with the promise of integration, black nationalists established free autonomous health clinics and challenged racism in the medical profession as well as exploitative medical research.[31] At the same time, many southern and immigrant black women in particular continued to birth against the grain, drawing on "motherwit"—intergenerational mothers' wisdom—to guide their birthing decisions. These women were perhaps also informed by what Washington labels black iatrophobia—a reluctance to trust white medical practitioners rooted in folk knowledge about the mistreatment of black patients and research subjects.[32]

In addition, granny midwives staged their own resistance to the suppression of traditional midwifery knowledge, deploying what Darlene Clark Hine describes as a culture of dissemblance.[33] By appearing open to and compliant with the arrogant intrusions of the white medical establishment, while simultaneously masking their continued use of traditional herbs, birthing positions, and rituals, granny midwives in the rural South negotiated a space within which they could practice their calling and retire with dignity.[34] Finally, building on the legacy of the grannies, urban black women played an important role in the emergence of the modern midwifery movement. These diverse strands in black women's resistance—including the microresistance of individual actions and covert as well as more visible forms of activism—laid the foundation for a very different politics of childbirth, one that is a matter not only of choice but of survival.

MY BIRTH MY WAY? CHALLENGING THE COMMODIFICATION OF EMPOWERED CHILDBIRTH

By the late 1990s, what started as a geographically dispersed potpourri of home birth collectives had coalesced into an organized movement with a national profile and significant victories. The development of the alternative birth movement into a sophisticated political lobby group and semiorganized social movement owed a great deal to organized medicine's efforts to stamp out home birth and midwifery.[35] Medical practitioners used a number of strategies to tempt, scare, or coerce unruly laboring women back into the hospitals. Hospitals incorporated some of the natural birth movement's demands by allowing family members to attend births, reducing the use of routine interventions such as enemas and forceps, and creating more hospitable birth centers. At the same time, physicians and medical societies portrayed home births as unsafe and unsanitary, despite evidence that midwife-attended home births had as good or even better outcomes as hospital births.[36]

Not satisfied with these indirect approaches, some physicians sought to eliminate the competition and thus force laboring women out of their homes. Addressing the "midwife problem" involved convincing legislators to tighten restrictions and impose physician supervision in states where midwifery was legal and reporting individual midwives to law enforcement in states where it was outlawed.[37] The surveillance and criminalization of their birth attendants outraged home birthers, generated favorable publicity for the movement against medical control over childbirth, and made the legalization and licensing of midwifery a priority. As a result, with the founding of the Midwives Alliance of North America (MANA) in 1993, midwives became organized as a national force. At around the same time, home birth mothers and midwives came together nationally to fight for women's right to midwifery care, founding Citizens for Midwifery in 1996.

When home birth mothers and midwives began to pursue their battles in the legislative arena, they engaged in what veteran civil rights organizer Ella Baker disparagingly called "legalism." According to Baker, making legal reform the primary vehicle for social change results in the alienation of ordinary people as the more educated and privileged become the only ones with the training and expertise to make strategic decisions. Baker advocated participatory democracy, involving direct action, minimization of hierarchy and professionalization, and participation of the marginalized and disenfranchised in society at every level.[38] As Baker might have anticipated, the alternative birth movement's shift in focus from building autonomous communities to influencing state legislative machinery has accompanied its increasing professionalization and stratification. Black midwives have remained on the margins of the statewide and national networks, and those who have gotten involved have complained of high levels of stress as they have sought to convince a predominantly white, middle-class leadership to take black women's concerns seriously. As recently as 2012, four leading members of MANA's Women of Color Council, including the chair, resigned, stating, in an allusion to the popular film on domestics in the Jim Crow South, "We are not 'The Help—2012 Version.' This treatment is not good for us, mentally, physically, emotionally and psychologically—this is the stress that kills us in so many ways, drains our energy and distracts our focus."[39]

Despite, or perhaps in part because of, this stratification, the alternative birth movement has successfully influenced lawmakers and popular opinion. Since 1976, twenty-eight states have legalized or licensed direct-entry or independent midwives, ensuring that women in those states who can afford one can have a midwife-attended home birth. In part, these successes have been due to the alignment of the movement with hegemonic ideas about race, motherhood, and consumerism. Rather than arguing for safe, empowering perinatal care as a human right that should be available to all women regardless of ability to pay, the movement mobilized popular ideologies about the rights of the consumer to position midwifery as an option for respectable women. As Craven explains, this strategic move enabled advocates to shed their radical, hippy, and feminist origins and to reinvent themselves as good citizen-consumers.[40] As a result, legislators opposed to feminism (because of its connections to choice—the right to choose whether to carry a pregnancy) and to left-wing countercultural tendencies have found it possible to support the consumer right of (white, middle-class) mothers to "purchase" the birth experience they desire.

Reducing birth justice to the right to shop has negative consequences, however, particularly for poor women, women with disabilities, trans/gender nonconforming people, and others who are constructed as recipients and dependents rather than consumer-citizens. If the right to a midwife depends on the ability to pay for one, then poor people, particularly those who receive welfare, are presented as having no rights. In fact, birthing parents who rely on Medicaid are often forced to birth in urban public hospitals, which are the least likely to have the resources to create more women- and patient-centered labor and delivery regimens. As such, they are perhaps the most in need of alternative midwifery care.

Black women as a whole are desperately in need of birth alternatives to address our disproportionate rates of pregnancy complications, lower likelihood of receiving adequate prenatal care, and poor breastfeeding rates. Yet black women are significantly less likely than white women to have the savings at their disposal to pay out-of-pocket for midwifery care. The median wealth of black women living with a partner is less than one-twentieth that of a white woman in similar circumstances; for single black women, the situation is particularly dire: even in their prime working years their median wealth amounts to a mere $5. The recession and housing crisis hit black communities particularly hard, and by 2010, 35 percent of black households had a zero or negative net worth compared to 15 percent of white households.[41]

An alternative birth movement that demands that the state legalize and license midwifery care but not that it provide that care to all regardless of the ability to pay is therefore irrelevant to the majority of black women. When our income is dedicated to our own and our children's survival needs, as well as to our commitments to struggling extended family members and friends, and our savings are little or nonexistent, the right to consume midwifery care is a hollow one. Traditionally, midwives lived in a subsistence economy with the women they served, and they could attend births for little or no fee, knowing that over time the family would pay them back by whatever means possible. Over time, modern lay midwives began to charge for their services, in part to cover the cost of maintaining the standards and records required by licensing boards. Today, a midwife-attended birth, as well as prenatal and postpartum care, can cost anywhere from $3,000 to $5,000, an enormous expense for a family living paycheck to paycheck and saving for baby essentials. Yet many health insurers limit coverage for midwifery, force women to have their babies in hospitals where midwives are not permitted to practice, or charge exorbitant copays. By accommodating the politics of consumerism, the mainstream alternative birth movement has surrendered the wider battle for birth justice in exchange for greater freedom for the privileged few. As David Barton Smith cautions, "Do not confuse market-driven reforms for real choice. When health plans and providers are more driven by market conditions, care becomes more fragmented and segregated by race and income. Consumer-driven choice ... amounts to an abdication of public responsibility."[42]

Although the fight to legalize and license midwifery has carved out space for midwives to practice in the United States and turned the tide against the hegemonic control of the obstetrical profession, it fails to challenge the entrenched inequalities rooted in the commercialization of health care and the rise of the medical-industrial complex. It ignores the most vulnerable pregnant people: incarcerated women and trans/gender nonconforming people, women in immigration detention centers, young women in juvenile halls who are subjected to practices—including shackling, denial of prenatal care, and inadequate nutrition—that endanger their pregnancies, and stigmatized birthing parents, such as people living with a mental or physical disability or drug addiction, who battle for the right to carry their pregnancies and to receive the support they need to raise their infants. The struggle for access to birthing alternatives is inseparable from struggles for racial, economic, and social justice and the fundamental transformation of global maternal-care systems. For the alternative birth movement to fulfill its stated goal of creating choices for all women, it must clearly change direction. The emerging birth justice movement, rooted in black and brown communities and informed by the stories, critiques, and dreams of marginalized, despised, and disenfranchised mothers and other birthing parents, is shaping a new vision of reproductive freedom.[43] It is a vision of a decolonized people, shaking off colonial and patriarchal legacies, challenging racial inequities, and building new relationships defined not by commerce but by commitments to social justice, community empowerment, and love as an insurgent praxis. It is to that vision and to the chapters in this book that we now turn.

OVERVIEW OF THE BOOK

In 2011, members of Black Women Birthing Justice put out a call for "critical essays and personal testimonies that explore African American, African, Caribbean and diasporic women's experiences of childbirth from a radical social justice perspective." Midwives, doulas, birth activists, breastfeeding advocates, home birth mothers, feminist and black studies scholars, and medical practitioners and researchers from across the United States and Canada responded. After reviewing the proposals, we identified voices that were missing or underrepresented—women with disabilities, incarcerated women, drug-using women, queer women, trans/gender nonconforming birthing parents, and women from Africa and the Caribbean—and made efforts to recruit contributors who could speak about these particularly marginalized experiences. As we did so, we sought to place black women's testimonies and analyses at the center of the conversation. Social science and medical researchers tend to examine, theorize, and discuss our lives but seldom ask us for our own interpretations of our lived realities. In contrast, we conceptualize black women activists, mothers, and birth workers as thinkers, knowers, and doers, not merely as research subjects or medical conundrums.

Even as we sought to center the lives and analyses of black women, we were also cognizant of the danger that so doing could erase the stories and experiences of those who do not conform to or identify with binary gender identities. Trans/gender nonconforming people of color are often left out of conversations about pregnancy and childbirth justice, which most often reify a binary division between pregnant and birthing women and male partners or medical practitioners. In compiling this book, we attempted to rectify that omission not only by including an essay by a transdad but also by being mindful about language and introducing gender-neutral terms, such as "birthing parent" and "pregnant people," that remind us that people who give birth do not universally identify as women.

The book has four sections that reflect our complimentary goals of examining historical and contemporary birth injustice toward black women, birthing parents, and communities and making visible individual and collective acts of resistance. The first section, "Birthing Histories," continues our historical contextualization of discussions about contemporary maternal health care. Darline Turner's oral history of her granny midwife grandmother provides an intimate insider account of childbirth during a period of transition from home to hospital. Alicia D. Bonaparte's detailed historical excavation of the role of physicians in suppressing black midwifery in South Carolina provides us with insight into the origins of the common belief that physician-attended hospital birth is the safest and best option for laboring women. Christina Mudokwenyu-Rawdon, Peggy Dube, Nester T. Moyo, and Stephen Munjanja's chapter explores the relationship between Western medicine and Indigenous birthing practices in postcolonial Zimbabwe. Their chapter refutes the romanticized images, promoted by some alternative birth advocates, of African women as "noble savages" birthing their babies alone in the bush, untouched by Western medicine and outside history.

In the second section, "Beyond Medical versus Natural: Redefining Birth Injustice," our contributors expand our understanding of birth injustice beyond the narrow medical/natural, male control/female empowerment dichotomy that is the focus of mainstream birth activism. Personal testimonies in this section push us to unpack the ways in which experiences of childbirth are shaped not only by patriarchal gender relations but also by race, gender normativity, class, nation, and geography. Viviane Saleh-Hanna and Iris Jacob encourage us to break the "deafening silence" around miscarriage and loss and to rethink the meaning of "natural." Marvelous Muchenje and Victoria Logan Kennedy highlight the complex relationship that black women living with HIV have with the medical system and call on birth justice advocates to stand in solidarity with these women. Jacinda Townsend provides a personal perspective on how the global epidemic in C-sections impacts black women. Syrus Marcus Ware explores what it means to be a pregnant man in hypergendered spaces like fertility clinics, midwife clinics, and labor and delivery wards. Ware's story interrupts commonsense assumptions relating to sex, gender, and pregnancy and challenges us to consider how a birth justice agenda can encompass a range of birthing genders. And Loretta Ross reveals how covert population-control measures target black women and argues that we need to expand our understanding of birth justice to include the right to have children, free of policies that restrict reproduction. At the end of this section, we honor black women who have died of pregnancy-related causes by reproducing quilt blocks sewn by family members and volunteers.

In medical literature, media, and public policy debates, black women are often represented as pregnant bodies to be policed, carriers of at-risk infants, or recipients of public health education. These representations suggest that our disproportionate risks for pregnancy complications and maternal and infant deaths are a result of irresponsible choices or unhealthy cultural behaviors. As active agents of our own lives, black women resist these depictions. In the third and fourth sections of the book, we foreground black women's acts of resistance to malign neglect, racial/sexual control, and the devaluing of black mothers and infants. In "Changing Lives, One Birth at a Time," we focus on individual and interpersonal acts of resistance. Rather than organizing demonstrations, lobbying lawmakers, or distributing popular education materials, the women in this section of the book manifest birth justice in their everyday lives. The authors, who include doulas, spiritual practitioners, birthing women, and a midwife, challenge powerful and widely held beliefs about where and with whom women should give birth, decolonizing their relationships with each other and with their bodies, healing trauma, and embodying self- and mother-love as a radical praxis. Their brutally honest, intimate accounts remind us that birth justice activism is far more than critical analysis and political organizing alone. Instead it is life-affirming soul work that has the power to move and change us deeply.

In the final section, "Taking Back Our Power: Organizing for Birth Justice," we begin to uncover the histories, strategies, and contributions of birth justice activists. Christ-Ann Magloire and Julia Chinyere Oparah explore possibilities for alliances between dissident ob-gyns, birth workers, and birth activists through a case study of Christ-Ann's VBAC activism. Ruth Hays explores how black midwives created moments of reproductive agency during slavery and after Emancipation and demonstrates how the contemporary black midwifery movement builds on this tradition in its work for reproductive freedom. Jennie Joseph, founder of the JJ Way, and Alicia D. Bonaparte describe how Jennie became a midwife-activist fighting for marginalized women and their children in Florida. Finally, Priscilla A. Ocen and Julia Chinyere Oparah document activism by and for pregnant individuals in prisons and jails and urge reproductive justice and natural birth movements to develop an abolitionist politics that seeks to liberate pregnant and parenting individuals from the prison-industrial complex.

This short collection cannot possibly do justice to the courage, creativity, and dedication of the birth warriors who are working to transform black women's experience of pregnancy and childbirth. We offer this book with humility about its inevitable limitations and omissions. We hope that the words gathered here inspire more black women, women of color, and other marginalized women and trans folks to document how we are decolonizing our bodies and remaking childbirth. We believe that in your hands, this book can become a powerful tool in the struggle for birth justice.

The rest is up to you.

PART I

Birthing Histories

CHAPTER I

Queen Elizabeth Perry Turner
"Granny Midwife," 1931–1956

Darline Turner

And there she stood, a stately and imposing figure, in a clean, pressed dress and starched white apron. In her bag she packed a few herbs, clean cloths, a bin in which to wash the baby, and very few instruments—all that she would need. They had come for her. A townswoman was laboring, and it was time for the baby to be born. She had to go, and there was no time to spare. So with a final word to her eldest son, Jethro, to "mind the others," my great grandmother, Queen Elizabeth Perry Turner, climbed into the buggy and set off into the night to attend a laboring townswoman as she delivered her baby.

Grandma Elizabeth was born of a black father and Cherokee mother in approximately 1894. According to family accounts,[1] she was quite the farmwoman, raising livestock, tending flower and vegetable gardens, and harvesting and preparing plants and herbs to heal the sick. Her mother had been an "Indian root woman," and it is assumed that Grandma Elizabeth learned much of her knowledge about herbs and healing from her. As a child, she said, she spent most of her time on her own around the barns and stables, and it was in this environment, one can only imagine, that she learned about birthing.

It was not until the mid-1920s that Grandma Elizabeth starting assisting at births. In the town of Inez, North Carolina, the first record of Grandma Elizabeth's presence as witness to a birth is on April 24, 1926, when she assisted Cealie Branch in the delivery of my aunt, Mary Ellen Turner, her own granddaughter. This is the first time that her signature appears on a birth record.[2] Her name does not appear again until 1931, when she "attends" the birth of E. Jasper Woodland on August 17, 1931. This is the first record of Grandma Elizabeth as a full-fledged midwife attending to the women of Fork Township, an enclave of Inez.

No one currently living knows what happened in Grandma Elizabeth's career from 1926 until 1931. There was no formal education of midwives at that time. A woman learned to be a midwife by assisting at births and over time assuming more and more responsibility in the delivery. Elders of my family and her last surviving daughter—who is now ninety years old—speculate that Grandma Elizabeth did intermittent training and apprenticeship during that time, as she herself was still having children. Grandma Elizabeth gave birth to eleven babies in all, from 1912 to 1928, and of those, eight survived. With so many children spanning such a wide age range, it is perfectly understandable that she could not pursue her midwifery training and apprenticeship full-time. Yet it is clear that she did in fact continue, and in August 1931 she attended a birth alone.

From that point on, Grandma Elizabeth was a respected and busy midwife to the women of Fork Township. She attended mostly to the black sharecroppers of the large plantations, but she also attended many of the white women's births in the town. Grandma Elizabeth was one of very few black women regarded as "Miss Turner" rather than "Aunt Elizabeth" by both the black and white clientele she served. She was very clear about her role. She provided midwifery and other well-woman and baby care. But if she was not related to you by blood, she was not your aunt and would not be regarded as such. In this way Grandma Elizabeth rejected a label that appeared to indicate intimacy but in fact upheld a system of segregation and black inferiority. She demanded and received respect from whites at a time when this was something that few southern black women dared to insist on—let alone expect.

In those days, the going rate for midwifery services was a mere $2 to $3 per birth. Grandma Elizabeth often provided her prenatal care and midwifery services in exchange for goods (chickens, fabric, or other items or services) or for free. Grandma Elizabeth was a savvy businesswoman, and she and my great grandfather owned a general store as well as the land upon which they farmed. Legend has it that my great grandfather had a very kind heart and was willing to extend credit to his customers, but Grandma Elizabeth was far less generous, maintaining a "cash and carry" motto. But she believed that delivering babies was her calling from God, and she could not deny a woman in need regardless of her ability to pay.

Grandma Elizabeth provided what would today be called preconception counseling and prenatal care. Meeting with women in their homes and often in the fields where they worked, Grandma Elizabeth would suggest herbs and tinctures if a woman was having difficulty conceiving or was stricken with morning sickness or other ailments. According to my cousin Evelyn, Grandma Elizabeth knew which women would have trouble conceiving based on the consistency of their menstrual cycles. And according to her daughter Arleemah, she would often send women in from the fields and home to rest "as their time drew near."

Great Aunt Arleemah shared with me a particular memory of her mother attending the birth of a townswoman. This woman was a field worker and showed signs of physical strain throughout her pregnancy. Grandma Elizabeth advised her to stop working early, but this woman was not able to do so. When Grandma Elizabeth was sent for, both mama and baby were in distress. The mama was only about eight months along, and it was a difficult birth. When the baby was born, neither he nor the mama was faring well. Grandma Elizabeth stayed with that family in their home for eight days, until the mama was stable, the baby was nursing, and she was sure that the family could care for itself. Midwives provided very personal health care to the women and children of the town, health care to which the poor black people (and poor white people) would not otherwise have access. Throughout the 1930s and 1940s, the childbearing women of Fork Township were attended to by my great grandmother Queen Elizabeth Perry Turner and by Mary Eggelston. There were a few other midwives available, but Grandma Elizabeth and Ms. Eggelston managed the bulk of the births in the township.

During the time that my great grandmother and other women were providing midwifery services, obstetricians were also available and practicing in Warren County. Their names are noted sporadically on birth records from the early part of the twentieth century, especially in the smaller townships such as Fork. Interestingly, they are noted to have higher maternal- and infant-mortality rates. It's hard to determine if they saw the more difficult cases or if they saw women when complications threatened their lives or their infants.

During the 1940s, birth practices in Warren County began to change, a process documented in the birth records available in the court house today. Up until the early part of the 1940s, births were almost exclusively attended by midwives, with sporadic and even rare attendance by a physician. By the middle of the fourth decade, shortly after the end of World War II, an increasing number of physician signatures appeared on the birth records—even in tiny townships like Fork. While Grandma Elizabeth and Mary Eggelston still attended most births at that time, more and more women—those who could afford to—were having their births attended by physicians. This shift coincides with the merging of obstetrics and gynecology as a medical discipline, the advent of antibiotics, the availability of antiseptic surgical techniques, and the use of sterilized instruments in medical practice.[3] The way midwives practiced was touted as "dirty," and the midwives themselves were deemed "uneducated" and "ignorant," even though many of these women had birthed more babies over a longer period than many of the physicians disparaging them.[4]

My great grandmother continued to deliver babies until 1956, when she attended her last delivery. In 1950 the Warren General Hospital opened its doors in Warren County between Warrenton and Norlina, North Carolina. This was a good distance from Inez and not accessible without a car or other transportation. During that time, the physicians and the health department went on an aggressive campaign to convince women to deliver their babies in the hospital. Their justification was that hospital births were safer and cleaner and facilities to handle medical complications were more readily available.

Midwives were required to take courses in childbearing and to register with the local health department in order to continue to practice—even if they were not doing hospital deliveries. Their bags were routinely inspected, and midwives were required to carry certain medical instruments and medications, not their own instruments, cloths, and the herbs to which they were accustomed. Midwives who chose to undergo a period of "training and certification" were granted privileges to perform hospital births under the supervision of physicians. My great grandmother was vehemently opposed to this. At fifty-six years old, with over twenty years of birthing experience, she was "not in the mood to mess with the doctors or the hospital." But more importantly, Grandma Elizabeth was vehemently opposed to the care that the women were getting. Women were placed in beds in wards to deliver. There was no privacy and no individual care. Women who had no complications were ushered out of the hospital within twenty-four hours, regardless of how the mother was feeling, how well the baby was nursing, or whether the family was ready to receive the mama and baby. Finally, women were charged $50 to give birth in the hospital. My great grandmother reasoned, if women could not afford to pay her $2 to $3 for home births, how would they ever afford $50 for a hospital birth? Rather than enter into a health-care system to which she was opposed, Grandma Elizabeth retired from midwifery. By the end of the 1950s, upward of 90 percent of babies were born in the hospital, and their births were attended by physicians.[5]

My great grandmother Queen Elizabeth Perry Turner died on December 29, 1970, from atherosclerotic vascular disease, commonly known as hardening of the arteries. She was a bilateral amputee and had been wheelchair-bound prior to her death, and that is how I remember her. I was five years old when she died.

As the history of midwifery in the United States is told and "granny" midwives gain appreciation for how they helped to birth, nurture, and grow our nation, the legacy of my great grandmother and other granny midwives will live on forever.

CHAPTER 2

Regulating Childbirth

Physicians and Granny Midwives
in South Carolina

Alicia D. Bonaparte

Throughout the Deep South, during the colonial and antebellum periods, "countless generations of poor rural women, both white and black, were attended in childbirth by granny midwives, mostly black women whose skills were handed down from mother to daughter over the centuries."[1] "Granny midwifery," a type of lay midwifery, derives from the term "grandmother midwife" because these midwives tended to be older. To become a granny midwife (hereafter referred to as a granny), a woman must have had a spiritual "calling" to the profession, served an apprenticeship until the older midwife retired, or followed a matrilineal tradition of midwifery. Grannies practicing in the United States in the early eighteenth through the late nineteenth centuries tended to be African American, menopausal or postmenopausal, and rurally situated. They served in pivotal leadership/religious positions within their communities and functioned as both birth attendants and healers due to an unmet need for health-care providers and a distrust of doctors in rural communities.

Research on granny midwives documents midwives' roles during the Transatlantic Slave Trade and post-Emancipation within black communities, illustrates how granny midwifery was not considered a true occupation because grannies lacked formal education and training, and discusses efforts

24

employed to eliminate southern black midwives from birthing work in the early twentieth century.[2] Importantly, granny midwives had decades of experience with successfully birthing black and white children and taught many newly minted doctors how to attend births.[3] In fact, black midwives successfully attended almost 80 percent of black and white births in the American South.[4] This chapter extends previous midwifery literature by examining physician advocacy for the elimination of granny midwifery within medical journals and noting the prominent arguments physicians used.

BRIEF HISTORY OF GRANNY MIDWIFERY IN THE UNITED STATES

Slaveholding American society valued granny midwives for their diasporic healing traditions and remedies. Their earliest role was to maintain a "healthy" labor force on southern plantations, particularly on rice plantations in South Carolina.[5] Grannies assisted most black and white births in the southeastern United States, and their respective communities considered them integral members. In some instances, grannies provided contraceptive and abortion methods to black and white women and served as spiritual healers and leaders within slave communities.[6] Grannies also assisted slave revolts by transporting abolitionist and rebellion messages between plantations. Grannies engaged in various social arenas unhindered thanks to the overall high esteem in which they were held within southern society. However, changes in the structure of US health care diminished this high regard toward grannies over time.

INSTITUTIONALIZED RESISTANCE TO GRANNY MIDWIVES

During the late nineteenth and early twentieth centuries, medicine became professionalized in the United States,[7] meaning that it became recognized as "a [special] body of knowledge, requiring extensive training [with its licensed practitioners] entitled to exclusive rights protected by law."[8] This shift imposed the requirement of a medical degree to provide health care and labeled nondegreed individuals, like grannies, as unqualified practitioners.[9] Women increasingly no longer viewed home birth as comforting or reassuring since hospitals were equipped with modern devices, anesthesia, and narcotics (like morphine and scopolamine) to assist in safe and painless deliveries. Furthermore, the professionalization of medicine by white male physicians pushed women into subordinated roles in birthing work during the late nineteenth and early twentieth centuries.[10] Consequently, granny midwifery became a minor subspecialty within the growing field of birthing work compared to the work of formally educated male and female doctors and nurses trained in the northern United States.[11]

Between 1900 and 1940, health officials and medical doctors depicted granny midwifery (and other forms of midwifery) as an unsafe and illegitimate form of health care by citing egregious mortality rates as a consequence of midwifery and castigating traditional methods of birth attendance.[12] Consequently, midwives suffered various criticisms and prosecution, allowing physicians to reduce the influence these black women held, elevating physicians in public opinion as superior birth attendants, and increasing the numbers of women seeking pre- and postnatal care from physicians.

INTERSECTIONS OF GENDER, RACE, AND AGE IN ANTI-GRANNY ADVOCACY

During the early twentieth century, Dr. Joseph DeLee, a prominent anti-midwife advocate, labeled birth as a risky and pathological process and stated that few women could escape damage during labor outside a hospital setting. His recommended procedure for a less risky birth received social acceptance and placed pregnancy and childbirth "under the control of the specialist." Unfortunately, this new practice undercut the practices of traditional birth attendants and allowed physicians to monopolize pre- and postnatal diagnosis and treatment.[13]

Women and men in the early twentieth century believed that women were the weaker gender physically and mentally. Therefore, the belief that women were delicate and medically incompetent compared to men trained in medical schools was a prominent theme in anti-midwife advocacy.[14]

This prior sentiment carried over into anti-granny midwifery advocacy. During the late nineteenth and early twentieth centuries, "racism and lack of economic incentives were major factors in medical tolerance of southern black midwives."[15] Many white physicians did not want to serve southern black communities, so granny midwives continued to serve rural areas. However, supervisory structures implemented by county health departments from 1915 forward initiated a shift of authority away from community-oriented midwives to local health departments and encouraged physician dependency. Physicians pushed black midwives to have mandatory attendance at midwifery training seminars, ostensibly to address concerns about infant and maternal mortality in the southern United States and to ascertain the number of practicing lay midwives. At these seminars, county health officials taught midwives—many of whom had successfully delivered hundreds of newborns—lessons about Christian attitudes and morals, along with the importance of cleanliness.[16]

To produce support for the new, formally educated midwife, physicians mobilized racist beliefs about blacks and their capabilities. Such persecution included linking diasporic approaches to healing by enslaved African Americans with granny midwifery practices and criticizing both as outmoded and primitive.[17] Some physicians labeled grannies "a cross between a superstitious hag and a meddlesome old biddy," an evaluation that drew on racist, sexist, and ageist stereotypes to denigrate black female elders.[18]

Public health lobbyists and physicians initiated campaigns against ethnic granny midwives (immigrant and black women) during the early twentieth century using circulars (or information pamphlets) that portrayed granny midwives as unkempt to indicate that doctors were preferable and more qualified birth attendants. Because their "likenesses [were] distorted and placed on circulars … grannies had to fight their own bodily representations in a society where only females who were delicate enough to require hospitalization were constructed as women."[19] Ageism was an important factor in these representations supporting the idea that grannies were obsolete and should be phased out. Unlike grannies, younger midwives had less social standing and desire for autonomy; thus "senior midwives were targeted for replacement by new recruits willing to accept the health departments' dictated standards for midwifery practice."[20] In South Carolina, the number of registered midwives decreased from 197 in 1900 to 124 by 1920 due to the spread of anti-midwifery legislation.[21]

LEGAL REGULATION OF MIDWIFERY

During the early twentieth century, medical doctors reasoned that midwife-assisted deliveries increased the mortality rates of mothers and infants. Subsequently, legislation specifically designed to limit or eliminate midwifery in its entirety birthed the persecution of granny midwifery. For example, physicians argued for "restrictive medical licensing laws and more rigorous medical education" and the removal of lay and granny midwives without the proper training.[22] This social persecution persisted on local, state, and governmental levels.[23]

Unfortunately, grannies had difficulty resisting the efforts of their largely urban-dwelling persecutors because they lived and operated primarily in isolated rural areas. So grannies could not form coalitions to fight for the continuation of their practice against well-coordinated physician criticism and maternal-health-care lobbyists during the early twentieth century. Midwives were also defenseless because this persecution and the subsequent prosecution were multifaceted. Critics published damning remarks in medical journals and medical association papers and advocated for granny midwives' clientele to use doctors as their birthing attendants within hospital settings. More interestingly, some female physicians and black physicians also lobbied for an end to lay midwifery in an effort to avoid being associated with granny midwives.[24]

Black Women's Positionality and Birthing Work

An analysis of black women's social position in the United States is critical to understanding why white male physicians targeted and labeled black granny midwives as interlopers in birthing work. Patricia Hill Collins writes, "African American women's status as outsiders [and that of women in general] becomes the point from which other groups define their normality."[25] Her work builds on that of scholars who argue that patriarchy created a system of oppression that branded women as deviants in comparison to men.[26] Their race and gender mean black women are the "other" and deviant; thus, they experience marginalization and social persecution via oppressive language and actions rooted in racialized patriarchy. I argue that physicians' negative commentary in professional medical journals and the characterization of midwives as deviant beings constituted social persecution of granny midwives and simultaneously created pathways for the "elevation of elite White male ideas and interests."[27] Once white medical men asked society to acknowledge their authoritative knowledge (or exclusive right to birthing work) and obtained legal backing via licensure requirements, the US social structure and culture embraced the necessity and "expertise" of white men in birthing rooms.[28]

The remainder of this chapter provides unique insight into the antagonistic and highly competitive environment that led to the medicalization of childbirth. Physicians used medical journals to advance their argument that only they could be trusted to deliver the nation's babies. "Anti-midwife physicians published scores of articles on the American midwife problem. . . . Between 1910 and 1930, the medical community and, to a lesser extent, the general public became embroiled in a vehement debate over the present and future role of the midwife in American society."[29] What follows is an exposé of physicians' anti-midwifery advocacy in South Carolina through an analysis of their own words.[30]

Given that the racist-sexist conditioning of American society in the early twentieth century colored black women's experiences, I expected physicians' opinions about granny midwives to reflect overt racism. However, my data revealed covert racism within physicians' commentaries, whereby physicians did not acknowledge or recognize how their statements contained racist sentiment. Although few physicians explicitly discussed granny midwives, their comments condemned midwives and the black populace in general.

Who Catches the Babies? Educating the Public about the Right Choice

In order to orchestrate the removal of midwives, physicians used convention and society reports to reflect on the impact of midwives in the *Journal of the*

American Medical Association (*JAMA*). For example, in 1910, Dr. Allen W. Freeman stated,

> There is no doubt that tens of thousands of women are being absolutely murdered by ignorant midwives. Every one who has ever practiced obstetrics knows how filthy and dirty, how officious and meddlesome these women are; and we know what a tremendous total of fatal and crippling illness they cause every year. . . . We must tell the people how many women these midwives are killing, and how much illness they are causing.
>
> I don't think people want to run the risk of being infected or killed by midwives; they run the risk because they don't know. The obstetrician and the health officers are the only people who apparently do know; and if we are going to be true to our duty, we must bring this information to them.[31]

Dr. James A. Haynes, in the same year in the *Journal of the South Carolina Medical Association* (*JSCMA*), also connected unregulated midwifery to maternal and infant deaths.

> We can see that for South Carolina to have ten times as many women to die during parturition and pregnancy means that something is radically wrong with our system. We allow dirty, ignorant women to proclaim themselves capable of taking care of mothers at this time when they should have the most skilled care and attention.
>
> There is no midwife law in South Carolina. No one, no matter how ignorant she may be is debarred from calling herself a midwife. *They are neither licensed, nor inspected, nor do they know anything in regard to what is necessary to preserve life under these circumstances.*[32]

By using the trope that midwives were "dirty," doctors engaged in demarcation strategies that informed the general public and other members of the medical profession that midwives were deviant and undesirable participants in birthing work. And their commentary included the assumption that education and training ensured that only physicians and other licensed health professionals would possess the necessary knowledge and authority to deliver babies.

PHYSICIANS' PERCEPTIONS OF GRANNY MIDWIVES IN BIRTHING WORK

Regarding physicians' specific commentary about granny midwives, I found one example of a physician using the term "granny." Dr. D. H. Smith, a South Carolina physician, wrote in *JSCMA*, "[We] are sometimes entertained with several 'Old Dippers'[33] of the community, who have come to see and encourage the patient; by telling of a similar case which they waited on, where the woman would have died, had she not put a pillow under her hips or given her pepper tea, 'Conceited old grannies' these are."[34] This text illustrates physicians' condescension toward granny midwives' expertise and asserts their professional superiority as younger and formally trained (white) men.

Black midwives comprised most of the midwife populace and tended to the larger black populace of South Carolina. Yet I found surprisingly few negative opinions about black granny midwives from 1900 to 1910 within *JAMA*. The one instance I discovered stated,

> Dr. Charles W. Kollock, Charleston, ... spoke of the large negro popula-
> tion in South Carolina, among whom eye diseases are rife and who are
> eminently careless in all health matters. He urged strict laws and education
> for these people. He quoted the number of births in Charleston from July 1
> to Dec. 31, 1909, that of 213 whites 155 were attended by physicians and
> 58 by midwives. Out of 225 colored births 30 were attended by physicians
> and 195 by midwives. He mentioned that those midwives were not only
> ignorant, conceited, dirty, but very superstitious, and that more stringent
> laws should govern them.[35]

Dr. Kollock's comments mirrored those of other medical officials who opined that midwives and African Americans required education in "all health matters."[36] Since most midwives in South Carolina were black women, physicians mobilized what Angela Y. Davis[37] calls the hidden logic of racism, allowing them to draw on popularly held stereotypes about African Americans without necessarily using overtly racist terminology. During their conference meetings, physicians argued that because South Carolina's black midwives practiced archaic techniques and used obsolete tools, they required further instruction. One example included in an editorial demonstrated approval of the boons associated with educating midwives: "Classes for the training of midwives have already been under instruction, and *especial attention is being given to the instruction of Negro midwives.* One of these classes has been under tutelage in Beaufort county and the islands on the coast. The instructor is a trained nurse of marked ability, well trained in good hospitals in the North, and capable of vastly improving the midwifery situation for her race."[38] This nurse, Mary Ruth Dodd, served as a training supervisor of black midwives for almost two decades, and the disproportionate resources dedicated to her instruction of granny midwives implied that black midwives required more tutelage than their white counterparts.[39]

The call for training for granny midwives drew on stereotypes of Afri-
can Americans and immigrants as unhygienic and lacking intelligence. For example, at a Louisiana physicians' conference whose proceedings were printed in *JAMA,* physicians stated,

> The State Board of Medical Examiners has recently made an extensive
> study of the midwifery problem. The report states that "midwives attended

approximately 50 per cent. of the births in this country," nevertheless the investigations prove that "with few exceptions the midwife is dirty, ignorant and totally unfit to discharge the duties which she assumes."

Reports show they are practicing in all states, mostly among immigrants and negro women. The board concludes that the first thing necessary is to insist on their being better trained, and a school for them has been opened in New Orleans.[40]

Doctors linked unregulated midwives to septic infections and birthing risks among their patients because

we permit, in many states without a question, an ignorant and dirty woman, such as depicted by Miss Crowell, "whose hands were indescribable, whose clothing was filthy, the condition of whose bag beggars description," to officiate in obstetrics, an important branch of medicine, and thus to slay and kill without one word of protest. . . . [Midwives are] carriers of disease and death, and it should be the especial concern of every physician having the welfare of his community at heart constantly to urge, in season and out of season, either the elimination of the breed, or, what seems more desirable, the creation of educational standards and state examinations and a supervision of midwives by legislative enactment.[41]

On the other hand, some doctors felt training was not the answer to the midwife problem. Rather, they believed the public should no longer use midwives as birthing attendants.

PHYSICIANS' ATTITUDES TOWARD THE BLACK POPULACE

Examining physicians' views of African Americans in general assists in understanding their advocacy for the elimination of black women from birthing work. Derogatory comments about African Americans occurred periodically throughout the forty-year period of my study. Some doctors made negative comments about African Americans' ability to provide health care, while others criticized African Americans' spiritual beliefs and questioned their physical and mental abilities. For example, in *JSCMA,* Dr. Robert P. Harris stated in his work on obstetrics, "We do not know, with certainty, when Caesarean Section was first resorted to. It was practiced among uncivilized nations, notably Uganda, in Central Africa. This fact was brought to light by Robert W. Felkin, F.R.S.E., of Scotland. . . . How old this operation is in Africa it is impossible to determine. It is remarkable that the African barbarian should be so far in advance of the Chinese and Japanese in operative obstetrics."[42]

Colonialism established a racial hierarchy casting people of African descent as naturally inferior, morally degenerate, and deserving of capitalistic exploitation and oppression.[43] Moreover, colonial racial dynamics provided substantial foreground for later persecutory considerations of black people in the United States.[44] Therefore, unsurprisingly, South Carolina physicians like Dr. T. H. Dreher stated, "Some time ago, a lady, sent by the government, dropped into my office and asked for my cooperation in *rounding up the old midwives* and teaching them some of the elementary modern principles of hygiene and antiseptics. I heartily recommended her work, and promised every assistance. I told her, however, that she and the government were short on one feature. That while teaching them how to bring young Hami-ites safely into the world, she should also post them on *legitimate* preventive measures, to keep a lot of them out."[45] Dreher's advocacy of birth control for black women mirrors early twentieth-century eugenics, which sought to reduce births among black, immigrant, and mentally and physically disabled women. By calling black children "Hami-ites," Dreher invokes biblical authority for his attack on black women and infants. The word "Hamite" is derived from the biblical story in which Noah curses Ham's son Canaan and suggests that black people originated as a "cursed," innately sinful race of people.[46]

Some physicians viewed African Americans as ignorant and superstitious. For example, in *JSCMA,* Dr. R. B. Furman argued, "The belief in witchcraft and the agency of occult forces has by no means died out. It is very common when a negro becomes ill in any unusual and to him inexplicable way to imagine himself tricked and even to be able to say who perpetrated the job. This state of mind of course sets up a vicious circle and the unhappy darky is liable to fall a victim to his own imaginings."[47] Doctors directed similar criticisms toward grannies in order to discredit them. For example, Dr. W. E. Simpson stated in *JSCMA,* "The superstitious and time-honored midwife customs are responsible for the death of many babies that survive the hazards of birth, and the first days of life. It is the rule in the midwife class of deliveries that the baby is purged and 'tea'd' to the point of almost extinction. Upon this handicap is engrated vicious habits as to feeding hygiene and care. The ludicrous remedies for sore eyes, thrush, hives, etc., are familiar to us all."[48] Referring to southern black spirituality as superstition reflects the colonial denigration of African religious practices. Physicians consistently deployed the racial stereotypes of superstition, poor hygiene, and ignorance in their battle to turn the public against midwives.

CONCLUSION

My investigation revealed that physicians used racialized and gendered criticisms of midwives and black communities as the basis for eliminating midwives in general from birthing work in South Carolina. Although few physicians explicitly named black granny midwives as the bane of birthing work, their opinions about who should and should not practice this work included clear racist and sexist biases. Physicians like Dr. Dreher viewed African Americans as nothing more than "bugbears" and "niggers" who hindered the medical attendance of white physicians and, further, were "overbreeders."[49] Claiming that African Americans as a whole were incapable of providing medical care because of their spiritual beliefs, traditional healing practices, and alleged lack of hygiene and ignorance, I argue, laid the groundwork for the persecution of southern black midwives.

Physicians linked black midwives to maternal and infant deaths in order to justify physicians' ownership of safe birthing knowledge. Moreover, several physicians opined that the public should not put itself at risk with a midwife-attended birth. As a result, doctors created a hierarchy in birthing work by labeling themselves as the best caretakers for pregnant women and their unborn infants. They also sought to reduce granny midwives' social standing, end their autonomy, and bring them under a doctor's and/or nurse's supervision.

This project contributes to midwifery research in three ways. First, midwifery researchers argue that physicians blamed the "midwife problem" for poor birth outcomes and pushed for the demise of granny midwives in the southern United States.[50] By focusing on South Carolina, a state plagued by high infant and maternal mortality rates, I demonstrate that South Carolina physicians' professional writings did not reflect a strategic effort to eliminate black midwives as previous researchers of southern black midwifery noted.[51] Instead, physicians tolerated South Carolina midwives in some instances so long as they adhered to new educational stipulations, training, and subordinated status. Second, previous midwifery researchers have not studied professional writings of South Carolina physicians to investigate how their opinions contributed to anti-midwife advocacy. Such an examination more clearly connects attitudes communicated via medical publications with the restrictive midwifery regulations instated during the early 1920s and 1930s. This important addition to midwifery research demonstrates the central role of prejudices toward African Americans, from both the medical profession and society at large, within anti-midwifery advocacy. Third, my examination of physicians' claim that birthing knowledge and practices required specialized training demonstrates how they were able to position themselves and other licensed health professionals (such as nurses) as birthing experts in American society. These findings are relevant for birth justice activists today and suggest a continued need to address the historically contested relationship between physicians and midwives.

CHAPTER 3

Between Traditional Knowledge and Western Medicine

Women Birthing in Postcolonial Zimbabwe

*Christina Mudokwenyu-Rawdon, Peggy Dube,
Nester T. Moyo, and Stephen Munjanja*

INTRODUCTION

Childbearing women in Zimbabwe are exposed to two main influential bodies of birth knowledge and practices of maternity care: the traditional system, which is based on experiential birth knowledge and practices, and the medicalized Western model. Though these coexist, there is an ongoing transition process from a traditional to a westernized culture mirrored within the field of women's health. Tensions between the two cultures are particularly notable in the area of reproduction, as the strongest beliefs and rituals in traditional life surround marriage, fertility, pregnancy, childbirth, and child rearing. The majority of childbearing women use Indigenous birth knowledge and practices during pregnancy, childbirth, and the postpartum period, even when they are simultaneously interacting with Western obstetric and midwifery models of maternity care. These women are born and brought up in communities where traditional knowledge and practices are commonly part of the family agenda, and the extent to which they are initiated into cultural birth practices varies from family to family and community to community.

34

This chapter provides a comparison of traditional birth knowledge, beliefs, and practices with contemporary obstetrics and midwifery. The authors have been involved in maternity-care services in Zimbabwe for more than three decades each and share over sixty years of clinical obstetric and midwifery practice. As Zimbabwean practitioners, educators, and midwifery advocates, we conclude this chapter with a call to strengthen and transform the biomedical model of care by studying and honoring traditional knowledge and good practices.

ZIMBABWE: CONTEXT AND HISTORY

The Republic of Zimbabwe is in central southern Africa, bordered by Mozambique, South Africa, Botswana, Namibia, and Zambia. Harare, the capital city, is in Mashonaland, while Bulawayo, the second-largest city, is in Matebeleland. Zimbabwe had an estimated population of 12.7 million in 2011, of which two-thirds reside in rural areas. Women of reproductive age (fifteen to forty-nine years) constitute 24.7 percent of the population. The literacy rate is high; overall, 94 percent of women and 96 percent of men are literate.[1]

The main cultural groups in the country are the Mashona, who live throughout the northern, eastern, and central parts of the country, and the Matabele, who live in the western parts. Other cultural groups include the Venda, Shangaan, Tonga, Kalanga, Ndau, Nampa, and individuals of European and Asian ancestry. The descriptions and discussions of traditional knowledge and birth practices in this chapter are mainly of the Mashona, as this group has been studied the most in Zimbabwe.

Zimbabwe was born from a system of colonization by the British, starting with the creation of the Federation of Rhodesia and Nyasaland in 1953, which lasted until December 31, 1963. In 1964, the federation broke up as a result of political unrest from Northern Rhodesian, Nyasalander, and Southern Rhodesian nationalists, with Nyasaland achieving its independence within the commonwealth as Malawi on July 6, 1964. Northern Rhodesia became independent as Zambia on October 24 that year. White settlers in Southern Rhodesia announced a Unilateral Declaration of Independence (UDI) on November 11, 1965, and the country became known as Rhodesia. But the UDI was not recognized by the British or any other countries. Rhodesia continued to face internal resistance from the nationalists, who waged guerilla warfare for over a decade. The Bush War, a conflict between the government and two rival communist-backed Black Nationalist groups, began two years later, and after several attempts to end the war, the Rhodesian government agreed to an internal settlement with nonmilitant nationalists in 1978. The country was then reconstituted under black rule as Zimbabwe-Rhodesia in June 1979, but this new order was rejected by the guerillas and the international community.

The Bush War continued until Rhodesia revoked the UDI as part of the Lancaster House Agreement in December 1979. Following a brief period of direct British rule, the United Kingdom granted independence to Zimbabwe in April 1980.[2] Robert Gabriel Mugabe, the current president of Zimbabwe, became the first black prime minister at national independence in 1980.[3]

TRADITIONAL CHILDBEARING IN ZIMBABWE

Zimbabwean traditional cultures have always placed great importance on a couple having children. A woman who has failed to bear children may be divorced and looked on as unworthy. Having children has a direct impact on the respect an individual acquires in society. Pregnancy confirms womanhood, and delivering a baby successfully is an important rite of passage. In the Matabele culture, it is considered unwise for a man to marry a woman who is not pregnant. Involuntary childlessness leads to devastating personal and socioeconomic consequences, especially for women. For men, childbearing is no less important. Impregnation is seen as a sign of manhood, and male childlessness is considered shameful and leads to extramarital affairs, domestic violence, and divorce. In traditional culture sometimes a male relative was asked to assist the childless man by secretly impregnating his wife. This was arranged and sanctioned by the senior members of the extended family but caused problems in the family if it became an open secret. Children are often associated with a sense of security in old age. They are born into the extended family unit rather than the nuclear family, and this is an important difference between African and Western cultures.

Preparation for motherhood in Zimbabwean traditional cultures starts in childhood and adolescence, when young girls observe older members of the extended family having babies. A girl is given chores to assist with baby care and may even be assigned a baby to look after. Aunts and married sisters are responsible for premarital counseling of adolescent girls. Having a child is a community event, but the period of pregnancy is risky, for the woman and her child are thought to be vulnerable to bewitchment by unkind people, especially those in the neighborhood.

Therefore, the pregnant woman may be given traditional medicine, early in or throughout pregnancy, which is believed to keep evil spirits away. In addition, a woman will not talk about her pregnancy until it is so advanced that she cannot hide it anymore or until she has felt fetal movements. With modern technological advances such as ultrasound, the young generation is transforming culture; a woman's pregnancy is a shared experienced with significant others.

Pregnancy is not perceived as an illness, and as a result pregnant women are expected to carry on with their chores in- and outside the house. Some women have been known to go farming in the morning and give birth in the afternoon or shortly thereafter. Despite this, older women in the family or the village pamper the woman by feeding her well as she is carrying another member of the family and community. Her husband is proud of her but does not demonstrate it openly in case the woman gets spoiled. In-laws and family take over decision-making and actively participate in the pregnancy and childbirth care. In the past, there was no formal antenatal care from traditional birth attendants (TBAs), but female in-laws or family members provided counseling, dietary advice, and herbs to make labor easier. Herbal medicine is believed to strengthen the woman's back and prepare the birth passage to ensure an easy delivery. A pregnant woman has to avoid any activity or foods that might compromise the health of the baby. Some dietary taboos lead the mother to avoid foods that are actually beneficial, such as eggs.

In the Shona practice, a woman pregnant for the first time was traditionally handed over to her parents for pregnancy and childbirth care. Her in-laws did not want to be responsible for the outcome of the first pregnancy, and this was an implicit acknowledgment of the risks involved. The origins of unfavorable outcomes are viewed in terms of the spiritual pathology within the family or community, such as bewitchment, angry ancestors, and direct poisoning by bad people.[4] The attitude to miscarriages is fatalistic. The most common statement said about miscarriages or stillbirths is "It wasn't meant to be my baby."

When a woman goes into labor, she is looked after by older women and a TBA in a hut secluded from the homestead. Men are not allowed into the room. She is told that she is on a long journey and is given food and drink to keep her strong. A woman starts pushing early, sometimes because of ignorance about the process of labor. No vaginal examinations are done, and all assistance starts when the head appears at the vulva. The TBA or female relative delivers the baby without cutting or any surgical procedures. A difficult labor is thought to indicate either that the mother is bewitched or that she has been unfaithful. She is required to confess the name of the co-adulterer for the child to be born.

Soon after delivery, the new mother is fed well. She is expected to rest. Close relatives come over to look after her. She has no opportunity for postpartum blues because she is always with one or more relatives providing support. She and the baby will not leave the house during the first week because evil spirits may enter her body while she is still weak. Until the cord has separated, evil spirits may also enter the baby through the cord stump. In most parts of Zimbabwe, mothers are discouraged from giving the baby colostrum (first breast milk), and the baby is given warm water until the "real" milk has started flowing. Colostrum is considered unclean. The baby needs protection from evil immediately after birth. Some herbal preparation may be applied to the weak spots: the cord and the anterior fontanel. After one week, the baby is given a name and leaves the isolation room with the mother to meet the rest of the extended family for the first time.

Child spacing is an important aspect of family life. There are taboos against sexual activity for several months if the woman has recently delivered, and breastfeeding is also known to have a contraceptive effect. Having properly spaced children is a sign of responsibility on the part of the man. If a family has a baby every year (*gore mwana gore mwana*), the husband is despised and considered irresponsible.

UNDERSTANDING THE MATERNAL-HEALTH-CARE SYSTEM

Before independence, Zimbabweans experienced inequalities in terms of health status and the provision of health care. The health system was based on a three-tier model: the missionary sector (private, not-for-profit, faith-based organizations); the private for-profit sector, including company-operated clinics; and the public sector. These systems existed alongside the services of traditional healers and birth attendants. The three-tier system was fragmented and uncoordinated. Maternity services, therefore, were and are still inaccessible to some women, particularly those living in rural areas. For many years women depended solely on TBAs for care during pregnancy and childbirth and between pregnancies. The TBAs acquire their knowledge and skills through experiential learning and observing their relatives, especially their grandmothers. This body of knowledge is passed on from mother to daughter or daughter-in-law, maintaining the intergenerational transfer of traditional birthing knowledge and practices. This knowledge and its associated practices have been maintained even in an era of rapid social and technological change.

Women seek the services of traditional birth attendants because of their accessibility and affordability. The TBAs, known as traditional midwives in Zimbabwe, live in the community, the majority of them at village level; they are respected members of the community who speak the local language and are familiar with the local cultural needs of the women they serve. They are considered authorities on traditional medicines and birth practices.

The traditional way of carrying and birthing infants in Zimbabwe has changed with the introduction and expansion of the primary health-care approach to maternity care. Consequently there is a progressive substitution of the TBAs' services with the fast-growing medicalized approach to modern maternity care, which attempts to integrate the positive contributions of traditional birthing practices into Western evidence-based practice to achieve better pregnancy and birth outcomes. Improved quality of care at health facilities and increased access to such care by women appear to be leading to the eradication of TBAs and their practices.

Zimbabwe experienced a significant decline in the maternal mortality ratio (MMR) following the adoption of the primary health-care strategy in 1980: there were 145 maternal deaths per hundred thousand live births that year versus 76 in 1988.[5] Adequate funding—which existed in Zimbabwe between 1980 and 1989—and governmental commitment to strengthening the health-delivery system paid dividends in improving the health status of women. However, these gains were reversed by the economic meltdown, critical shortage of health-care resources, and challenges associated with social discontent. This later led to land invasion and occupations by the Indigenous Zimbabweans, political instability, global disapproval of the current government, and limited funding for health services from the donor community between 1990 and 2008. The economic crisis, compounded by the HIV burden, decreased funding from international partners, and multiple other factors, contributed to a dramatic decrease in health-care resources and an increase in maternal and child deaths.

The estimated maternal ratio was approximately 520 maternal deaths per hundred thousand live births in 1990, 680 in 2000, and 470 in 2013.[6] The 2013 statistic's downward trend possibly reflects extensive training of maternity-care providers in emergency maternal and neonatal care. But the number of women dying from pregnancy- and childbirth-related complications is still too high. Zimbabwe is therefore making insufficient progress toward Millennium Development Goal 5: improving maternal health. HIV prevalence is reported at 18 percent among women ages fifteen to forty-nine,[7] and HIV/AIDS is identified as the leading indirect cause of maternal death, accounting for 26 percent of all maternal deaths.[8]

Even during this expansion of Western-style maternity services, many women continued to turn to traditional pregnancy and childbirth practices, some by choice and others because of lack of access to health-care services. Women's continued preference for TBAs makes it imperative that practitioners of westernized obstetrics and midwifery commit themselves to understanding more about traditional birthing practices, the people who offer traditional care, and how this understanding can inform Western-style maternal care. Every woman has a right to survive pregnancy and childbirth and to enjoy motherhood. Without this understanding, some women will continue to die in the hands of caregivers, and the blame game between traditional and Western-style caregivers will continue, without benefitting either women or health-care professionals.

TRADITIONAL VERSUS CONTEMPORARY OBSTETRICS AND MIDWIFERY

The last three decades have witnessed a shift toward primary health care and adoption of rights- and competency-based approaches to maternity care.

Training programs for TBAs, introduced in the 1980s as part of a response to the Alma-Ata Declaration of 1978, were later aborted because evidence from around the world has shown that training TBAs has not reduced maternal mortality. Instead, all women are deemed to require skilled attendance—defined as the presence of a skilled birth attendant and an enabling environment—to prevent maternal deaths as a result of pregnancy complications. A skilled attendant is a professional who can be a midwife, doctor, or mid-level provider, such as a clinical officer or nurse, trained to perform the following critical functions: intravenous administration of antibiotics, sedatives, and oxytocic drugs; manual vacuum aspiration (of retained products of conception); assisted vaginal delivery; manual removal of the placenta; and basic neonatal resuscitation with bag and mask.[9]

These trends, strengthened by the thrust of evidence-based medicine, have entrenched the biomedical model in the care of women and sidelined traditional birth attendants. Millennium Development Goals 4 and 5—to reduce child mortality and improve maternal health—will only be achieved by greatly increasing skilled attendance during pregnancy and childbirth in developing countries. The complex care that women need for most complications cannot be provided at the community level by upgraded TBAs or other lay workers, and this is the reason why maternal mortality ratios are not decreasing at the expected rate in sub-Saharan Africa. The MMR in native populations without any scientifically based medical care is estimated to be two thousand deaths per hundred thousand live births, a level no country can accept.

The TBAs were unknown to their colonial masters; however, the communities they served appreciated their work and service to childbearing families. As colonialism took its toll, there was a gradual loss of traditional culture, and some women sought medically based maternity care. With the introduction of the primary health-care model, the Zimbabwean government recognized the TBAs' contribution toward maternity care and their popularity among the communities they served. In an attempt to reclaim traditional birthing, the Ministry of Health introduced a training course designed to upgrade TBAs' knowledge and skills in caring for women during pregnancy and childbirth in the early 1980s. The course was later abandoned. Any improvement in pregnancy outcomes was attributed not to TBA training but to new initiatives in the Western model of maternity care. The loss of traditional birth practices stems not only from erosion due to colonialism but also from the demand that biomedical care should become better and more accessible to save lives as some traditional practices have been deemed harmful to the health of the mother or baby.

We still need, however, to study and assess the impact of traditional knowledge and practices on current biomedical care. Both the traditional and biomedical health systems are used by a majority of women during pregnancy and childbirth in Zimbabwe and nearby countries because TBAs are readily accessible and afford women continuity of care.[10] TBAs also ensure that women receive traditional food that is highly nutritious and assist with breastfeeding, although some prohibit women from feeding their babies colostrum—first milk—which contains various substances beneficial to the newborn. It is acknowledged that while some traditional practices are beneficial, others, such as herbal treatment for the cord, can cause serious harm to the baby. Table 3.1 shows that this is often due to traditional knowledge or practices that conflict with recommendations by medical practitioners. Table 3.2 shows the potentially beneficial effects of some traditional knowledge and practices (this is not an exhaustive list).

A systematic study of the knowledge and practices in this area of all the ethnic groups in Zimbabwe still needs to be conducted. However, this brief survey demonstrates that practitioners of the biomedical model need to construct effective health-education messages based on the Indigenous knowledge of women and their families. These issues should be reflected in midwifery and medical training curricula. In addition, advocacy, health-education, and behavioral-change strategies should be underpinned by detailed studies of cultural norms in order to have maximum impact.

Table 3.1 Effects of Traditional Beliefs and Practices on Modern Management of Pregnancy

Belief/Practice	Effect
Pregnancy and prenatal period	
Delayed acknowledgment of pregnancy	Seeking antenatal care later in pregnancy
Belief in spiritual/social pathology	Poor acceptance of biomedical explanations and interventions
Return of pregnant woman to her mother's home at seven months	Beginning antenatal care at one facility and delivering at another
Labor	
Belief in need for strength	Large meal in early labor
Belief in strong pushing	Pushing before the cervix is fully dilated
Belief in fundal pressure (manual pressure on upper uterus)	Late referral for failure to push out the baby
Lack of vaginal examinations	Late diagnosis of abnormal position of fetus
Postnatal period	
Early traction on the umbilical cord	Detachment of cord and retained placenta
Need to bury placenta secretly	Decision to avoid birthing in a facility (currently unsafe in rural Zimbabwe)
Isolation of mother and infant for one week	Delayed referral for maternal and neonatal problems
Taboo on sex	Reluctance to use birth control
Prolonged lactation	Reluctance to use birth control
Applying preparations to cord stump	Infection in the newborn

Table 3.2   Selected Traditional Beliefs and Practices and Their Potentially Favorable Effects on Pregnancy Outcome

Belief/Practice	Effect
Pregnancy and prenatal period	
View of pregnancy as an extended family event	Encourages involvement of partners and significant others
Return of pregnant woman to her mother's home at seven months	Highlights risks of pregnancy and childbirth
Encouragement of pregnant woman to eat more	Emphasizes nutrition and diet
Labor	
Belief in need for strength	Demonstrates understanding of need for nutrition, which can be provided via small meals in labor
Belief in strong pushing	Encourages squatting during pushing
Postnatal period	
Early traction on the umbilical cord	Can be used to increase awareness of postpartum hemorrhage
Isolation of mother and infant for one week	Can be used to increase awareness of origin of neonatal sepsis and hygienic steps needed for prevention
Taboo on sex	Can be used to promote contraception using the knowledge that the taboo arose from the need to space pregnancies
Prolonged lactation	Can be used to promote contraception using the knowledge that prolonged lactation was used as birth control
Applying preparations to cord stump	Can be used to promote replacement of preparations with detergents

WOMEN'S PARTICIPATION IN CARE

Women's participation in care is critical for their own satisfaction and better health outcomes. Advocates for safe pregnancy and childbirth encourage women in Zimbabwe to attend prenatal care and deliver at a health facility to reduce the risks associated with home delivery. Health-care providers are assumed to offer women a better opportunity to participate in decision-making about their care. But observation shows that some women living in rural areas cannot afford transport to health facilities and maternity fees. They often rely on the expertise of traditional midwives for maternity care. Home birthing has the advantage of occurring in a familiar environment, with the woman and her family participating in decision-making about care. The problem arises when complications occur, such as bleeding from the womb before or after birth of the baby. TBAs are not skilled in managing obstetric and new-born complications; hence home delivery is associated with increased risk of maternal or neonatal death.

Modern obstetric and midwifery care has the potential to involve women in their care based on choices, preferences, and a partnership model. Unfortunately, the critical shortage of modern maternity-care providers in the public health sector results in a "conveyer belt approach" to care. Women are often not consulted about the care they receive, especially during labor and childbirth, because too many women require care at the same time from too few practitioners. The service women receive is provider rather than patient driven. As a result, a woman is more likely to accept care from a TBA whose workload allows time to discuss care and attend to a woman's choices and needs.

This means that traditional pregnancy and childbirth practices offer an environment more conducive to women's comfort and satisfaction than health facilities do. Evidence from a South African study indicates that women trust the knowledge of traditional birth attendants and prefer their care and expertise to the inconsiderate treatment they receive from midwives at health facilities.[11] For women to benefit best, an eclectic model of care drawn from the best practices of both traditional and modern maternity care would be a worthwhile approach. Women's participation in their care gives priority to their wishes and health needs, emphasizes the importance of informed choices, and considers women as equal partners in the planning and delivery of maternity care.[12]

CONCLUSION

There is a worldwide surge in advocacy for safe pregnancy and childbirth. In developing countries, this most often takes the form of advocacy for Western medical approaches. The role of TBAs is being eroded as Western practices of maternity care progressively take over traditional birthing practices. In Zimbabwe, government policy requires every woman to deliver at a health facility where skilled health care is available. But women know so well that skilled care is often unavailable and therefore may make a conscious decision to seek the services of a TBA. This means that traditional birthing knowledge and practices will remain the choice of many women, challenging policy makers to devise maternity-care initiatives that will work best for women and their families. The influence of women's perceptions of pregnancy, traditional beliefs, and health on their choices and decision-making must be understood to enhance collaborative partnerships between traditional and Western birthing knowledge and practices in the provision of maternity care.

Every woman deserves high-quality maternity care at a time of need, and no woman should die giving birth. In order to achieve a significant reduction in maternal and child morbidity and mortality, every woman must have access to skilled attendance at birth and emergency obstetric care if and when pregnancy and childbirth complications occur. As Zimbabwe shifts from traditional to Western birthing practices, we must create collaborative partnerships that learn from both traditional and Western birthing practices for all women to realize their right to a safe pregnancy and childbirth.

PART II

Beyond Medical versus Natural

Redefining Birth Injustice

CHAPTER 4

An Abolitionist Mama Speaks
On Natural Birth and Miscarriage

Viviane Saleh-Hanna

I am a black feminist, the child of Coptic ancestors and Palestinian refugees. I am a criminologist turned abolitionist who for most of her adult life has worked to challenge and dismantle the coercion and exploitation of black communities by colonial institutions of labor, punishment, and surveillance. I see this work as deeply rooted in historic and unfinished struggles to abolish slavery and colonization in Canada,[1] the United States,[2] and the world over.[3] Up until my first pregnancy, my abolitionism had mostly taken place in solidarity with people in prisons in West Africa,[4] Canada,[5] and the United States.[6] With the onset of this new chapter in my life, I found myself face to face with a new site of institutional oppression. In this chapter, I look through a black feminist abolitionist lens at my experiences of pregnancy, miscarriage, and medical violence and share my journey to reclaim my power.

VOICES OF MY ANCESTORS: IN A LOUD NATURAL BIRTH

During my first pregnancy, my baby and I were medically categorized as "high risk." Despite that, I pursued a natural birth. I wanted a birthing experience that was neither determined by chemical interventions and induced paralysis nor reliant upon blind, uncritical submissiveness to medical protocols. I

46

wanted a birth that was as loud or quiet, messy, active or still as it needed to be. I wanted a birth that was not institutionalized and predictable, not conquered or colonized, but instead self-determined and free. I wanted my black child to enter this crazy world on his own terms, in his own time, if he could. I wanted that for him. For myself I wanted to be part of a larger ritual and practice that women have performed for centuries. I wanted to allow my body to do what it needed to do, and I wanted to learn about and experience my own body's potential.

At first I decided to work with a midwife. I called the only midwifery practice I could find in my region. On my first call I spoke to a receptionist who asked me to call back after I was at least eight weeks along: "A lot of women lose the baby before that and we wouldn't want to waste our time." I was shocked by this introduction to midwifery and decided to speak to my obstetrician, a black woman who had birthed her children naturally. She recommended her own midwife, a white woman who worked in the same practice. I met her and several others because in this clinic the on-call midwife would attend my labor. During each consultation, the midwives, who were all white women, wore white doctor's coats and spoke through highly medical frameworks, which made me question whether the move from doctor to midwife would really protect me from an overly medicalized and colonized pregnancy. It was evident that midwifery had been conquered in this setting, but I stayed because I believed that I did not have other options. Early on I made several boundaries very clear: in the clinic and hospital I did not want any men to examine me or to be involved in my reproductive health care, I wanted as little chemical or medical intervention as possible, and I expected to be briefed and included in all decisions.

During my second and third trimesters, one of the midwives consistently pressured me to take the H1N1 flu vaccine. I told her that I had done my own research, learned that this vaccine had never been tested for detrimental effects on pregnant women or unborn babies, and decided against it. She responded, "You're letting your politics make bad decisions for your baby," adding at the end of her tirade, "You're not being a very good mother." After that incident, a few days before I went into preterm labor, I ended all relationships with the midwives in that practice and went back to working only with my obstetrician.

When my water broke, I called my obstetrician's clinic and spoke to her directly. She informed me that she was the doctor on-call that night and would most likely be at the hospital when I arrived. I labored at home for the first few hours until my contractions were a few minutes apart. When I arrived at the hospital, I heard my obstetrician's voice behind curtains giving instructions to nurses and residents, but I never saw her, and she never spoke to me directly. In the meantime, residents casually approached me with needles and IVs, saying, "This will help move things along." I responded, "No, thank you," and insisted that I would only take drugs if they were necessary to save my or my baby's life. I had to fight for a natural birth in that hospital, and I won. I was prepared because the fight began long before I went into labor. The majority of friends and family members who learned that I was pursuing a natural birth mocked me, jeering, "Wait until the pain starts. You'll be begging for drugs." They were wrong. The possibility of being immobilized on a hospital bed nauseated me. Allowing latex-covered hands to insert a large needle into my spine to squirt chemicals that would paralyze me from the waist down seemed worse than any labor pain I would endure.

I went into labor during the devastating 2010 earthquake in Haiti, and throughout the night I kept all the women who were laboring through unsafe and dangerous conditions in my heart. Due to my categorization as "high risk," the hospital staff would not allow me access to the hospital's Alternative Birthing Center. I maintained autonomy and continued to reject unneeded "assistance" well into my labor. The hospital staff gave up on trying to intervene or even communicate with me. They eventually brought in a nurse from the Alternative Birthing Center who was trained to assist in natural births. They informed me she could stay with me as long as another woman pursuing natural labor did not come to the Alternative Birthing Center. She stayed with me throughout the duration of my labor, and she was wonderful. Music and hot showers sustained and carried me through labor. I had composed a playlist that played a random selection of Coptic hymns, classical Egyptian music, Palestinian and black hip-hop, soul, R&B, folk, West African Afrobeat, and Jamaican reggae. We played the music on a small stereo and asked to be left alone. My memory of my first labor is musical: drums, strong voices for liberation and rap during intense contractions, gentle a cappella and hymns in between.

> I'm a African, I'm a African, never was a African American
> Blacker than Black I take it back to my origin
> same skin hated by the klansmen
> big nose and lips, big hips and butts dancin'

by dead prez was playing when I entered the "ring of fire," that transitional moment in labor that feels like you have entered a new dimension somewhere between worlds.[7] In retrospect I wonder how the all-white hospital staff who came in and out of my room felt about Peter Tosh's call, "Arise Black man arise! Arise and know thyself,"[8] or Nina Simone's declaration that

> There's a million boys and girls
> Who are young, gifted and Black!
> And that's a fact.[9]

The significance of this music in that setting was not lost on me. I was inside the belly of the beast in my most vulnerable state. The violence that the medical industry has inflicted upon black and colonized women's bodies was in the forefront of my mind as I walked through the hospital's mechanical doors that night.[10] My music was a shield, with artists like Spiritchild reminding me,

> We cried for peace, you would not listen
> so now we walk with ammunition
> I'm for peace but soldier listen
> I will not see another victim of
> your democracy
> your insanity
> your child brutality
> your inhumanity
> your corporate policy
> my philosophy
> rid the world of your system.[11]

I felt accompanied by the music and hymns throughout labor. When it was time to start pushing, Leonard Cohen's "The Great Event" announced, "It's going to happen very soon" and reminded me of "the majesty of creation."[12] When my son entered this world, Faith Nolan was singing,

> Well we're livin' in one world
> And we're breathin' the same air
> Water's for us all
> Like the food everywhere
> And we all have a right to our share.[13]

After sixteen hours of labor, Biko Ajani was born. The sun was setting, and the entire room had taken on the orange and pink hues that bathe the start and end of each day. The doctor did not reach us in time. She was putting her gloves on when Biko was born. Ashanti, his father, caught him, was the first to hold him in this world, the first to hand him to me. Biko had one eye wide open and a dimple on his cheek. Peter Tosh's live acoustic performance of "Get Up Stand Up" played while the doctor patched me up, and as she stepped away, the playlist ended.[14] Ashanti and I sat in silence with a brand new life in our arms. It felt as if the ancestors had spoken to me through our people's music, carried me through labor, and "moved us along" without the labor-inducing drug Pitocin. My son was born free of chemical interference and on his and my own terms. For just one moment, his first moment on this earth, we had achieved self-determination.

THE SILENT MISCARRIAGE

When I got pregnant two years later, I uncritically followed the protocol of secrecy. Almost all pregnant women in the West have been warned, "Wait for the first trimester to end before announcing your pregnancy, *just in case* something happens." I did not seriously consider the implications of these words until "something" did happen. My worst nightmare became a reality toward the end of my first trimester, when it became clear that I was having a miscarriage. I entered into immense grief that I had to hide, while continuing life as if nothing happened, because as far as the majority of people in my life were concerned, nothing had.

It was the spring term, and in my classes at a local university, I had assigned *Beloved* by Toni Morrison[15] and *Kindred* by Octavia Butler.[16] Both books depict the racialized violence of birth injustice and trauma and the significance of kinship in identity formation. We were also learning about historic memory and Middle Passage trauma[17] and black women's historic and ongoing struggles against medical violence and sterilization.[18] I asked my students to reflect upon the concept of social death and the blurred boundaries between life and death under slavery;[19] after all, *Beloved* is a book inspired by the life of Margaret Garner, an enslaved African who killed her daughter to save her from white supremacist–patriarchal violence. As I challenged my students to confront patriarchy's racist conquest of our bodies, I carried my own silent shame and my perceived failure to carry this pregnancy to term. The strength I eventually found to cope with my miscarriage came from the knowledge I had gained through Biko's birth. My labor with him had instilled in me an ability to listen to my body and to trust it, despite the devastation of miscarriage. I was backed by an abolitionist rejection of authoritative domination and a black feminist endurance despite patriarchy, and these foundations helped me find the words I needed. My miscarriage allowed me to hear the unbearable, at times deafening silence that surrounds this issue.

I came into this miscarriage knowing that I needed to pursue a natural process. When my bleeding started, I tried to get a doctor's appointment to find out what was wrong. My doctor (the same obstetrician) postponed my appointment twice and eventually left town for a short vacation, so I had to consult with a new physician from her practice. I knew that something was wrong, but no one believed me. They claimed that it could not be a miscarriage because I was not describing physically painful cramps.

When I finally got an appointment, I waited almost two hours before being seen. Despite intense emotions, I maintained a stone-faced silence that was becoming the theme of this miscarriage. The nurse who brought me to the examination room said, "He will be right in. Get undressed. We have you scheduled for a pap smear." I asked why I had to see a male obstetrician and if I really needed a pap smear. She responded, "That's who is available, and according to our records, you are due for a pap smear." I asked if they knew I was pregnant and bleeding. She responded yes.

I walked out and fought with the receptionist about refunding my copay because, damn it, that was the only thing I could get back from this day. As things got progressively worse, I went to the emergency room. An ultrasound revealed that my embryo was less developed than it should be for that stage of pregnancy. I was told that either everything was fine and I was a few weeks off on the actual date of conception, or the embryo was "never healthy" and is now "dead" inside me. The words "never healthy" and the way the doctor's voice sounded when she said "dead" still resonate in my head as I write this. I paid my $100 deductible and went home devastated.

I finally started to seek alternative care. With my family doctor's assistance, I found an obstetrician whose philosophy of health and health care was compatible with mine. She ordered blood tests and within a few days confirmed that my pregnancy hormone was decreasing rapidly. I was without a doubt having a miscarriage. The entire process, from the first signs of trouble through the end, took seven weeks. It was finally time to say good-bye to my vision of the baby I had imagined from the moment I learned about my pregnancy. When it was finally over, I was simultaneously relieved and devastated.

Reflecting on my miscarriage for seven weeks brought to the surface deep-rooted fears of loss. As an African and Palestinian woman, I carry heaviness, a fear of loss of loved ones intensified by my inability to find "home." I have wandered from city to city and continent to continent for the majority of my adult life. I was surprised at how much I thought about the loss of Palestine during my miscarriage. I was grieving the loss of a potential, a life I had never met or known, yet one that was mine, was within me, was a part of me. I have never been to occupied Palestine, and I found myself unexpectedly confronting the impact of that loss of family, land, and life during my miscarriage.

SPEAK UP: SOUNDING OUT THE SILENT VOICE OF MISCARRIAGE

In US society, patriarchal pressures accompany womanhood. Central is the pressure to produce babies. When we do have babies, so many mindlessly ask, "When are you going to have another one?" The prominence of this question was highlighted during my miscarriage. One day, a neighbor sitting on her porch across the street was chatting with me as I sat on my second-floor balcony.

"So," she asked loudly, "are you planning on having more kids anytime soon?"

I shouted back across the street, "I had hoped to have one on the way but am going through a miscarriage, so ..."

She looked at me with large eyes and an awkward silence. I thought, Much better. Finally I'm not the one being quiet. For the rest of my miscarriage,

I responded in this way every time someone asked me that question. I had filled the silence with word and truth, and it was liberating.

The more I spoke about my miscarriage with women in my life, the more I learned that many of them had endured at least one. Most amazing was the openness with which so many talked about their miscarriages once I shared my own. When it was out in the open, miscarriage became a part of life. Many of my friends had undergone medical procedures to speed up their miscarriage, and I understand their need for it to end quickly. We each had our own journeys and philosophies, and being able to share all of that was empowering.

"Wade in the Water, Children"

Very shortly after my miscarriage, I got pregnant. I was simultaneously excited and cautiously terrified: I could not endure another loss. I decided to break the code of silence by telling my family and friends about my pregnancy from an early date. The response I got from some regarding such open disclosure was ridden with shame. People expressed anger, one asking with annoyance, "What if you have another miscarriage? Then what are you going to do?" Some did not speak to me for months after learning that I was not respecting the code of first-trimester secrecy. These same people were appalled to learn that I had spoken openly about my miscarriage. The process was very tense and full of resentments that I had not expected.

My third pregnancy concluded with natural labor, despite being classified "high risk" again. Although I found a gentle, attentive, and caring doctor who respected my autonomy and birthing desires, her colleagues did not always understand why I made certain decisions. A handful of residents and interns acted entitled to access my body as an educational tool. They appeared confused, even outraged, when I made any decisions at all about access and my care. One of the residents spoke about me in derogatory ways while examining me and assumed I would not understand her technical jargon. Unfortunately, she was on call the night I went into labor.

When I arrived at the hospital, that resident insisted on performing a vaginal exam before calling my doctor. I told her I was not comfortable with *her* doing it. In the midst of contractions, the last thing I wanted to endure was a vaginal exam performed by this woman. Despite the misogynistic imagery of laboring women as comically angry and unreasonable, the reality is that we are extremely vulnerable. She took advantage of this vulnerability by insisting that I had no choice but to consent to her examination if she was going to call my doctor at all that night. I unwillingly "consented," and the experience was horrible. The pain I felt during her examination was excruciating. When I told her she had induced very painful contractions, she responded with a chuckle, "You should be grateful I'm helping move you along." I felt violated, as if I were being hazed into accessing my doctor. I was also jarred into the memory of my first labor, when doctors and nurses insisted that I needed assistance "moving along" in labor. I had experienced natural birth, survived a natural miscarriage, and reflected on the fragility of life and the realities of loss. The irony and the relationship between forced migrations and this need of Western medical professionals to "move us" and our babies "along" were not lost on me.

In all I had thirteen hours of natural labor with a baby who was posterior: face up instead of face down. When a baby enters the birth canal in this position, labor is typically extremely difficult due to the intense back pain and closely spaced contractions it causes. I had about seven hours of closely spaced and sometimes overlapping contractions. I did not experience back pain because my daughter was born in the caul: she came down my birth canal and entered this world with her water bag intact. The water cushioned us and shielded me from back labor. I was not able to carry my baby to term due to pregnancy complications. My doula, Gina, helped me pursue natural induction. Had my doctor broken my water to induce labor, as we had considered doing the week before, I do not believe that I would have been able to achieve a natural birth.

I had been pushing for about forty-five minutes when the doctor told me that she could not find my baby's heartbeat. I did not panic because I could feel the baby moving and knew that she had to have a heartbeat to be active. The doctor informed me that if the baby did not make it through the birth canal soon, she would have to insert a screw into the baby's head to monitor her heart. I was petrified as images of people entering the room with a drill, putting it inside me, and blowing through my precious baby's head entered my mind. With Ashanti and Gina holding me, I pushed so hard that Yasmeen Grace literally burst out of me. My husband explained that first they saw a water bag, then our daughter's head full of hair inside the sac: I pushed so hard after that, she burst through the sac, and it was all the doctor could do to put her hands out to direct the flying baby toward me. She came soaring into my arms while Sweet Honey in the Rock revived black resistance in their rendition of the amazing Underground Railroad song:

Wade in the water
Wade in the water, Children
Wade in the water.[20]

My experiences of birthing my children and surviving a miscarriage have been among the most significant in my life. I have witnessed firsthand the power and potential of our minds and bodies and have acquired a better understanding of how white supremacy is inseparable from patriarchy and why these systems of oppression encourage women to stay removed from experiences that would allow us to encounter our true strength and resiliency. Coming into motherhood as a black-feminist-abolitionist allowed me to consider options for birthing and miscarriage that went beyond the expected protocols of dominant institutions. Through these perspectives motherhood has empowered me to think even more critically about the ways we are supposed to behave. That midwife was wrong; my politics had not made me a "bad mother." My understandings of this world have strengthened me, allowed me to consider anticolonial options for birthing and miscarriage, and enabled me to build stronger sisterhoods along the way.

CHAPTER 5

Mothering

A Post-C-Section Journey

Jacinda Townsend

My older daughter and I are at Bloomington Hospital. In radiology. Radiology has a huge saltwater aquarium, laminate wood flooring, and CNN on the wide-screen television. It's all quite calming. This is because if you're in radiology, something's likely gone wrong: something is inside you that should not be. A piece of glass is embedded in my right foot. It's been there for weeks, ever since I accidentally stepped on a large shard of picture glass under my bed. I pulled the largest piece out myself, but I'm told that sometimes, smaller pieces break off in the flesh. They hang out. They cause problems. Still, I've preferred to walk with a limp, engaging in the hope that the glass will somehow magically work itself out of my foot. Why? I fear hospitals. I don't trust physicians. I deeply loathe the medical establishment. "Hug me," I tell my daughter. She's eight. "I'm afraid of hospitals."

I wasn't always a person who shrieked at the sight of a tongue depressor. Until my daughters' births, I was bold—ballsy, even. The slicing of skin didn't scare me. I endured dental procedures with no Novocain. After two traumatic, unwanted cesarean sections, though, I've come to see hospitals as places where the unexpected can happen on the turn of a dime, places where callous medical professionals order procedures simply so they can line their pockets, places where vibrant life can quickly turn into death. I limped around on my injured foot until a friend of mine said, "This is unacceptable." Bless

55

her heart, she didn't send me to a doctor: she referred me straight to radiology. This friend, whom I trust absolutely, will look at the X-ray herself.

My daughter hugs me. It's a moment of normalcy between us. I'm reminded, at such moments, of all the years when every single act of my parenting was tinged with the feeling of having failed my daughter from the first instant of her life. I wonder, as I often do, whether as long as you carry the memory of living an event, you ever really get past having lived it.

*****

Four years before I became pregnant with my first child, I spent a weekend at The Farm in Summertown, Tennessee. The Farm is one of the longest-standing intentional communities in the United States. In 1971, a caravan of brightly painted school buses and Volkswagen vans left San Francisco and crossed the country to settle there. When I visited in 1999, some of these original buses were still there, resting amid the pristine pines and grasses of The Farm. The Farm is home to the legacy of Ina May Gaskin, a mother of modern midwifery. "Birth is a holy sacrament that belongs to the family," reads a page on The Farm's website. "Birth is a natural process best performed at home surrounded by family and supportive midwives." Ina May's daughter-in-law, helping her daughter lodge her feet on her chair and turn a flip, said to me, "By not letting women push their own children into the world, we're depriving them of their power."

It wasn't a new idea to me. My mother, a ferocious caregiver and a fierce advocate for her children, had told me that she felt at her most powerful when she gave birth. Despite being a black single mother in a racist community in rural Kentucky, she sent one child to Harvard at age sixteen and another to Stanford at age seventeen. She always asserted that much of her mama bear instinct, her courage to divorce my father, and her will to take on a system that was stacked against her as a mother came from the moment of my birth. "You'll see," she told me. "After you go through all that pain and pushing, you turn into something else altogether."

*****

I became pregnant in 2003 and almost instantly fell ill with an intense nausea that was with me all day, every day, for the entire nine months. I had other, more painful complications, including a necrotizing fibroid that sent me into contractions during my sixth month, and by the time I went to the hospital to give birth, I was worn out. Ready for my pregnancy—which a close friend had called "the absolute shits"—to be over. Ready to push my child into the world.

I found a doula in Springfield, Missouri, where I was likely to give birth. I attended natural childbirth classes in Wisconsin, where I lived. I read book after book and website after website about the process and signed all the forms saying I didn't want an epidural.

Here's what I knew: I didn't want my child to be exposed to the toxins flowing through an epidural. I didn't want my daughter to be weighed down with drugged grogginess during her first moments in this life. I wanted to experience the joy and self-fulfillment of pushing my child into the world. I wanted to feel and be present for each moment. I wanted to meet my daughter immediately. I wanted to hold her. I wanted to breastfeed her. I wanted to smell her. I wanted to sing to her. I wanted to say, "Hello, baby. Welcome to the world."

Here's what I didn't know: The World Health Organization recommends that C-sections should occur in no more than 15 percent of births.[1] In this country, C-sections are given to a third of laboring women. Often, they are forced on those women (which technically makes them assaults). C-section rates differ from hospital to hospital, they differ among obstetric practices (and they usually differ among physicians in the same obstetric practice), and they differ among regions of the country. When I called later to find out what the epidural rate was at the hospital where I gave birth for the first time, I was stunned to find that it was well over 90 percent: as the nurse told me on the phone, "If you make it to this hospital before dropping the baby out, you're just going to get an epidural."

And this is what happened to me, there in Missouri, far from the birth balls and walking walls I'd taken for granted while touring the progressive maternity ward in the hospital in Madison, Wisconsin. I moved to Springfield a week before giving birth, and I didn't know that my doula did not have a very high natural birth success rate. Early on in my twenty-seven hours of labor, when things were going well, I asked if I could have my ECG monitor removed so that I could walk freely and help my labor along. "No," said the rather unfriendly nurse on duty. And to my doula, she said, "Make sure that woman gets an epidural." My doula nodded. My heart sank.

I resisted an epidural for the first day of my labor, and only when my cervix dilated from four to eight centimeters over the course of a couple of hours, when the doctors in attendance said I would be ready to push in short order, did I agree to an epidural. I was worn out by then, almost semiconscious. My doula and my husband had listened to me moan in pain. They'd watched me sob and vomit bile. After a day of this, both were happy for me to have an epidural.

What did this magical epidural do? It stopped my labor. Altogether. That epidural became the anesthesia I'd need to undergo an emergency C-section. My daughter was removed from me not long thereafter. I didn't get to see her for hours. When I did, it was painful to have her lying on my chest, so close to where I'd been sliced open. I couldn't even hold her, so it was a good thing that she was asleep and I was completely unable to move. We both just lay there while I hummed to her. I couldn't sing. It would have hurt too badly.

*****

Five years later, I found myself pregnant with my second daughter in the same kind of rural, conservative community where I'd given birth to my first. The last practicing midwife at the hospital had just had her privileges revoked after a dispute with a doctor over her advocacy during a birth. Only one practice in my health insurer's network did vaginal birth after C-section (VBAC). A colleague recommended one of the doctors, the only woman, in that practice.

My second pregnancy was no less difficult than the first. Nine more months of persistent nausea and grotesquely swollen feet from the fifth month. I had another necrotizing fibroid that caused me to cut short a vacation in Brazil during my eighth month and suffered numerous other discomforts. Emotionally, the pregnancy was also difficult—it was happening during the revision of my debut novel and in the middle of a divorce. Once again, I found myself eager to push the child out into the world so that my body could return to normal. When I interviewed my obstetrician about VBACs, she seemed genuinely supportive. I never thought to ask her how many VBACs she'd actually done in recent years.

As I approached my thirty-eighth and then my thirty-ninth week of pregnancy, my obstetrician's support for my VBAC waned. "She's breech," she said of my daughter. My other daughter had been breech, I told her, until the fortieth week, when she responded to my putting headphones across my abdomen and turned around beautifully. I expected this little music lover to do the same. Still, the obstetrician scheduled me for a C-section. "It has to be on a Thursday," she told me. "I only do these on Thursdays." And she scheduled the surgery for September 3, a few days after my due date.

The contractions I had at the end of my first pregnancy had been induced. They hadn't started coming until I'd had my cervix chemically ripened, almost two weeks after my initial due date. At the end of my second pregnancy, however, my body began to remember what it had done the first time. It got into place earlier, this wonderful body of mine, and it did things fast and furiously. The second time, I began having contractions in week thirty-nine. They went on for days, until they were only three minutes apart. Still, I didn't instinctually feel that I was about to give birth. I avoided the hospital and I avoided my obstetrician because I knew that a slow laborer seeking a VBAC didn't belong anywhere near a hospital.

My contractions became more intensely painful and frequent on September 2. I knew that my regular obstetrician didn't do rounds on Wednesdays, and I knew by then that the other doctors were more supportive of my VBAC plans. "I'll wait for that baby," one of them said. "I'm not sure Schneider will." My then husband and five-year-old daughter had already packed up the house and moved to Iowa, where I was going to spend my maternity leave, so my mother drove me to the hospital. My mother had missed the first child's birth and was looking forward to being a part of this delivery. She knew how depressed I'd been after my first failed attempt, and because she will never stop being a mama bear, she wanted to help me succeed this time around. She wheeled me onto the elevator and up to the maternity ward nurse's station. The first thing the on-duty nurse said was, "Oh. You're scheduled for a C-section?"

"No," I told her. "I'm going to give birth."

*****

According to *Child Health USA 2013,* one in every three babies in the United States—32.8 percent—was delivered surgically as of 2012.[2] Between 1996 and 2009, the C-section rate rose by 60 percent.[3] Accepting these statistics as anything other than troubling means accepting the notion that somehow many of us have evolved into creatures that can no longer deliver babies through the natural processes of our own bodies. It also means accepting the idea that black women in particular have lost the ability to give birth naturally: in 2008, black women had more C-sections than any other group (34.5 percent, compared to 32 percent of white women and 31 percent of Latinas). These disparities are sometimes explained away by pointing to black women's alleged poor diet and health, leading to more at-risk pregnancies. However, even among low-risk first births, a 2005 study showed that black women had a better chance of having a C-section.

*****

My obstetrician wasn't making rounds September 2, but she was there, dressed to the nines under her white coat at 6 a.m. After examining me and determining that my cervix hadn't dilated, she kept me there on the grounds that my feet were swollen. My feet had been swollen for months, but she said we had to do a twenty-four-hour protein test for preeclampsia. When that test came back negative, my obstetrician said she had to keep me another twenty-four hours because my blood pressure was elevated. I resisted the urge to laugh out loud. My five-year-old was seven hours away from me, in Iowa, starting kindergarten. My mother had misplaced my house keys. My obstetrician was clearly trying to slice me open. *Of course my blood pressure was elevated.* Nonetheless, at the end of that twenty-four hours, I had managed to watch enough mindless television and drink enough water to lower my blood pressure. I had also lost my mucous plug, and during the course of a stress test, my daughter had actually tried to take a breath, revealing that she was in no fetal distress whatsoever. We were nowhere near two weeks after my due date, and my body was working beautifully. My daughter was doing beautifully. Things were working.

My obstetrician had an external fetal monitor on me during those forty-eight interminable hours, and my daughter's heart rate had been miraculously steady. Shortly before I was to be dismissed from the hospital, however, my doctor brought in a chart showing that it had done one deceleration. One deceleration. One. "You keep throwing things at me," she said, though it was clear that she was the one throwing things at me. This one was going to stick, unfortunately, because when she said she'd have to keep me in the hospital until I actually gave birth, I lost all resolve. There was simply too much mindless television, too much soulless food. When told that I wasn't going to be on the C-section schedule that day, the anesthesiologist came to try to talk me into having the surgery. When I said no, he sat there, at the foot of my bed, crossed his arms, and simply stared at me. This strengthened my resolve momentarily, but when he left, practicality won me over. The sweet little daughter I'd already met was away, in kindergarten, and because I'd had to drop her off for her first day of school and then drive back down to Illinois, I hadn't even gotten to talk to her teacher. "Fine," I said, and I called my husband, who immediately loaded my daughter in the car and drove the seven hours down to Illinois so he could be present for the surgery.

I remained angry during the surgery. I was hostile to my obstetrician when asked questions, hostile to the anesthesiologist who'd come to my hospital room to intimidate me. Even as my precious, beloved daughter was being surgically removed from my body, I felt an overpowering aura of hostility. I felt love only at the moment I heard my daughter cry for the first time. I felt a tear running down my cheek, but then I realized that, mid-surgery, I couldn't even wipe it myself.

*****

Before my second daughter's birth, I had asked to have my tubes tied in the event I needed to have a C-section, because my pregnancy had been so awful. But in the moment, I was so angry at the medical staff that I had a hard time saying yes when they asked me about it. They would profit from my decision, after all. Doctors have come to manage the process of giving birth for their own financial gain and convenience.

"Your body's just not going to do this," my obstetrician had told me during the twenty-four-hour protein test, even as I was telling her about my lost mucous plug. What she meant was that my body wasn't going to do it on her timetable. She needed for my body to do it—or not do it—on a Thursday.

Health insurers pay an average of $18,329 for vaginal births and $27,866 for cesareans, while Medicaid pays $29,800 and $50,373, respectively.[4] Since the attending doctor is often paid according to the type of delivery, there is a huge incentive for doctors to find reasons to perform these surgeries.[5] My tubal ligation would just be gravy for her.

*****

My husband at the time of my second daughter's birth was abusive. Not in the dumb way of men who punch their wives' teeth out but in the smart way of dishing out abuse with a huge psychological component. As he drove me home from the hospital after our daughter's second birth, we got into a fight about our pending divorce. He screamed and cursed at me. As I watched our sweet little daughter sleep through it, I felt at once a sense of cognitive dissonance that this was happening on her first ride home and relief that she couldn't hear it. When I asked him to stop, he began driving faster, accelerating at speed bumps. I was in so much pain already. I started sobbing. "I can't believe you're doing this to another human being," I told him through tears. I've often wondered if he knew just how deeply he cut into my psyche. His abuse added another layer of pain and anger to my already traumatic birth experience.

As I drove to Iowa a few days later, in pain because I had cut my Vicodin dose in half so that I could stay awake for the drive, and as I hobbled up the stairs of my house to try to comfort my crying newborn, I wondered what kind of carefree life my obstetrician was living with her own two children at the expense of the birthing women she treated like commodities.

My obstetrician, as it turned out, lived a quarter of a mile down the road from me. We were distant neighbors in this way for the eighteen months I continued to live in Illinois: every time I drove my children to school, I caught a glimpse of her house. In the winter, when the trees were bare, I caught a better glimpse of her house. I eventually had to make myself stop looking. But what I'd already seen was the pool and the construction work on the nice brick terrace with built-in recessed lighting that surrounded it. When that terrace was finished, I wondered how much of the profits from my own C-section had gone toward her beautiful backyard. How many bricks she'd put into that terrace when she sliced into my abdomen.

*****

The first time I gave birth, I did not feel that I had actually become a mother. For a long time, I did not feel that way. For the first few years of my first daughter's life, I was very timid about my parenting and open to advice even when I knew it was wrong. "You should start her with jarred fruit," they adamantly told me at day care when I sent her with Gerber's spinach, and I let them give her their own jars of peaches, even though I'd read widely that babies should be started on vegetables in order to lessen their risk for childhood obesity. I let teachers and even other parents talk me into anything. I was pretending to be my daughter's mother, waiting for her real mother to show up and take over. I felt that I'd failed her in the most important moment possible—that ultimate moment of her entrance into the world—and that I was therefore doomed to be an inadequate mother in the moments that followed.

Gradually, I began to change. First came small moments of advocacy, tiny moments of mama bear. I removed her from a preschool when I felt that things weren't going well. I confronted children who weren't playing nicely with her on the playground, children whose parents were sitting nearby, allowing their own sons and daughters to behave badly. I doggedly pursued a diagnosis of gluten intolerance when I suspected it but no doctor would believe me. Finally, I accepted that somehow, somewhere along the way, I had become, quite solidly, two girls' mother.

*****

My daughter and I hold hands on the way out of radiology. My friend hasn't seen the X-ray; I don't know, just yet, what is in my body that's not supposed to be there. But it's a warm spring day, and my eight-year-old is somehow, impossibly, as high as my shoulder. She's just tested into the city's gifted program and received praise from her cello teacher. We're on our way to pick up her three-year-old sister, who is already reading like a pro, who is as funny as any comedian, and who is also thriving.

On days like these, days when I know that my children are happy and healthy, I almost forget how they came into this world. And I realize that some of us become mothers not at the moment of birth but in the treasured moments of love that follow.

CHAPTER 6

Confessions of a Black Pregnant Dad

Syrus Marcus Ware

Last weekend I gave a talk to a group of Lesbian, Gay, Bisexual, Transgender, Transsexual, Intersexed, Two Spirited, Queer, and Questioning (LGBT-TI2QQ) would-be parents. The group was diverse and included several trans parents-to-be. As I sat among them describing how we started our family, I was struck by how much has changed since we began our process. Our family journey began during a time with few resources for racialized trans parents; yet only a few years later, I was speaking to an entire classroom full of people and preparing to write a chapter about my experience as a black trans man. In 2009, I published an essay about my experience as a trans man considering getting pregnant.[1] Since I wrote that piece, a lot has happened to advance the public's understanding of trans parenting. When I first began writing, there were few resources about trans parenting: few films, few articles, and very few resources for prospective trans parents. For instance, in 2006–2007, when we were working on a new course for trans would-be dads, there was so little information generally available that we had to call doctors and surgeons and seek out trans dads and trans-friendly midwifery practices across the continent.

We first taught the course during the year that the sensationalist media pounced on the story of a pregnant dad named Thomas Beatie—thereafter referred to by most media outlets as "the Pregnant Man." This kind of sensationalist reporting about trans issues was not new, and neither was the framing of "pregnant" and "man" as mutually exclusive. But the rendering of Beatie's experience as unimaginable, his body as unintelligible, and his life as impossible was a refocusing of transphobia, heteronormativity, and sexism into an intense warning to all other past and future trans dads. We had begun working on our course about a year before Beatie's story broke, and as we started the first run of the curriculum, it felt all the more vital following this harsh sensationalization of trans parenthood. In a way, this also pushed me to write about my experience of being a dad who gave birth. Our stories are often untold, yet likely much more plentiful than previously imagined. Since 2009, several brave masculine-identified butches and trans guys have come forward with their stories and shared their experiences with the world.[2] Several films and anthologies have been created about trans parenting.[3] On a more personal note, my partner and I became parents—I carried our child—and we found ourselves in a small community of trans parents.

In a world with so few other pregnant and parenting trans men to act as role models, our journey entailed a million unknowns. We anticipated that being trans dads would be a huge hurdle on our road to parenthood and therefore prepared by planning how we would deal with transphobia and gender expectations. In the end, our experiences of racialization as black men raising a baby who reads as white to many has been by far one of our biggest sources of external curiosity and often frustration. What follows is a consideration of the personal and political, a contemplation of gender, parenting, and the many other things that come up when parenting outside gender- and race-based expectations.

INSEMINATION, OR "YOU ARE GOING TO STICK WHAT IN WHERE?"

My partner and I both wanted children and felt ready to become parents—as ready as you can be! We carefully weighed out our options for starting a family—fostering, adoption, using a gestational carrier, and getting pregnant. I realized that I wanted to try to get pregnant. As a trans guy, I did not feel conflicted about the idea of being pregnant and a man; in fact, I had been curious about pregnancy for a while. Once this was decided, we had another series of questions to answer: Would we use a known or unknown donor? Would we go to a fertility clinic? Would we try to do it at home? It seemed like an endless series of choices. Of course, choices are tied to many things: financial resources for buying sperm and paying for insemination at a clinic, personal connections with folks who have sperm, access to legal advice for crafting known-donor contracts, and so on. We had access to some but not all of these things. In the end, we decided to borrow some money and try the clinic route. We lovingly referred to the reproductive endocrinologist at the clinic as Dr. Baby Maker. The following is an account of our first appointment.

A few months ago we had our first appointment with Dr. Baby Maker at the Baby Making Clinic (BMC). A week before the appointment, a nurse at the clinic that referred us to the BMC called us to let us know that our application had been red-flagged. The query: "How could two men be in need of insemination?" I'm not sure why I was surprised by this; fertility clinics are still very gender-specific places where men produce sperm and women carry babies, despite the reality that in this world this is only true some of the time. I wondered if the clinic would be prepared to help a trans woman with sperm immobility to successfully get her trans male partner pregnant despite his ovarian cysts. Perhaps, perhaps not … I worried that this early interruption in the process might be a warning sign for future complications with the clinic, but Nik and I bravely decided to continue on and give the BMC another shot. Thankfully, the nurse who referred us did some previsit advocacy on our behalf. In addition, shortly after we began at the BMC, a group of queer parenting advocates did some great trans-specific training with the clinic staff to help get them ready and up to speed to provide excellent care to their future trans clients. The clinic welcomed us and set our first appointment date for early spring 2008.

We went to our first appointment at the BMC full of anxiety and excitement. What could we expect? How long would it take? Would they call me "she"? Would I be recognized as the father, along with Nik? And, perhaps most pressing, would they have to (eep!) probe me? I had already decided that I was willing to put up with a certain level of confusion or misinformation about trans bodies if it would help us reach our goal: to get pregnant with our baby. Yet, as we sat in the waiting room, I wondered if I would be able to handle being "she'd" or having a frank discussion about my "ovaries" or menstrual cycles with a doctor. I felt confident that despite wanting to be pregnant, I was definitely still a man. I worried about the staff's ability to recognize and respect my beliefs. I believed that as a man about to carry our child, I had a lot to offer our child in terms of questioning gender rigidity in our society and teaching the world about alternative ways of parenting. Perhaps it was this hope that got me through that time in the waiting room, unsure what to expect.

The previsit advocacy clearly worked, because during the ultrasound, the technician asked me which washroom I would prefer to use. I explained that I used the men's washroom. She led me through a back door to the hallway by the elevator. "This is the only men's washroom on the floor," she said apologetically, as she led me through the twists and turns. "We don't have too many men getting ultrasounds in this clinic." This seemed like an extreme understatement. I would guess that I was one of the first men ever to be a client in that part of the clinic.

PREGNANT MAN CLAIMS HE IS A PREGNANT MAN

My second encounter with the BMC was later in the spring of 2008, a few weeks after Thomas Beatie burst onto the global scene with his story of insemination and pregnancy, becoming widely known as "the world's first pregnant man." Of course, there have been other pregnant trans guys before Beatie, but his decision to share his story brought to light the reality of male pregnancy for many people for the first time. Media headlines exclaimed, "The Pregnant Man: Is This a Hoax?" and "Man Claims He Is Pregnant"—as if this was clearly an impossible and preposterous idea. Even Oprah got in the mix with a long interview with Beatie. I suppose it is a mark of some progress that the headlines questioned the pregnancy rather than the fact that Beatie was a man. My experience of pregnancy was very much reflective of this. My being pregnant seemed to call into question my gender identity and my preferred pronoun not only among strangers, which was perhaps understandable, but also, surprisingly, among those closest to me. The idea that pregnancy is an experience exclusive to women is reinforced over and over in the media, the classroom, and everyday conversation. In fact, not all people who identify as women can get pregnant, and many people who do not identify as women can. To return to the media headlines, it is worth considering the fact that the media questioned whether Beatie was pregnant rather than accepting his pregnancy and then questioning his gender.

Absent from much of the reporting about Beatie was any discussion of race or his experience of racialization. I feel this is indicative of the ways that racialized LGBTTI2QQ people are often forced to separate out our experiences rather than being able to talk about the interconnected and multiple identities that make up who we are. I'm not suggesting that Beatie had much say in the reporting about his pregnancy or about the initial telling of his story. The media homed in on his trans identity and used this as the hook to sell a sensationalized version of his story. He went on to write an autobiography, perhaps in part to reclaim control of the telling of his story.[4] I read his book because I wanted to understand more about his experience as a mixed-race person. Beatie doesn't talk too much about his own experience of race-based thinking and racialization in the book.[5] This omission left me feeling that a crucial part of this discussion about trans parenting was missing. My experience of being a trans parent is intimately connected to my experience of being a racialized parent and a parent of a mixed-race child. I'm not suggesting that Beatie should have to talk about his experience of racialization because he is in a racialized body—far too often racialized folks are expected to talk about race as always already central to our experiences of the world. I am not trying to replicate this process. However, as a reader, I was looking for some reflection of—or contrast to—my own experience.

I am not alone in noting this absence. Mitsuru Mitsuru, a guest writer for the online publication *Racialicious,* writes about this omission in a review of Beatie's book: "So I heard a while ago that celeb transman Thomas Beatie is a mixie much like myself. He too has a white mama, an Asian daddy, and originally, an Asian surname. He too was born with all the plumbing to make and be pregnant with a baby. And like me, he too made the decision to get folks to recognize him as male."[6] Like Mitsuru, I identify as a mixed-race trans man, and like Beatie, I chose to get "pregnant with a baby." And I too wanted to find more connection on all of these grounds with Beatie—with someone (anyone?) else who might share the experience of being of color, trans, and a parent. I yearned for this because in the end, my family's experience of racialization has affected our daily interactions with the public much more than gender.

Our child has very light brown skin and blue eyes—blue, the color of my grandfather's eyes. Strangers ask us, "Why are her eyes blue?" while we are in line at the supermarket. They say, "Wow, she sure is a different color than you," when we are trying to get our stroller onto the bus. They question, "Where are her parents?" when we are feeding her in the park. Although this doesn't happen in every interaction with people outside our family, it happens with such alarming frequency that it seems to me that it has become a weekly, if not daily, occurrence. It's funny how much we prepared for the potential transphobia that could threaten our future family. I spent so much time trying to be prepared for being a pregnant man and then a trans dad. I didn't think to prepare for being a black man raising a baby who reads to many as white. I wanted to be ready for those who would challenge our family because of the fact that Nik and I are trans guys. Instead, it turns out that not much has changed since my early childhood as a mixed-race kid in the 1970s. I remember people staring at us brown kids with our white mum and black dad. I remember them asking unwanted questions about our family and expressing concerns about how being mixed race would be too confusing for us—leading to a "life of angst and worry."

In 2012, it seems that we are facing many of the same issues. We prepared for being challenged because my body might look different from those of other dads in the playground. Now we are preparing for a future in which we are also challenged because our skin colors look different from our child's. And I'm sure we will one day face challenges based on an intersection of these two experiences of difference.

Things have gotten a lot easier now that Amelie is talking, running up to me, shouting, "Papa, papa!" But the questions continue. On the way home from her day care last week, a man stopped us at the bus stop. He asked, "Is this your baby, or are you the babysitter?" I confirmed that I was Amelie's parent. He said, with palpable disdain and sadness in his voice, "No! She is *so* white! And you are . . ." his voice trailed off, and he gestured with his hand disapprovingly at my face. And I wanted to scream. The implication was that I am "too black," that black is awful, and that Amelie, reading as white, deserves to be in a better family than ours, a family of color. Instead of screaming, I looked at Amelie. She smiled at me, said, "Papa. ABCD?" and launched into her jumbled version of her favorite song. We walked to the next stop, and along the way I wondered how we were going to manage these kinds of interactions, especially as Amelie becomes more and more conscious of "grown-up" conversations. As we learn how together, I find myself seeking kinship with other trans dads of color, and Thomas Beatie's story becomes all the more relevant to me.

The story of Beatie's first pregnancy came out about a year after we ran the first session of "Trans Fathers 2B," a fourteen-week parenting course for trans guys considering parenting, run through the Queer Parenting Program at the 519 Community Centre and the Parenting Network in Toronto. The course was run by a trans man who had practiced midwifery for years and was working as a labor and delivery nurse at a local hospital. There were seven people enrolled in the course. We—a group of people who were going to become parents, something that bonded us all together—met in a child-themed playroom at the Metro Central YMCA. Our discussions focused on how to talk to other parents and family members about our decisions to parent, how to handle transphobia on the playground, and how to advocate for ourselves around our gender preferences and identities while, say, in the throes of labor. We also worked with our course facilitators to push for the inclusion of a session focused on the experience of racialization and things to consider when parenting children who look different from you or adopting/fostering kids from different communities than your own. In retrospect, I wish that we had spent more than one session talking about this, brainstorming with other parents-to-be. I guess it's true that you can't anticipate the kinds of questions you may have until you have them. At the time, I couldn't imagine what our child would look like and couldn't anticipate that she would look so much like my mother. As a mixed-race person, I was very aware that any donor we chose would affect what our child looked like. I had always experienced being "different" in both my parents' families—"too black" in my mum's family and "too white" in my dad's. But during our course, I couldn't get past thinking about gender and pregnancy. I wrote this about my early pregnancy:

> I have realized that to be a pregnant man is to be a spectacle. Male or not, public attitudes about pregnancy render the pregnant person an object of public display. Every stranger you meet is likely to touch your belly without asking and give you a laundry list of suggestions for what you should be doing throughout your pregnancy. But being a pregnant man adds a new level of publicity. Not only are you pregnant, but you might, like me, have a short beard. I've had top surgery and have a man's name. When I

meet other people who have been pregnant, they usually spend the entire conversation staring from my belly to my lack of breasts to my beard and back again, which can make for distracted exchanges. I'm really excited to be able to carry our child, but it is not without the challenge of feeling ultimately different in this world, connecting two puzzle pieces that don't belong together. I am torn between wanting to proclaim my pregnancy to the world, inevitably rendering me female to even my friends and family, and wanting to remain seen as masculine, thus seeming inevitably not-pregnant. I suppose that's why I am so enamored and in awe of Thomas Beatie. His willingness to publicly announce his pregnancy has brought the concept of men being pregnant to the general public. His publicity has made pregnant and man no longer oxymoronic, but rather something that happens in this world. Of course, there were and are many men before him who became pregnant. He is not the first and is not the last pregnant man. But his very visibility has created a shift in our understanding of who it is in this world who gets pregnant, and has made it easier for me to explain my situation to other people, simply answering their blank stares with the phrase, "You, know, like Thomas Beatie, the Pregnant Man!"

Despite the fact that I am not the first trans guy to be going through this, the world still sees trans male pregnancy as a highly unusual event. And at least at this moment in history, it's not the most common way to bring a child into the world. But that doesn't mean that the systems in place to help people have families should be any less welcoming or prepared for trans parents-to-be. Over the past several months, Dr. Baby Maker has been a supportive and encouragingly optimistic part of our health-care team. He may not fully grasp all the terminology and concepts related to trans bodies, but he has truly put all of his efforts into helping us begin our family. For this I am eternally grateful.

I am thankful for the many sessions in the Trans Fathers 2B course in which we practiced dealing with other parents, with strangers, with our families, with other children who might not understand our genders, or who might be critical of trans parenting. Through scenarios, discussions, and workshops on self-advocacy, I feel more prepared to deal with questions like: "Hey … Is that your mom or your dad?" at our child's best friend's third birthday party. I am also thankful for the ever changing, ever growing network of trans parents out there who are sharing resources, support, creativity and resilience; through face-to-face meetings, online forums, and courses like Trans Fathers 2B.

Now I realize that if I could ask Thomas Beatie anything, it would be this: What do you say to people who impose race-based thinking immediately upon meeting your children? How do you talk to your kids about race?

LABOR PAINS

I developed preeclampsia and had to deliver our child early. We rushed to the hospital with trepidation—we had been planning a home birth, complete with candles, a warm tub, and a few rounds of Scrabble. Most importantly, our plan allowed us to have some control over who would be present at the birth of our child and to sidestep the potential pitfalls and transphobia we might experience as trans dads in labor at a large public hospital. Yet here we were, en route to the hospital, with no hospital bag, no Scrabble board, and no idea what to expect in the coming hours. Our midwife sensed our concern when we met her in triage. Because of the seriousness of my health condition and the fact that I was going to require extensive medications and a possible C-section, she had to transfer care to an attending physician. I was terrified. I worried about the preeclampsia, I worried about the baby, and I worried how I was going to deal with the hyperfeminizing world I was about to enter: the Mom and Baby Unit of a big hospital. Before leaving us in the care of our new doctor, our midwife went around to the entire team we would be working with to advocate for us—to ensure that we were called by our chosen names and addressed as our preferred gender. I will be forever grateful that she did this. As each round of nurses, doctors, and anesthetists came in and out of our room, they consistently referred to us correctly—it was incredible. Our identities were not just respected; in fact, they were validated in new and interesting ways. I ended up having to have an emergency C-section after thirty-four hours of induced labor. The surgeon who performed the operation told me when I was in recovery that he believed my having a "male pelvis" had resulted in a longer surgery than expected. Rather than sounding disparaging, he said, encouragingly, "It's great news, really. It means the hormones are do-ing what they should!" I was not prepared for this somewhat misplaced but well-intentioned support of my body, my life, and our family.

POSTSCRIPT

After my labor, the other questions began. It wasn't whether I would be Dad or Mum that predominated our first family outings; instead, they were shaped by a society bent on racialization and vocalized amazement about difference within family groupings. I wrote this shortly after having Amelie:

> Now that we have had our baby, I realize that, though there are many wonderful and difficult things about being a trans dad, some of the biggest issues we face on a near daily basis are not related to gender at all.
>
> As a trans dad, my gender identity is challenged in several ways. Two particularly difficult challenges are being called mum a lot instead of dad

by strangers and loved ones alike, and regrowing chest tissue as a result of chest-feeding my baby. We are under a particular kind of scrutiny about how we are raising our baby in relation to gender: We were recently questioned by a family member if we are putting Amelie in pink enough—enough to show that we are not making gender "confusing" for her. We are required to show that we are not making gender confusing to our five month old by instilling in them a clear sense of pink, blue and two distinct genders. These experiences are frustrating.

But none of these examples have affected our family as much as the way that race-based thinking is projected on the tiniest of humans. It's truly terrifying to watch. It propels me to imagine a different world, one where we could live in communities that did not impose the notion of two genders and two sexes on our children, and one where race-based thinking and racialization was not a principal organizing factor for our society. I feel pulled to create this kind of home, this community with every fiber in my body, not only for us but for our children's children.

We are part of a growing network of trans parents, many of whom are from racialized communities, and among this group we are seeking solace. Within our trans and LGBTTI2QQ parenting community, we have had a chance to celebrate our new family, our differences, and our identities as trans dads.

CHAPTER 7

Birth Justice and Population Control

Loretta J. Ross

Not everything that is faced can be changed; but nothing can be changed until it is faced.

—*James Baldwin*[1]

LINKING BIRTH JUSTICE TO POPULATION CONTROL

The purpose of this chapter is to expand our definition of population control, to examine its ubiquitous processes through the lens of reproductive justice, and to explore its significance for the birth justice movement. Most critiques of population control focus on strategies for manipulating the growth rate of a population or subset thereof through reproductive measures and means. But as a reproductive justice activist who also advocates for birth justice—the human right to birth with dignity and to parent in safe and healthy environments—I urge attention to the multiple ways that Indigenous peoples and communities of color are constrained through a constellation of public policies that aim to maintain white supremacist economic, social, and political hierarchies. The following assertions illustrate how proponents of population control engage and affect multiple domains, including food distribution, labor patterns, migration, and domestic and foreign policies:

The world is overpopulated.
Population pressure is destroying the environment.
People go hungry because there is not enough food to go around.
Poor people keep themselves poor by having too many babies.
If we don't get population growth under control in the Third World, those people are going to migrate here and take our jobs.
Whatever your cause, it's a lost cause without population control.[2]

To challenge supporters of population control, one must address the myth of overpopulation. This myth is laced through our culture and politics (both feminist and otherwise) and leads to ethical relativism: human rights abuses are justifiable to save the environment, alleviate hunger, or reduce fertility. The overpopulation myth, in fact, disguises the maldistribution of wealth and resources like food and water and distracts from environmental destruction caused by overconsumption, neoliberal capitalism, and the military-industrial complex.[3]

This chapter examines how population-control measures, far from saving the planet from catastrophic overpopulation, bring together apparently disconnected public policies and stereotypical attitudes to constrain communities of color. I wish to emphasize the dialectical connections between our communities and our reproductive decision-making by bringing land-use policies and gentrification into the conversation as one example of contemporary population control. This offers a fuller exploration of the intersectional potential of the reproductive justice framework and the human rights violations we experience collectively.

It is ironic at this historical moment that antiabortion conservatives are taking credit for the fight against population control, attempting to seize the moral high ground from people of color who have fought it for centuries. Today's ultraconservatives claim that the Affordable Care Act (ACA), aka "Obamacare," is a government conspiracy to promote population control. For example, Family Research Council president Tony Perkins argues that the government will eventually encourage infanticide and same-sex relations as a form of population control, because the ACA "not only includes abortion, contraception and sterilization" but pushes an "unbiblical view of children and of life."[4] In supporting the Hobby Lobby challenge to contraception coverage in the ACA, Andrea Lafferty of the Traditional Values Coalition asserted that the contraception mandate is part of a larger attack on Americans' freedom that also includes imposing Islamic sharia law in the United States.[5] In a pseudodocumentary titled *Demographic Winter: The Decline of the Human Family,* "cradle competition"[6] reemerges through graphic alarmism that predicts white "demographic suicide" through reduced births.[7] This claim evokes President Teddy Roosevelt's warning about "race suicide" and his support for the eugenics movement a century ago and further echoes today's white supremacists' opposition to abortion and birth control—at least for whites.[8] It is difficult to give serious credence to the notion that ultraconservatives, who oppose every racial, sexual, and immigrant justice measure ever conceived, are now concerned about the fate of all babies, including brown, black, and Indigenous ones. The irony is that these same anti–human rights leaders previously promoted population control as a conservative social-control strategy to fight communism, racial unrest, terrorism, immigration, and desegregation. Birth and reproductive justice activists must not cede the fight against population control to the Right. Instead, we must create an antiracist, feminist critique that places this struggle at the center of our efforts to protect our reproductive autonomy and build self-determination for communities of color.

Historically, population-control measures in the United States, including sterilization abuses, promotion of dangerous contraceptives, and separation of family members, employed reproductive strategies to control communities of color.[9] The construction of the hierarchies of white supremacy depended on preserving white "purity" and separating and subjugating Indigenous peoples and enslaved Africans, processes that required the "constant purification and elimination of racialized enemies within the state."[10] Authorities maintained racial boundaries by placing the regulation of reproduction and policing of interracial sexual relations at the center of their project. These processes continue today with assaults on sex education, abortion, and birth control.[11] This is population control through reproductive oppression, a process that leads to what Rickie Solinger calls the "racialization of reproductive politics."[12]

Reproductive strategies are key to controlling entire communities, but they are not the only strategies, and as such, they must be examined in the context of a larger analysis of systemic coercion. Population-control measures not only overtly threaten our reproductive freedom and self-determination but also manifest through institutions, policies, and processes that at first glance appear disconnected. These include

- restrictions on freedom of movement
- immigration restrictions
- the prison-industrial complex
- racial profiling and police brutality
- racist and sexist media portrayals
- resource allocation
- welfare
- health care
- housing segregation
- food insecurity
- underfunded public education
- zoning regulations
- internal displacement through natural disasters or eminent domain
- voting rights

- credit and finance regulations
- restrictions on civil liberties
- environmental racism

While not exhaustive, this list does illustrate how public policies that do not overtly target our reproductive capacities achieve the unstated goal of population and community control. For example, in 2014 the US Supreme Court let stand a Nebraska city's ban on renting residential housing to undocumented immigrants. Claiming that the ordinance does not discriminate against Latinos, the city of Fremont, Nebraska, requires potential renters to prove they are in the country legally.[13] Similar policies exist in Pennsylvania and Texas. This is an example of population control through land-use and zoning policies, comparable to the Alien Land Acts of the nineteenth century that forbade even legal Japanese immigrants from owning land. While this type of community exclusion is largely unrecognized by the mainstream pro-choice movement, it is vital that policies that affect whether an individual may choose to start or rear a family be included in discussions of reproductive justice.

The phrase "population control" is loaded with assumptions, stereotypes, and hidden values. Historically, many people associate population control with reproductive oppression by the eugenics movement of the 1920s to the 1950s and sterilization abuses in the 1960s and 1970s. As reproductive justice activists, we should question that narrow view. Eugenicists in the past did not limit their scope to hereditarian biological processes, and neither should we. Eugenicists addressed a wide range of subjects, including immigration and demographics, economics, environmentalism, state surveillance, land-use policies, scientific racism, the mental health and criminal justice systems, foreign policy, and militarism.[14] Similarly, when US politicians used the term "population control" during the Cold War, they were alluding to the fight against communism, dominion over natural resources, and expansion of the military. Proponents frankly recognized that controlling land, resources, and labor is key to controlling the world.

Population control in North America, of course, did not start in the twentieth century when the term was first popularized; it began with the genocide of Native Americans in order to colonize the continent. Settler colonialism in the United States, as in other countries, requires the disenfranchisement of Indigenous peoples and their obliteration from the land and its history. Most devastatingly, it must eliminate consciousness and memory of Indigenous peoples in order to tell a fictional story about the land, its "emptiness," and the newly constructed rights of the settlers who must, perforce, violently resent the righteous sovereignty claims of native people in an unending performance of genocide. According to Genocide Watch, the final stage of genocide is genocide denial.[15] Joined with reproductive oppression, this whitewashing process imposes itself on the bodies of Indigenous people in numerous ways, effecting what I call "reproductive disappearing." Settlers plowed the corpses of Indigenous and enslaved Africans into the foundations of this country.

With the development of the eugenics movement at the beginning of the twentieth century, African Americans opposed the targeting of their communities for population reduction.[16] In the 1960s and 1970s, feminists of color organized to oppose sterilization-abuse policies and urged activists fighting for abortion rights to work together with black, Latina, and Indigenous women for full reproductive freedom.[17] Perhaps inadvertently, many of us overlooked the wider definition of population control that the state employed and focused narrowly on sterilization abuse as the logical corollary to abortion rights. This oversimplification of population control minimized government and private efforts to restrain politically restive brown and black communities that were challenging white supremacy.

This limited view continues to have consequences today as many feminists fail to incorporate the myriad ways peoples of color worldwide are targeted for containment and elimination in order to control their land and natural resources. More recently, some advocates of population control have responded to allegations of racism and neocolonialism by adopting an approach euphemistically named "population stabilization." Under this ostensible women's rights banner, advocates call for increased access to fertility regulation through birth control and abortion to mitigate climate change. They champion anticonsumerism and women's rights as solutions to environmental problems—a rationale that reinforces, rather than challenges, eugenicist thinking. Our rights are worthy of protection in and of themselves and should not be positioned as stepping-stones to a broader agenda. When adopted as a basis for policy development, funding decisions, and research, these neosexist points of view mask the large structural causes of environmental problems, degrade women, and dismiss more radical feminist of color opposition to population and community control.

Reproductive justice activists seeking to understand the extent of population control in the twenty-first century must analyze the ways our communities are restricted today, rather than simply focusing on birth control, abortion, and sterilization. By making visible the web of apparently disparate policies that together form a totalizing system of containment, we expand the meaning of population control to recognize and include practices that, regardless of intent, limit reproduction for women of color and Indigenous women.

ECONOMIC, SOCIAL, AND POLITICAL FACTORS DRIVING POPULATION CONTROL

In the 1950s and 1960s, the mechanization of agriculture drove some 11 million people off the land and into cities searching for a way to support themselves and their families. For African Americans, this coincided with a mass movement against Jim Crow segregation in the South that began in the 1920s and continued a huge migratory shift from the South to the North. These developments concentrated black and brown voting strengths in many urban areas, defining subsequent fights for control of the political machinery of these cities as well as struggles over local jurisdictions with large black populations in the South. These fights affected all levels of government and city services, including the racial composition of the police and fire departments, and support for public services such as schools and health care. The battles for integration and opportunity also determined how city contracts were awarded, how land was used, how taxes were raised, and who benefited from these decisions. Authorities looked for newer ways of controlling urban populations, particularly after violence erupted—usually following police brutality, as was the case with the many riots of the 1960s.

The 1968 Kerner Commission Report, a study of black civil unrest spurred by the 1967 urban riots, is considered liberal for its acknowledgment of white racism as the source of violence.[18] But some of the report's other observations ominously presaged population control; for example, the report noted that the largest central cities "will have Negro majorities by 1985, and the suburbs ringing them will remain largely all white, unless there are major changes in Negro fertility rates, in-migration, settlement patterns, or public policy."[19] The report also called for an expansion of police surveillance and intelligence to contain further racial unrest.[20]

The Kerner Commission's recommendations also resulted in what housing activists called "spatial deconcentration"—the deliberate breaking up of large concentrations of black voters in urban areas.[21] In order to convince African Americans to leave their urban communities, a series of "push" policies had to be implemented: the closing of schools, hospitals, fire stations, social services offices, grocery stores, and other basic services that make communities viable.[22] Public housing was destroyed or neglected and made unlivable. "Pull" factors were also important in persuading African Americans to move out of the cities into the surrounding suburbs. The first housing voucher program, Section 8, was created to provide subsidized housing assistance for low-income families, but the vouchers could only be used in suburban locations. To persuade suburban officials and landlords to accept this influx of low-income renters, the federal government created two programs, the Areawide Housing Opportunities Plan and the Regional Housing Opportunities Program. These provided federal grants to suburban governments to increase the funding for their police departments while guaranteeing federally protected high rates of return for landlords participating in Section 8 programs.[23] Taken together, these push and pull factors set the stage for the waves of gentrification and dilution of black voting strength we see today in urban areas. The racial reorganization of New Orleans after Katrina typifies a contemporary implementation of the policy of spatial deconcentration.[24]

The Kerner Commission report also referenced "Negro fertility," reflecting the federal government's belief in the inexorable relationship between "overpopulation in the … black community and social chaos."[25] The Office of Economic Opportunity, launched in 1964 as part of President Lyndon Johnson's War on Poverty, began spending money on population reduction as an antipoverty measure. In 1970, President Richard Nixon urged Congress to increase its spending through Title X on birth control and sterilization as a strategy for containing the growth of the African American, Latino/a, and Indigenous populations in the United States. He notably reversed his support during his 1972 reelection bid when family planning was rejected by the social conservatives of the Republican Party.[26] When family planning was offered as a way to reduce black and brown populations in the 1960s—as a strategy of population control—Republicans like George H. W. Bush and Richard Nixon embraced it.[27] When it was perceived as a way to increase women's freedom and autonomy in the 1970s, they quickly opposed it, fearing that white women would voluntarily reduce their fertility. This echoed the concerns of some eugenicists from the 1930s who shared the same sexist and racist fears and opposed Margaret Sanger's campaign for birth control.[28] Both points of view pivot on the same fulcrum of population control: some babies are more valuable than others.

By the 1980s, urban job opportunities were in steep decline. Industrialized cities experienced a rapid increase in the use of labor-saving technologies. Corporations transferred millions of jobs overseas to developing countries in globalized labor markets with "cheap" labor. These factors, plus privatization and corporate deregulation, caused job loss and devastated the social fabric of communities in the inner cities. Neighborhoods, housing, clinics, hospitals, schools, and local grocery stores were further destroyed or shut down under spatial-deconcentration plans implemented by Ronald Reagan as part of the transition from Fordism to neoliberal capitalism. The result was a tremendous increase in homelessness, lack of accessible and affordable medical care, food deserts, and lowered standards of living for millions. At the same time, ascendant neoliberal politicians demanded the destruction of the social safety net, including dismantlement of the welfare system, and concentrated on destabilizing Social Security, limiting unemployment insurance, and keeping the minimum wage at subsistence levels.

The federal government today encourages urban gentrification through land-use policies, tax codes, and subsidized finance. A new dimension of older deconcentration strategies includes the decimation of funding for public transportation, limiting mobility for people who must travel between city and suburb without cars. Such policies control communities in ways that rerationalize eugenical thinking and manipulate targeted populations. However, because they seldom use overt measures to curtail reproduction, opposition to these human rights abuses is often severed from conversations about reproductive oppression and birth injustices. But whose interests are served when we separate our movements in this way?

REPRODUCTIVE OPPRESSION TODAY

As a black feminist, I questioned the isolation of abortion from other social justice issues. This separation left little space to consider other reproductive health issues, such as the right to give birth and parent with dignity, a problem that led my African American colleagues and me to create the reproductive justice framework in 1994. We focused on how our community experiences reproductive oppression and ways to counter it.[29] Reproductive justice is not difficult to understand. It is both a theoretical paradigm shift and a model for activist practices. It is about three interconnected sets of human rights: (1) the right to have children, (2) the right not to have children, and (3) the right to parent the children we have in safe and healthy environments.[30] Reproductive justice includes our right to mother and parent in radical opposition to thinly disguised race- and class-based manipulation and thus encompasses the struggle for birth justice. However, reproductive justice does not privilege the production of babies as the only goal of women's biology; nor does it insist that only biologically defined women experience reproductive oppression, because it includes transgender individuals and has been expanded to include bodily autonomy. Instead it insists on the human right to make personal decisions about one's life and the obligation of government and society to ensure that individuals have access to the resources necessary for implementing those decisions. In particular, reproductive justice draws attention to the lack of physical, reproductive, and cultural safety that constrains "choices." Reproductive justice focuses on oppression—the structures of injustice and inequality—and on resistance—the development of new theories and strategies for change.

Contemporary reproductive oppression facilitates the neoliberal economic system. For example, the nation's elite deploy the myth of the undeserving welfare-dependent black or immigrant mother to justify austerity measures that are destroying our social safety net. Corporate leaders transfer industrial production abroad to avoid US labor force costs and maximize profits. Both the poor and middle class are under assault. Demagogues attack mothers who are not native born, middle-class, and heterosexual. Former Arizona Senate president Russell Pearce (R), proposing the state's draconian anti-immigration law, asserted, "You put me in charge of Medicaid, the first thing I'd do is get Norplant, birth-control implants, or tubal ligations. Then we'll test recipients for drugs and alcohol, and if you want to [reproduce] or use drugs or alcohol, then get a job."[31]

Despite the "Age of Obama" and the racial symbolism this presidency carries, the white supremacist hierarchical system continues to organize and distribute resources and punishments along racial, class, and gender lines. White supremacy continues to devastate communities of color through mass incarceration and police violence. Elites manipulate technological developments like genomics and assisted reproductive technologies, once again using science in the service of racially deterministic practices.[32] Media and public policy define women of color and poor women as "bad" mothers and hold our families responsible for all the ills of society, from the Wall Street mortgage crisis to environmental degradation.[33] Because our children are defined as products of "morally impoverished" upbringings, they become disposable cannon fodder for US imperialism around the world or neoslaves in the prison-industrial complex.[34] To be worthy of existence, our children must either protect, or produce more wealth for, the 1 percent. In this context, it is essential that we work collectively to counter the forces arrayed against our survival.

CONCLUSION

Reducing population control to sterilization abuse is analogous to reducing racism to the gutter epithets of overt racists. Neither includes the range of oppressive policies and microaggressions that we experience. This reductionism relieves the rest of society of accountability for the harmful continuum of policies and practices that constitute contemporary population control. As reproductive justice activists, we need to explore the full potential of our new critical framework and move beyond past narrow interpretations. As birth activists, we need to expand our understanding of birth justice to include the right to have children, free of population-control policies that denigrate and restrict our reproduction. Our ancestors fought against population control, and we have to be equally ready to reconceptualize population control to include a much wider array of public policies. This will enable us to bring together many social justice movements to protect our human rights to birth justice and self-determination.

CHAPTER 8

Beyond Silence and Stigma

Pregnancy and HIV for
Black Women in Canada

Marvelous Muchenje and Victoria Logan Kennedy

I had my first sexual experience after I was engaged. Practicing safer sex was not something that crossed my mind, as I was already cohabiting and talking about marriage. I remember vividly that one of my friends warned me about my partner's promiscuous behavior and that one of the girls he was in a relationship with had died of AIDS. I asked my partner, and he denied everything, including the question of HIV and the relationship. I believed what he told me. I was so much in love and told myself that if he was having relationships, they would end once we got married. My eyes opened wide the day I received my HIV diagnosis. I had no doubt how I had gotten infected as he was the first man I had been with, and I had never used drugs or had a blood transfusion. The words my friend told me kept flashing in my mind. I was devastated. I blamed myself for not listening to my friend and my instinct. I felt ashamed, lonely, and used. —Marvelous

Marvelous's story as a black woman living with HIV provides a starting point for this chapter. Indeed, hers is one illustration of the stories of millions of women who navigate the stigma of living with HIV. Dominant representations of HIV suggest that it is a death sentence, rather than a condition that people live with. Even where progressive media and social justice organizations challenge this image, people living with HIV continue to be seen as white, gay men. Black women living with HIV are often invisible, and those who experience pregnancy and motherhood are doubly marginalized due to their lack of white privilege and HIV stigma. Where their experiences are recognized, they are viewed as a homogenous group, with their identity as people living with HIV superseding their identity as women of color. In contrast, Marvelous's experiences of life, pregnancy, and motherhood have also been shaped by her identity as an African woman and as a migrant. Understanding the complexities in the lives of black women living with HIV in Canada requires us to look beyond the hegemonic biomedical fixation with HIV and explore the impact of culture, race, class, gender, migration, and sexuality on women's pregnancies and birth experiences.

WHO ARE BLACK WOMEN LIVING WITH HIV IN CANADA?

Black communities comprise only 2.5 percent of the Canadian population.[1] It is estimated that 62 percent of black people in Canada live in Ontario, where 4 percent of the population is black.[2] In contrast, black communities within Ontario are disproportionately represented in the province's HIV statistics.[3] The primary mode of HIV transmission within black communities remains heterosexual intercourse.[4] From 1998 to 2008 black women accounted for approximately 18.8 percent of new cases of HIV in Canada, where ethnicity is reported, compared to black men, who represented 6.6 percent.[5] This is in distinct contrast to all other ethnic groups—except Canada's Indigenous populations—where infection rates are higher among men.[6]

Black women living with HIV include migrant women and women born in Canada.[7] Most black migrant women living with HIV in Canada have come from eastern and southern Africa and the Caribbean in search of better opportunities for themselves and their families, including better access to health care, which may be required to manage HIV among other conditions.[8] More than 50 percent of all mobile women are fleeing persecution and other forms of trauma as refugees.[9]

> After eleven years living with HIV in my home country, I became a human rights activist passionately and tirelessly participating in initiatives in the HIV movement. I came to Canada for better opportunities, and I was fleeing my country of birth, which at that time was unstable. I also sought access to HIV treatment. While I was in my country, access to HIV treatment was costly, and the only way I could afford to get medication was to participate in a drug trial. Since the study I was in was coming to an end, I knew it would be a challenge to access medication and routine laboratory monitoring from

government institutions like I had received throughout the study. Making a decision to migrate to Canada was not easy as it meant starting a new life without any of my support systems, including my common-law partner. My hope was that he would join me in Canada as soon as possible. Little did I know that eight years later we would still be apart due to systemic immigration barriers. —Marvelous

Canada has seen a steady rise in the number of migrants coming from HIV endemic countries, now thought to be about 8 percent of all migrants.[10] Most of the migrant women living with HIV in Canada are black. Black migrant women living with HIV are often unsure about immigration policy regarding applicants with HIV, and those whose status is unknown experience the stress of mandatory immigration HIV testing.[11] This means that many immigrant and refugee diasporic women in Canada do not get tested for HIV of their own volition.[12] Immigration HIV testing rarely adheres to protocols related to pre- and post-testing counseling.[13] Consequently, newly diagnosed applicants can end up with little support and limited understanding of what HIV means for their health and their admissibility to Canada. They are often left to grapple with the troubling reality of a new HIV diagnosis on their own.

THE "S" WORD: STIGMA

An HIV-positive woman's experience of stigma is complicated by intersecting realities in her life. These intersections include racism, poverty, sexism, HIV-related stigma, and stigmatization of newcomers.[14] These identities cannot be dismantled and need to be considered in concert. This is particularly important for black women living with HIV since a variety of determinants of health and stigma shaped HIV acquisition and their general health; these factors continue to shape their current health status.[15]

The stigmatization of black women living with HIV often begins at the moment they are diagnosed. In a culture where HIV remains highly stigmatized, assumptions are made about promiscuity, and in some instances the diagnosis is seen as a punishment from a higher power for untoward behaviors.[16] These early experiences of stigma are not fleeting; they persist in interactions with family, partners, friends, and even care providers. Black women living with HIV report feeling increasingly marginalized from long-standing circles of support, love, and protection over time. This loss of support is exacerbated by the experience of systemic barriers related to gender, race, class, and sometimes immigration status.[17] These experiences of stigma are often further exacerbated during pregnancy, when women are required to access high levels of medical care.[18] The real or perceived risk of stigma has been found to be a barrier to accessing care, which can have serious consequences in pregnancy.[19] Pregnancy can also be a time when expectations of privacy change, given family and community investment in an unborn child. Black women living with HIV can find themselves further isolating themselves to avoid unsolicited questions about the pregnancy and to avoid unintended disclosure of HIV status.

PREGNANCY AND HIV: TESTING, TRANSMISSION, AND TRENDS

I got pregnant in May 1996 before my HIV diagnosis. My gynecologist dismissed the idea of testing me for HIV, even though I requested one as I had other sexually transmitted infections. He indicated that I was looking healthy and I should not worry. Since I was not practicing safe sex with my partner and he did not agree to go and see the doctor for STI treatment, I continued to have infections. For the sake of my baby, I decided to leave my partner. I gave birth in January 1997 to a bouncy premature baby girl. At six months she developed pneumonia. She died. I suspected she might be HIV-positive, but I was too afraid to ask. During those days, a lot of children were dying of AIDS as testing was rare, treatment was difficult to access, and knowledge was scarce. At that time I developed a rash, which I assumed was caused by stress. During one visit the doctor dismissively told me to have my rash checked. It was then that I noticed that the friendly doctor and other nursing staff had changed their attitude towards me and the baby, and they had stopped giving any medications. Soon after the burial I went to see a different doctor, and I requested an HIV test. The test came back positive. —Marvelous

Routine HIV testing in pregnancy has been considered a best practice in Canada since 2002.[20] The result has been greater than 90 percent uptake of HIV testing in pregnancy among women in care.[21] However, populations of women at highest risk of HIV infection may not have the personal agency to test for fear of violence or societal disapproval.[22] This high uptake also only takes into account those women in prenatal care. Given the structural barriers to health care that exist in the lives of women at greatest risk of HIV, including black women, there is concern that testing rates may be lower.

Between 1984 and 2008, black infants accounted for the largest proportion—46.8 percent—of infants perinatally exposed to HIV.[23] This proportion has increased over time, from 43.2 percent between 1984 and 2000 to 49.8 percent between 2001 and 2008. Pregnancy rates within a population are influenced by many factors.[24] The first factor is migration. More black women living with HIV have migrated to Canada in the last decade, resulting in overrepresentation in the general HIV statistics. It is also thought that more black women living with HIV are electing to become pregnant or maintain pregnancies due to greater access to HIV care, resulting in extremely low rates of vertical transmission[25] of HIV among women who access care in Canada (0.4 percent).[26] Cultural expectations are another salient factor.[27] When cultural pressures to mother compete with personal fears related to HIV, cultural expectations seem to prevail.[28] This is particularly true among black women, given the widespread recognition that fertility and motherhood define womanhood.[29] Women may even desire to get pregnant in order to conceal HIV status, and others may see pregnancy as an opportunity to avert suspicion.[30] The immense cultural pressure to become pregnant can be a normalizing experience in the midst of exclusion and othering.[31] Access to treatment and a risk of vertical HIV transmission that is approaching zero may allay fears of passing HIV to the unborn child.

Rates of mother-to-child transmission remain an important example of racial inequality in prenatal and HIV care. HIV-exposed infants in Canada are at highest risk of transmission if born to a black mother. Between 2002 and 2009, seventy-five infants were confirmed to be infected with HIV. Of those, forty infants (53.3 percent) were black.[32] Disproportionate rates of infection, alongside greater rates of transmission in utero, collectively suggest ongoing injustices in access to care and disadvantages within the system.

ACCESS TO CARE

Higher rates of poverty, less access to information, culturally insensitive services, lack of knowledgeable service providers, and transportation issues illustrate some barriers faced by black women living with HIV who are attempting to access care during pregnancy. The results are disproportionately negative birth outcomes for black children born to HIV-positive women. This in turn perpetuates assumptions that medical interventions do not adequately reduce the risk of vertical transmission and/or stereotypes that black women with HIV are less likely to seek in care.

Fears pertaining to immigration have been noted as a particular concern in pregnancy among HIV-positive black women migrants.[33] Disclosure could lead to deportation, loss of employment, stigma, and intimate partner violence. Women may avoid health care to prevent disclosure. The situation for black migrant women with HIV is even further complicated by varying insurance coverages. Most pregnancy services in Canada are covered through universal health-coverage programs available to citizens, permanent residents, and landed (documented) immigrants. The Interim Federal Health Program (IFHP) exists for resettled refugees, refugee claimants, certain detainees, and other specified groups not eligible for the government health insurance plan. IFHP offers short-term financial coverage for a limited number of health-care services. Nonstatus (undocumented) and other migrants who fall outside IFHP eligibility and universal coverage remain uninsured. Some will be referred to community health centers that provide care to low-income uninsured women in pregnancy.[34] Without such a referral, women cobble together solutions, including accessing midwives, who sometimes provide services to the uninsured and marginalized in an attempt to achieve optimized care for all women; avoiding prenatal care and only seeking medical aid at the time of delivery; and in some instances avoiding formal health care altogether.

Access to fertility services represents a unique facet of HIV and pregnancy. People with HIV have used fertility services to prevent the horizontal transmission of HIV to their HIV-negative partners. Routine procedures used in infertility treatment can be implemented in serodiscordant HIV couples.[35] Eliminating unprotected intercourse also eliminates the risk of HIV transmission. In Canada, fertility services are privatized and costly, preventing some black women with HIV from even considering this harm-reduction approach to conception. Cases of black women living with HIV who have undergone coercive sterilization and now desire a child are also emerging.[36] In these instances, fertility services are their only option to conceive. Privatized fertility services are often out of reach as they require a high level of financial security, they are offered in limited places across Canada, and awareness of the use of these services in cases of female sterilization is limited.

The voices of black lesbian, gay, bisexual, trans*, and queer (LGBTQ) women living with HIV are largely silenced in the discourses about fertility and HIV. The threat of violence and persecution for sexual orientation has brought many LGBTQ black women to Canada, some of whom have acquired HIV through acts of sexual violence for identifying with the LGBTQ community.[37] Fertility remains a pressing issue within this community with an enhanced need for access to fertility services for donor sperm and insemination. Little is known about how the intersecting identities these women possess may come together to influence access to and decision-making about pregnancy care. What is known is that the further a woman's reality is from hegemonic norms of heterosexual, white privilege, the more challenging access to care becomes and the less decision-making power a woman possesses.

PREGNANCY LOSS FOR BLACK WOMEN LIVING WITH HIV: BROADENING OUR UNDERSTANDING

In 2003, I fell in love again. I was taking HIV medication, and my health had improved. I decided to have another baby. In the midst of worry about the possibility of vertical transmission, I also developed other medical complications. These issues did not resolve, and I had to deliver the baby prematurely. In that moment of panic, the same gynecologist who delivered my first baby told me that it was best for me to have a tubal ligation as I was going to have a cesarean section. He told me that with my health complications and HIV, I was risking premature death by continuing to get pregnant. I was tired, afraid, stressed, and hopeless, so I agreed to sign the consent form. My son died when he was ten days old. I have no reason to think that my baby's death had to do with HIV since I was in treatment and responding well. I believe that he died because he was very premature. I was so devastated, after losing two babies and having a tubal ligation, how could I call myself a mother? As an African, to be a woman, a wife, you have to bear children. Knowing future pregnancies are not possible for me is an endless experience of loss. When I came to Canada, I imagined the possibility of having more children through fertility procedures. But hope quickly turned to despair when I learned how expensive it would be. I grieve the loss of my two babies and any hopes of getting pregnant every time I see other women who are pregnant, or when people ask me how many children I have. —Marvelous

Loss does not have to be synonymous with death. For many black women living with HIV, the experience of pregnancy loss is related to the potential to bear and parent children. This loss exists across a continuum dating back to the moment of diagnosis. Addressing this sense of loss must happen in stages. It begins with discussing reproductive potential at the time of diagnosis and at ongoing intervals early in care for women in their reproductive years. Grief and loss may continue as women face the awareness that the ideal of an unmedical-ized pregnancy and birth is likely impossible. Decisions are quickly stripped away. Pregnancy becomes yet another encounter with the medical system that potentiates stigma. The loss is also related to a lack of understanding among health-care professionals about how empowering motherhood is for black women and why personal agency to make reproductive decisions must be preserved.

Reproductive losses have been imposed on many black women living with HIV. Prior to widespread access to effective anti-HIV treatment, inter-ventions to eliminate the reproductive potential of women with HIV were not uncommon.[38] Women in developing countries, where the HIV epidemic began to unfold, and in low-income communities in Canada and the United States were counseled not to have children.[39] Some women were in the early years of their reproductive potential when they were sterilized to prevent pregnancy, a widespread practice particularly in sub-Saharan Africa.[40] Abor-tion has also been used to prevent women with HIV from having children.[41] Stories of black women feeling pressured to abort pregnancies persist today in the echoes of community dialogues. Reproductive health violations of women with HIV appear to have been most common among black women and are human rights issues that urgently need to be addressed.

The opportunity to honor the death of a child from AIDS is not always afforded to black mothers because of HIV stigma. The death is marked by shame. For black migrant women, grieving the loss of a child is further complicated as traditions around death change postmigration. Grief is understood within a very Western mentality of tearlessness as strength. This has led many women to feel that their grief experiences, real or potential, are forcefully truncated. Fortunately, today in Canada few women experience the loss of a child because of HIV, and unique supports for black women who have lost a child to AIDS remain absent. Instead women must reach out to general support services for bereaved parents, where their identities as HIV-positive and/ or black women are unacknowledged. Access to these services is even more compromised among newcomers who may not possess the knowledge of their new context and who express immense fear of disclosure and stigmatization. Like so many women who lose a child, black women living with HIV are often silenced after a short, socially normalized grieving process without any ongoing support.

AGENCY AND RESILIENCE: FIGHTING BACK, COMING OUT AHEAD

The word "AIDS" is so scary to most people, but to me the word reminds me to ask myself, "Am I doing something?" Throughout my journey living with HIV, I have worked with great mentors. It is because of their words of encouragement, their struggles and resilience, that I soldier on tireless in the HIV movement. I have devoted myself diligently to ensure policy-makers, service providers, and researchers understand that women living with HIV have unique needs and rights that change through each stage of their life, from childbearing years to menopause. My role as the Community Health Coordinator at Women's Health in Women's Hands [WHIWH], Community Health Centre in Toronto, Canada, gives me the opportunity to be the voice of the voiceless and giving a face to HIV. I have the privilege of openly and shamelessly disclosing my HIV status in public, as I know most of my black sisters living with HIV cannot do so due to various reasons beyond their control. Working at WHIWH has empowered me to work from an inclusive feminist, pro-choice, antiracist, anti-oppression, and multilingual participatory framework in addressing the issue of access to health care for black women living with HIV.

Women living with HIV must be the driving force behind policy and program changes. My experiences as an activist include digital stories and videos that identify the stigma, discrimination and oppressive policies, attitudes and practices that hinder access to adequate care for HIV-positive women.[42] The videos have been screened in conferences, service organizations, and community forums and influenced policy changes. The birthing movement must stand in solidarity with black women with HIV. HIV-positive women's voices and actions alone cannot address some of the systemic and structural issues that impede the human rights of black HIV-positive women. We need everyone to jump on board and break down these barriers: United we stand, divided we fall. —Marvelous

While mainstream discussions about birthing justice have emancipated many women from the oppressive medicalization of pregnancy, the experiences of black women with HIV have been all but ignored. And yet the voices of black women living with HIV echo across Canada. Recognizing their interconnectedness with one another, black women with HIV have developed community support at grassroots levels and worked tirelessly to call on privileged decision-makers to honor their right to the same sexual and reproductive health rights afforded to other women, regardless of race or immigration/citizenship, marital, or HIV status. These include the right to make informed decisions around childbirth without coercion or judgment; to receive accurate, accessible, and comprehensive education and evidence regarding pregnancy; and to access pregnancy-planning services that recognize the multiple, intersecting dimensions of oppression that impact the health of black women.

CHAPTER 9

What I Carry

A Story of Love and Loss

Iris Jacob

My daughter's birth was beautiful. She was born at home, on the same bed where she was conceived, to the sounds of Fela and my screams of pain. We had chosen her name as soon as we found out she was a girl: Ifétayo, a Yoruba name that means "Love brings joy." Nothing could better describe how we felt about our blessing. Ifé came out with her fist up and didn't make a sound. No tears, just hunger and a need for sleep after her long journey.

Ifé's father was elated. Mike bragged to everyone about his new baby girl and her mother who had pushed her out completely naturally. I told him not to say that, because although I knew it was an accomplishment, I also knew that it would be painful for some women to hear. Their own childbirths may not have gone according to plan or may have been completely outside their control, and they might have feelings of failure or inadequacy. But still to this day, he says the sexiest, strongest, highest moment he felt was when I pushed for an hour, reached down, pulled out my baby, brought her to my chest, kissed her, and put her on my breast. Right after her birth, when the midwives left, he held us, and we celebrated our family's accomplishment. His support, my hard work, and Ifé's traveling abilities united us.

Ifé's birth was not completely magical. The midwife did not arrive on time, my birth assistant and doula got into a heated argument, and my labor pains were out of this world. If an epidural had been available, I would have taken it, but having a home birth was a preplanned trick I played on myself. I knew that if I gave birth in the hospital, I would most likely succumb to the pressure of doctors and end up with unwanted medical interventions as a result of the close relationship medicine has with capitalism in this country. My contractions were never really equidistant, my labor went on for twenty-one hours, and I react to pain in a pretty dramatic way. Hearing stories of my friends—strong women who had planned natural childbirths but went to hospitals that didn't seem to care—scared me. C-section rates are ridiculously high in this country.[1] Although doctors, hospitals, and expectant mothers are often more comfortable with vaginal births, the hospital industry, which functions as part of a patriarchal and capitalist society, is more interested in predictable outcomes, as well as avoiding lawsuits and maximizing insurance payouts; it is not interested in the varying needs, desires, and lives of women.

Not only is having a natural birth, well, natural, but it also just felt safer.

Our plan has always been to have a tribe in our home. Ifé is the leader and takes that role with pride. When we found out we were pregnant again, we were ecstatic. Ifé was sixteen months old, and we believed that our timing was perfect. The baby would come just after Ifé turned two and the siblings would be close. This time around, my pregnancy felt different. I had started working again, or perhaps I should say hustling. I taught yoga, did some community organizing, led teacher trainings, consulted with various organizations on social justice initiatives, wrote curricula, and taught a woman's studies course at a local college. I was working to save so that I could take a year off, just like I had with Ifé. But this time, I would not be eligible for unemployment.

It was not just my work that made this pregnancy feel so foreign. It was my spirit. I did not feel as invigorated this time. Thankfully I did not have any morning sickness, but it seemed to be replaced with anger. I was upset and mad and lashed out at others with little provocation. Mike received the brunt of this, and although he tried to be understanding, everyone has limits. We fought more, and everything seemed harder. When we went in for our eleven-week nuchal screening, I was looking forward to finally leaving the first trimester.[2] As we read the results with our midwife, she seemed confused. The likelihood of trisomy 21, also known as Down syndrome, came back as one in ten thousand. This had been the same for Ifé. Below those results were those for trisomy 13 or 18. Instead of the typical slim odds, the ratio was 1 in 360. Although the midwife didn't seem sure, she said that we shouldn't worry because only ratios like 1 in 100 were cause for concern, and we were nowhere near that.

I did not understand what any of this meant, and it did not seem like anyone else did either. We went home and did some research. We found that trisomy 13 or 18 means "incompatible with life." There are cases where babies survive for a day or maybe even a year, but they have almost complete organ failure and cannot function in this world. I did not know what to do with that information. According to the experts, all we really needed to do was wait. Our risks were not that high. Why worry?

I stopped doing research and tried to look for other sources of support. I knew all the facts and the signs to look for; now I needed reassurance. A spiritual leader told me to speak with my baby. To thank my baby for being mine, for being a part of our family, and for coming to us. He said to thank each one of my baby's cells and pray for each one. To speak to my child, to love my baby. We made it a new nightly ritual to rub cocoa butter on my belly and talk to the baby as a family. When the baby started kicking back, we knew we were getting through.

Finally, we went in for the twenty-week ultrasound. We brought Ifé so that she could see her little sibling and we could all be a part of the process. She lay on the bed with me as they scanned my belly and then inside my vagina. The technician was so sweet. She talked and joked with us about our children and collected lots of information. When she asked us if we wanted to know the sex, we knew we couldn't wait. As soon as she said, "You're having a boy," I saw Mike's face light up. We secretly had both wanted a son, and her words were music to our ears.

After about an hour of measuring and collecting data, she said she still had to get his complete height. She told us to take a walk and come back in half an hour, and he would have definitely moved. We walked around the complex with Ifé, talking about boy names and imagining our life with our new son. At that point, he could not arrive soon enough.

We went back and got into position again. The technician came in, and as she started checking, she got quiet. She excused herself and left suddenly. A few moments later, a different woman came in. She said she was the doctor and wanted to discuss some results with us. She said that during the screening, they found that the baby had a cleft palate, as well as extra toes and fingers, and that his spine was not developing. I burst into tears. She kept talking, as if she didn't see me, in a positive tone they must have taught her during medical school. She said that there are many things like speech therapy that can be done, but we knew the truth.

I called my midwives and asked them to be honest with me. Did the ultrasound folks tell them that the baby had a trisomy? They gave me the same runaround, saying they couldn't be sure, but suggested that I should probably have more tests. I finally spoke to the head midwife, and she helped me schedule an amniocentesis a few days later.

We were broken. I cried for what felt like days, until the amniocentesis. My life felt blurry. I did not do what I needed to for my jobs and did not feel like moving. We sent an e-mail to our family and friends, asking for prayers, but I didn't want to talk to anyone. No one really seemed to understand. They did not know what it was like to have your son living and moving inside of you, yet in the process of dying.

The amniocentesis confirmed what we already knew. Our son had trisomy 13, the rarer kind, which meant he could not possibly survive. The emotionless doctor told us our son actually had an extreme case and that his kidneys were full of fluid. At twenty-one weeks, he would not be alive much longer.

Now we had a choice. We could either stay pregnant and see how long he lived, abort him, or be induced into early labor. In all cases it was certain that he would not survive. Never in my life have I had to make a harder decision. For a few days Mike wanted to stay pregnant. I could not imagine holding my baby in my womb, feeling him kick, and knowing that at some point he would pass away. Once Mike found out that a second- or third-trimester miscarriage could be dangerous, he quickly changed his mind.

I knew that I could not go through labor. I could not do twenty-one hours of the kind of pain I vividly remembered to have a dead baby. We decided on having a "D and E," a dilation and evacuation, a fancier term for an abortion.

During our days of decisions and tears, we picked a name for our son. Kamau. It was perfect. Our quiet warrior.

After having Ifé at home, I never thought I would have a baby in a hospital; I never wanted to. But instead, this birth, this transition, was both in a hospital and incredibly medicalized. It was a two-day process: first I went in to have my cervix dilated; then the next day I had the operation. In all of my research, I could not ascertain how the baby would actually die. At that point I could still feel him move, and I still spoke to him. They told me on the day of the dilation that he would die in the evacuation process. I felt sick. Not my son.

I told the doctor that was not going to work. My son was not going to die by being sucked out of me, limb by limb. She said that was what always happened, but she recognized my concern. By a clear act of the creator, she asked me, "Do you have any other children?" We said, yes, Ifétayo. She looked at us, stunned, and told us that she was a Yoruba priestess and had a dear friend named Ifé. She then informed us that there was one solution, but it could be risky: I could get a shot in my stomach that would go directly into Kamau. It would take his life over the next few hours in a much more peaceful way. She would be able to justify this to our insurance as a spiritual need.

We got the shot. Over the next few hours, we prayed over our son and held him. I could feel his life drifting away. His kicks got lighter and eventually completely stopped. My son died inside of me. He was twenty-two weeks of wonderful growing in me. My womb, which was once supplying his life energy, was now cradling his corpse. I knew the difference. I could feel every part of the change and transition. He was now a part of the spirit world again—he was no longer my little baby in his little home.

The next day was a blur. We went into the hospital, had the procedure, and went home. It all went well; people were pleasant, and I had lots of drugs.

I came home and slept for days, waking up to cry and to eat chocolate. Mike was trying to let me know how much he appreciated me and us and our love. So he fed me, and I ate and slept, and I cried.

Mike took care of everything else related to Kamau. We got his body cremated, and Mike ordered a beautiful urn. We set up an altar for him, with his pictures, candles, his urn, and a memory book. Mike was our rock during that time, taking care of Ifé and explaining to her that her brother wasn't inside of Mommy anymore but in the spirit world.

Eventually life was supposed to return to normal. We told our friends and family what had happened. People offered support and love, and we were so appreciative but had no idea what to do with it. We had become so close and dependent on each other that inviting others into our pain felt more beneficial to them than to us.

One comfort was that I had never stopped breastfeeding Ifé. When my milk came in, as though my son had been born, Ifé picked up the slack. Her milk intake allowed my uterus to shrink back down to size incredibly fast, shocking the doctor during our two-week follow-up. The magic of babies and healing is incredible.

I returned to work, yoga, consulting, teaching, and organizing. People asked why I had been out or how the baby was doing and then got uncomfortable when I told them the truth, so I learned not to talk about it. At the same time that people didn't want to hear my story, they all had a few of their own. They themselves or people they knew had lost babies. I began to hear story after story of miscarriages, abortions, child deaths, or problems conceiving. I always thought I had entered a secret club when I became a mother, one that no one really talked about but whose rules every mother seemed to know. This was a different club—one that was really top secret, yet had more members than I could have imagined.

I began to think about birth and death and life and choice. I was incredibly fortunate to be able to have Ifé at home. I had the insurance, the education, the ability, the health, the support, and the option to do so. I live in Washington, DC, where home births are allowed and midwives are legally able to practice them. I was able to have the birth I wanted with Ifé not just because of our good health but because of the politics of the city and the privilege I hold.

I was also able to choose the kind of death I wanted Kamau to have. Again, because of my education, my insurance, my ability, my support, and the city I live in, I was able to have a second-trimester abortion. If I had lived in many other states that do not allow this, I would have been forced to carry Kamau as long as he stayed alive, at risk to my life. The similarities between my two birth experiences, which had seemed so incredibly different before, now became evident. In very different ways, both of my experiences were natural. I was in charge, leading the way in decisions related to my body.

It has not been that long since Kamau died. Ifé is now two and a half and full of energy and love. Mike took our son's passing as his own wakeup call and has prioritized his health in a whole new way. I think we were all jolted into the realities of life and death, and he recognizes now how he wants to be around as long as possible. And I am pregnant again. Excited, but incredibly cautious and intimidated.

I am still healing emotionally, and I am not really sure when or if I will ever fully get better. I teach bell hooks, Audre Lorde, and other black women writers who emphasize the importance of self-love and healing, but I am still learning what that really means for me. Some days are better than others. Mother's Day was horrible. I expect the anniversary of his death will be hard, but a month later our new baby girl is expected to arrive. I am still struggling with saying that she will be born. I know better now.

Going natural or having a natural childbirth, I've realized, is not a specific way of giving birth without medical interventions. Rather, it is a practice of recognizing life, celebrating love, and listening to our bodies. Ifé's birth was magical, but so was Kamau's death. His transition into the spirit world and Ifé's transition away from it were natural. It was their time. It was filled with confusion and fear and pain, but in the end, it was what they both needed. In the process of recognizing their experiences, I am coming to see the truth in mine. I respected my body, I recognized my choice, and I was heard.

I love my children, all three of them. I love them for who they are and what they brought and are bringing me. I am who I am because of them, and I would not change any of my time with them. I am different now than I was, but it's okay. Life is not only about living; it's also about death and change and love. It's mostly about love.

CHAPTER 10

Images from the Safe Motherhood Quilt

Ina May Gaskin and Laura Gilkey

The Safe Motherhood Quilt Project is a national effort developed to draw public attention to maternal death rates in the United States, as well as the gross underreporting of maternal deaths. The project honors women who have died of pregnancy-related causes since 1982 and is the vision of midwifery pioneer Ina May Gaskin. The Safe Motherhood Quilt Project is the voice for mothers who can no longer speak for themselves.[1]

Tatia Oden French, thirty-two, entered a well-respected hospital to deliver her first child in December 2001. She was in perfect health and looking forward to a natural childbirth, without any interventions or drugs. According to her doctor's calculations, she was a little under two weeks overdue, and so she was given Cytotec—a drug not FDA-approved for labor induction—to start her labor. Ten hours after being administered Cytotec, Tatia suffered severe complications, and an emergency C-section was performed. Both Tatia and her baby, Zorah, died in the operating room. This quilt block was created by Ina May Gaskin.

Tameka McFarquhar, twenty-two, bled to death in her Watertown, New York, apartment several days after giving birth in December 2004 to her first child, Danasia Elizabeth McFarquhar. Tameka's cause of death was placenta increta, meaning that she was discharged from the hospital with the placenta inside her uterus and the deaths of her and her daughter could have been avoided with proper medical care. Tameka and Danasia Elizabeth McFarquhar's bodies were flown to Jamaica for burial. This quilt block was created by Elizabeth Maxen.

Trishawna Quarles, thirty-four, suffered from sickle cell anemia through-out her life, and she and her husband knew that pregnancy would be a high-risk event for her. Nevertheless, they decided to try to have a baby. Late in her pregnancy, Trishawna began to have complications, and her doctor performed an emergency cesarean. Her son, Dorian, was born on September 10, 2011, in Santa Maria, California. After delivery, Trishawna developed blood clots and kidney problems. On September 16, 2011, she died of heart failure. This quilt block was created by Hayley Boultinghouse.

Corrine Johnson died on May 5, 2009, in Pittsburgh, Pennsylvania, of medical complications following a cesarean. Her baby survived. This quilt block was created by Laura Gilkey.

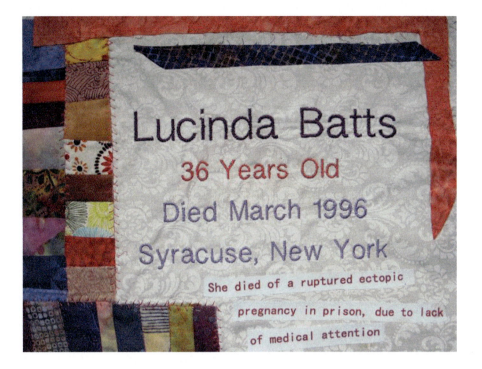

Lucinda Batts, thirty-six, died of a ruptured ectopic pregnancy in March 1996 while in custody at the Onondaga County Justice Center in Syracuse, New York. A state commission found that Batts's death occurred as a result of indifferent or incompetent medical care, and in 1996 the county health commissioner vowed to adopt new standards for medical care of incarcerated women. Despite these measures, Chuniece Patterson died of the same complications in the same jail in 2009. This quilt block was created by Jan Lapetino.

Kalilah Roberson-Reese, twenty-nine, died on Christmas Day 2006. Pregnant with her first child, she went to a hospital in Houston, Texas, complaining of leg and chest pains and shortness of breath but was repeatedly sent home. During her last visit, she was transferred to a medical center, where doctors performed a C-section in an unsuccessful attempt to save the life of her unborn child. At that time, Kalilah suffered a potentially fatal amniotic fluid embolism. She suffered extensive brain damage a month later when medical staff failed to notice that her breathing tube had been dislodged. This quilt block was created by Barbara Resendes.

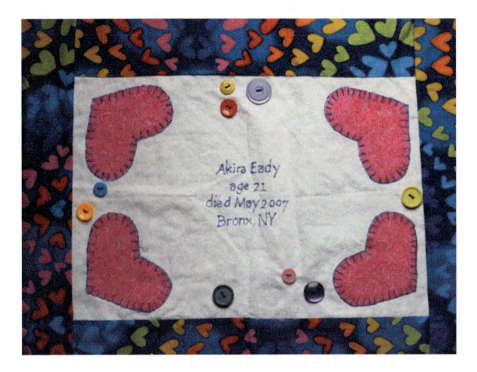

Akira Eady, twenty-one, suffered postpartum seizures and heart failure shortly after giving birth to her third child at Mount Sinai Center in New York. Akira bled heavily after receiving an epidural and complained of headaches after giving birth. The hospital released her nevertheless, and she was brain-dead within four days of giving birth. Akira's two-year-old son later died of internal injuries while in her boyfriend's care. This quilt block was created by Michelle Connor.

Lesley Ann Marshall Spencer was born on Mother's Day, May 11, 1969, in Philadelphia, Pennsylvania. Pregnant with her first baby, she was induced for two days and then underwent a C-section. One month later, on July 9, 2002, she died. According to her doctors, she suffered from postpartum cardiomyopathy while being treated for what they had thought was pneumonia. Her sister Cecily Harris remembers her thus: "Lesley Ann Marshall Spencer was a phenomenal woman, a caring, intelligent, funny, outgoing woman, and my little sister. After giving birth to her first child, a daughter, only God knew that Lesley and Jayda would have three weeks to bond during countless breastfeedings, while gazing into each other's eyes and souls. After Lesley transitioned, Lesley's husband became 'mom' and dad, in caring for their daughter; from rocking Jayda to sleep at night, to braiding her hair, adorned with the most beautiful beads, and coaching her basketball team. As Jayda's auntie I feel blessed and privileged to share that Jayda has grown into a beautiful, sweet, intelligent (straight As) pre-teen."

PART III

Changing Lives, One Birth at a Time

Birthing Sexual Freedom and Healing

A Survivor Mother's Birth Story

Biany Pérez

> I carry my fears on my body because I don't want to leave them laying around.
>
> —*Warsan Shire*[1]

Poet Warsan Shire discusses what it means to carry the weight of one's fears in order to avoid being exposed. What does it mean to live in a body that has experienced trauma or assault? The body carries the histories of past pains and present assaults. Unresolved trauma, abuse, and fear are carried in our minds, spirits, and bodies. This imprint of fear becomes a part of our lives, so much so that we hold onto it tightly. This comfort, this illusion of safety, becomes our shield from the world. Our bodies no longer belong to us. We carry the fear so tightly that we do not recognize who we are. We learn to disassociate from our minds and bodies. Our emotions no longer carry meaning while we inhabit our bodies. We are foreigners, looking at our bodies from the outside. Disassociation from our bodies becomes our way of life. We dissociate from the fear of knowing our bodies because we are afraid of what that knowledge will reveal.

My journey from pregnancy to childbirth led me on a quest to wrestle with tough questions concerning my past. What does it mean to survive sexual trauma and abuse? What happens when black survivors of sexual abuse become pregnant? How do I, as a childbearing black woman survivor, deal with the extra challenges related to my trauma and cope with the changes to my body involved in pregnancy? This chapter takes you on my journey of transition from victim to survivor-mother. I invoke the spirit and words of black queer feminist poet Audre Lorde, who calls for women to search in that deep and dark place within us, to use the erotic as power. Pregnancy and childbirth became that place for me. They allowed me to search deep within, to fight against disassociation in an effort to unite my mind, body, and spirit while I prepared for my son's arrival.

Toni Morrison writes, "Each story has a monster in it who made them tough instead of brave, so they open their legs rather than their hearts where that folded child is tucked."[2] I learned early that my body was something to be despised. I thought I deserved what happened to me at the age of ten—that I deserved to be robbed of my innocence and sense of self-worth. So when my mom's boyfriend called me to the master bedroom while my mom was out making her weekly run to the supermarket, I was intrigued by the extra attention I received from a man who "filled" the empty shoes of my absentee father. A part of me was curious, enthralled, and frightened. He asked me to sit on my mother's bed. So I did. Then he asked me to lie down. And I obeyed for fear that he would physically hurt me, like my mom's alcoholic former boyfriend had hurt her the year before. Then he began to touch my legs. As he reached to my inner thighs, my voice expressed my disgust. He spoke in a quiet, threatening voice. "Now you don't want me to call your sister in here. Be quiet. Everything is going to be fine." And I did what he said. As he touched my face, kissed my lips, caressed my thighs . . . I just lay there like one of the dolls in my bedroom: lifeless.

From that moment on, through secrecy, silence, and self-judgment, I would carry this pain and shame. At ten, I would experience a permanent numbness, separating myself from my body in the hope of never feeling this pain again. I would walk away from this experience hardened by the shame of what had happened but never brave enough to confront the incident and the trauma that lingered. At this point I learned to navigate the world as a victim, using my tough exterior as a shield to push people away so that I would never feel that pain again. My childhood trauma, left unresolved, gave birth to more pain, disappointment, and shame.

I met him my first semester of my freshman year in college. He was a nice guy, popular, and we shared mutual friends. He seemed noncommittal, and I was insecure and fascinated by the attention he gave me. A few months later my friend and I went to a party off campus, had a few drinks, and decided to pay him a visit. My friend went back to campus, and I decided to spend the night. He was a good guy, or at least I thought he was. We cuddled in his bed and kissed—until he held me down. Flashbacks of my past resurfaced. I said no. But he ignored me. He acted like I was not there. He was not physically violent; yet he was stronger than me. He made me invisible. All I could do was return to the ten-year-old girl in the master bedroom in the 1990s, numb and motionless. As he penetrated my body, I slowly left my "self." I could not allow him to see me break. I had to be tough. In my near comatose state, while he remained on top of me until he was finished, I imagined my soul/spirit leaving my body and just walking away. But my spirit didn't walk away; it stayed in the room with me, outside my body, watching me. I felt ashamed, angry, and guilty. This time I believed I would walk away from those feelings for good, never to relive this pain again.

Insight mediation teacher and emotional wisdom consultant Ruth King discusses her walk with trauma and abuse: "I realized that while I had physically walked away from the traumas of childhood, I still carried them with me. The cruelties and disappointments were thriving, sheltered inside my body, mind and heart. I did not know how to love and was too afraid to learn."[3] Like King, I physically ran away from my past, hoping to leave it behind, but the trauma and pain were living inside my body and mind and hovered over my heart and spirit. This tough and hardened exterior that I created not only pushed people away but made it impossible for me to know and give love. It was evident to me that I had never really abandoned my past but buried it and let it invade my body like a disease. I was slowly beginning to see that I had spent my life running from my true self because of the agonizing shame, disappointment, and pain I felt.

"Vulnerability sounds like truth and feels like courage. Truth and courage aren't always comfortable but they're never weakness."[4] Brené Brown shows us how to embrace vulnerability as a space where we reclaim truth and courage. In our society, we have been taught to see vulnerability as weakness, but it is the opposite and is the only way to tap into our strength and infinite power. I ran away from my story of abuse because I did not want to be a casualty of my past, but in running away I became a prisoner and a victim. Pregnancy allowed me to tell my story, embrace vulnerability, and take a courageous step in becoming a survivor and embark on the journey to sexual (erotic) freedom. I came to learn that in order for me to be free from the pains of my past, I would have to share my story.

Upon discovering my pregnancy in August 2011, I was in denial. I knew that pregnancy would offer me the opportunity to confront the traumas that I have kept in hiding for far too long. But I was not sure that this was the time for self-discovery. I reached a breaking point that year. My demons were confronting me, and my unborn child was invading my life. Despite intensive therapy sessions and daily doses of antidepressants, I felt hopeless and even considered ending my life. I was getting pretty close to exploring and unpacking my fears, traumas, and suicidal thoughts. I believed that I was emotionally unprepared and too broken not only to bring a child into this world but to raise a healthy one. In the thirty-nine weeks of my pregnancy, I learned that growing inside me were two "children": (1) my baby, and (2) the inner child I had kept tucked under the pain of my trauma. Thus, both would inspire me to heal and seek the freedom I yearned for. Gradually, I learned to forgive myself for not being able either to change or to accept my past. By practicing emotional release, therapy, yoga, meditation, and mindfulness and embracing vulnerability, I would be able to walk the road of love and freedom.

My pregnancy was an educational, spiritual, emotional, and transformative voyage. Early into my pregnancy, I spent a great deal of time reading and absorbing literature on the topic of pregnancy and birth. As a radical woman of color, one of the issues that resonated with me pertained to the ways the US health-care system denigrates, violates, and abuses women's bodies, especially those of pregnant and expectant persons. Learning about the medical establishment's view of pregnancy as a medical condition and the frequency of superfluous medical interventions led me to choose an out-of-hospital birth, one that valued women's inherent knowledge of pregnancy and childbirth. After watching the documentary *The Business of Being Born,* I affirmed that I could not have a birth in a hospital unless it was medically necessary. This education served as inspiration for me to spend the next couple of months working on myself physically, emotionally, mentally, and spiritually to prepare for a vaginal, nonmedicated labor. This quest for self-awareness and readiness allowed me the opportunity to tap into my inner strength and awareness about the type of birth I wanted for my baby and myself.

Having spent half of my adult life disguising the pain of my past and not knowing that I recreated the suffering that I was seeking to avoid, I knew that only by being present in mind, body, and spirit while in labor would I be able to birth with awareness. I viewed pregnancy and childbirth as a sacred passage and not a medical event (even when medical care is necessary and a part of birth). For me, this sacred passage required preparation rooted in self-discovery, emotional release, and looking within to be able to give birth rooted in mindfulness. I was concerned that the unresolved pain I was dealing with would have a negative impact on my pregnancy and labor. My journey revealed that my past trauma deserved my attention and respect and that I could not be fully liberated until I had healed my relationship with my self. In other words, labor would be the act that helped me to tap into my inner strength and courage. This would be a labor of love, strength, and courage. It would allow me the opportunity to seek freedom from within and to trust my body in a way that I never could have done before.

We have been taught to fear the feminine power that lies within us, and in turn we continue to fear pregnancy and childbirth. Birthing my son, Zen, gave me the courage to embrace vulnerability and unlock the trauma that lived within my mind, body, and spirit. The path of a vaginal and nonmedicated labor and birth allowed me to tap into my inner awareness, the site of power and pleasure known as the erotic. Audre Lorde calls for women to recognize the power of the erotic within our lives because it allows us to touch our most deeply creative source and obtain the energy we need to pursue genuine change within our world. She further states, "For as we begin to recognize our deepest feelings, we begin to give up, of necessity, being satisfied with suffering and self-negation, and with the numbness which so often seems like their only alternative in our society. Our acts against oppression become integral with self, motivated and empowered from within."[5]

The return to the erotic is a reminder of our capacity for feeling and our right to reclaim joy. To recognize our profound feelings is to no longer be determined by external forces and to seek and reclaim the power that lies within. Our erotic knowledge empowers us and becomes the lens through which we reclaim our right to love and be loved. The erotic allowed me to tell my truth, trust my body, and love myself so that I could have the birth of my choosing. The erotic way of knowing helped me to birth with love, strength, and courage. No longer was I a prisoner of my past. Birthing in the presence of my partner and wise women who believed in the power of the erotic and the power of women to birth the way they want helped me to reclaim my own power.

My birth story will forever leave an imprint on my mind and body and will forever touch my heart. I gained a sense of freedom with my body, sexuality, and self that I could not imagine before giving birth to Zen. On the early morning of Saturday, March 17, before the sun rose, I felt my first contractions. I spent the day using movement, breathing, and meditation to get through each contraction. With the support of my partner, breathing exercises, and positive words that affirmed the trust I had for my self and my body, I was able to endure labor until I was ready to go to the birth center. Later that evening, the contractions were stronger and closer together. I was in active labor, and my partner and I were headed to the birth center. When we arrived, our midwife and an on-call nurse welcomed us. My friend and doula arrived about an hour later. While I was in active labor, the pain was unbearable, and there were moments when I considered pain medication. My support team reminded me that I was close to meeting my child, reminded me to breathe, and reminded me of the ancestors who were present, supporting me through this trying time. I did not feel alone. I was surrounded by love. With each contraction, I tapped into my erotic knowledge, which allowed me to trust my body and to surrender. The contractions became stronger; it felt like they were coming every minute, and at that point I claimed the erotic. I was doing the birth dance of breath, movement, and looking within that deep, dark, and strong place within me.

In claiming my power, I also was able to embrace the miracle of surrendering. Surrender is an active life energy that flows through us. Spiritual teacher Eckhart Tolle defines surrender as "the simple, yet profound wisdom of yielding to rather than opposing the flow of life. The only place you can experience this is in the Now, so to surrender is to accept the present moment unconditionally and without reservation."[6] The power of surrender allowed me to be one with the present moment. It allowed me to become in tune with my body, my emotions, and the pain and the sensations of the unknown that came with labor. In surrendering to labor, I no longer resisted the sensations of the unknown. My mind, body, and spirit were in sync. The power of the erotic and the miracle of surrender gave me the strength to birth my son the next morning. I could trust my body. When labor became difficult and the pain intolerable, flashbacks of my past came to mind, but my support team reminded me to look within, to trust my body, and to simply surrender. I experienced surrender as a site that allowed me to gain erotic satisfaction and sexual freedom, to love and accept my body in the present moment.

Birthing Zen gave me an astounding and lasting sense of power, increased self-awareness, greater intimacy and openness with my partner, unbelievably beautiful memories, and a new and improved relationship with my own body and sexuality. The labor, while challenging, gave me confidence, strength, and power that I never knew I had. A vaginal, nonmedicated birth was important to me because I needed to feel and be in the moment. It allowed me to trust my body in ways I never was able to before. This birthing story will forever erase the past and the ways I allowed my pain and childhood trauma to haunt and perpetuate the anguish I wanted to escape. Birthing is a spiritual, emotional, and physical journey that allowed me to embrace the erotic and my own strength. It allowed me the power to love myself again.

What does it mean to be a survivor-mother? I have learned that I am more than a collection of events that have happened to me and that I have agency over my life. In choosing the erotic, I tapped into the deep place within me where my inner awareness led me to strength, courage, and the wisdom to have a memorable birthing story. The power lay within me, and I was able to tap into the inner spiritual force of my ancestors who supported me during labor. I learned to be present, to embrace courage, to work to understand fear-based beliefs, and to trust my body to help birth my son. I no longer birth the pain of my past. I have birthed sexual freedom, and I will continue on this path of healing so that I can help my son gain the same freedom and awareness. As a survivor-mother, I remember my past as a place of strength, but I am not controlled by it. Instead, I look within for love, courage, and sexual freedom.

CHAPTER 12

Birth as Battle Cry

A Doula's Journey from Home to Hospital

Gina Mariela Rodríguez

As I studied to become a doula,[1] my personal experiences with medical violence started to make sense. When I was younger, an ob-gyn cut me with a speculum during an exam and sent me home with a pad without apologizing. It happened twice more after that. Each time I felt more ashamed of my body and more afraid to ask questions.

I thought something was wrong with me.

I was told it wouldn't hurt, that it shouldn't hurt.

But it did.

My first—and last—male ob-gyn told me he didn't test for sexually transmitted infections "unless you have reason to believe you have something." He assured me he wasn't worried because Rhode Island "has a small gay population and all the IV drug users are locked up." I was infuriated and horrified as he examined me and never again returned to his office.

The more I learned about the history of obstetrics, the more I connected that institution to my everyday experiences and to our collective historical experience as women of color living under patriarchy and racism. I was reminded of Saartjie Baartman, the Khoikhoi woman put on display, in life and in death, to demonstrate European beliefs that Africans were an oversexed, inferior race.[2] I learned that the so-called father of gynecology developed his surgeries by experimenting on enslaved women, without anesthesia or their consent.[3] I learned about the forced sterilizations of Puerto Rican and Indigenous women across the United States and Canada. I came to understand the hospital as a place that continues the colonization of our bodies, our wombs, our first breaths.

*****

By the end of 2010, I had assisted in three births as a doula. All were with working-class women of color. Two were hospital births—one without medication, the other medicated with Pitocin and an epidural. The third was a home water birth under the watchful eye of candles and midwives, sistahs and Oshún.

I was honored to have been a part of each of these women's journeys. Each time, I was overwhelmed by the all-knowing power of these sistahs' bodies, minds, and spirits. Nevertheless, there was something particularly special about Tsedaye's home birth. It was far longer than the two hospital births I attended. Three days long, in fact. And although she might say otherwise, it felt throughout those long days and nights that she wasn't suffering but enduring. And it came to me—in that space created and protected by women's energy, in the calm and encouraging presence of the midwives, the candles, the incense, the struggle—that birth is an act of self-determination.

Four months after assisting at Tsedaye's home birth, I was pregnant. I made decisions. Other than my husband, there would be no men. No sterile beds. No clocks. No timeline. No interventions. No needles. No fingers. No speculums. No IVs. No monitor and no paper. No shared bathroom down the hall. I would not end up on my back in the white man's hospital. They would have to take me kicking and screaming.

Like Tsedaye, I wanted a certified professional midwife (CPM) to attend my home birth, but none were able to practice safely in Rhode Island. Although it is not illegal to have a home birth in Rhode Island, a midwife's licensing determines whether or not her presence at a home birth is legal. Unfortunately, at the time of my birth, CPMs were not yet licensed to attend home births in Rhode Island as they were in neighboring states. For decades, midwives have crossed into Rhode Island from Massachusetts to assist at home births, but in the case of hospital transfer, they may not accompany women for fear of heavy fines or potential jail time. Some have even been threatened with cease-and-desist orders. Preventing women from having home births forces them under the control of the colonial medical establishment and increases their vulnerability to medical violence. Rhode Island's laws present women with few options but to birth in a hospital.

I wouldn't take no for an answer. So I waited. I went to my ob-gyn for initial ultrasound and blood work, told her not to expect me back for care, and went home to do more research. And then I found Mary, a certified nurse midwife (CNM) who had built a practice paving the way for women to have home births with legalized providers. As a CNM, she had hospital privileges, which meant she could accompany me if I should need to transfer.

My appointments with Mary were lovely. We got to know one another and built authentic trust. She knew Jen, my doula. And Mary worked with Camille, a midwife I saw years ago who didn't use stirrups. I was thrilled! As a doula, I knew there would be no guarantees, and my midwives and doula reminded me of that often. They told me to pack an "in case" hospital bag. Still, I did not consider the hospital as an option. I believed I needed to avoid it to survive.

*****

My water broke on Tuesday, December 13, 2011, at 1:45 a.m. I was asleep and felt the trickle through my dreams. I woke, felt it again, and got up to go to the bathroom. I reached down. Yes. It was my water. I put on a pad and went back into the bedroom. Leaning into my husband, I said, "Julian, babe, I think my water just broke."

"Really?" His voice was so gentle, so elated, it brought tears to my eyes. We were too excited to go back to sleep. Instead we kissed, wrote in our journals, and talked until dawn.

In the morning, I called Jen and Mary to let them know about the slow leak from my bag of waters. I was concerned that Mary would start counting hours since my water had broken. Instead, she was laid-back and encouraging. "Yup, okay," she answered to each point in my report: my water had broken, I was going through a maxi pad every couple of hours, and I had mild contractions about fifteen minutes apart. She asked me to call her when I called my doula to have a sense of when she and her team might be coming.

My mother came by with goodies and hugs. We cleaned the house, Mom made a marinara sauce, and we fielded calls from my aunts and uncles and friends. I knew it wasn't easy for Mom to be there—she was nervous about me having a home birth—but she came to support me despite her own fears.

Jen came over around 5 p.m. By that time the contractions were five to seven minutes apart and hard to talk through. Mom left after Jen arrived—we knew she would be too anxious to stay for the birth. Jen and Julian supported me throughout the evening. I squatted or leaned against the couch with my knees on pillows, but I liked standing most. I felt most of the pain in my lower back.

After a couple of hours, I got into the shower. Julian stayed with me in the bathroom, but I bathed myself, allowing myself to let go, to submit to the pain of the contractions. It was the first time I felt truly empowered, and calm, during the labor. I have no idea how long anything took or how long I was in any particular stage or position in my labor at home. That was perhaps one of the most beautiful aspects of being able to labor at home for so long—the lack of a sense of time, the complete ability to be in my zone. Each contraction felt helplessly infinite and frightening, but I had no sense of how long or how far apart they were. They were simply there, gone, and there again.

My team set up the birth pool, a kiddie pool we had bought for $25. Jen asked if I had a tank top or bathing suit to wear. "I'm going in naked," I said. This was a very significant and empowering moment. I rarely reveal my body and don't even like wearing shorts. Labor and birth helped me let go of that inhibition. I didn't struggle. I just stripped off and got right in without even thinking about it. I love that I was able to do that.

Oshún's healing waters gave me a chance to rest between contractions. As I knelt in the pool, my friends Viviane and Dara poured warm water over my back. My doula looked me in the eyes, working with me through the contractions. The women-womb energy brought by their presence and by being in the water was emotionally, physically, and spiritually grounding. Julian held my face in his hands quietly and attentively. At one moment, I asked everyone to moan with me. It was by far one of the highlights of labor—sitting naked in a kiddie pool in my writing room while we moaned and laughed together at the absurdity of the scene.

After a while we decided to get out of the pool to speed things up again. Standing brought the contractions on back to back. I had a feeling something was off and kept asking if I was "doing it right." Everyone assured me there was no right or wrong way. But I knew I wasn't "progressing" the way my contractions seemed to indicate. I vomited throughout the labor. Too many times to count. In cups, in the bathroom sink, in bags, in my hands. I couldn't keep sips of water down. Every time I vomited, I felt a release in my bottom and in my mind. I don't remember my midwife arriving, but I do remember her standing in my living room quietly and simply bearing witness.

*****

By Wednesday morning I was exhausted. My baby was posterior, so we did everything we could to change the baby's position. This included inversions over my huge Spanish and Portuguese dictionaries (by far the worst part of labor), lunges on the hall stairs two at a time, and squats with Julian holding me from behind.

We stood at my altar, and Dara prayed. I got lost in prayer, calling out to ancestors, Oshún, the Orishas, God, the Virgin Mary, all the women before me who have done this. "Assata did this in prison," Dara said. I felt uplifted, out of body, lost in an energy beyond myself, beyond everyone in the room with me. It was love. Love for life, for the womb, for family, for community, for struggle, for this baby, for the pain.

"Walk," they encouraged me. We walked.

Midday Wednesday, my midwife checked me. She pulled her hand out. Looked at me. "Three to four." I flipped.

"I hate myself! What's wrong with me? I can't keep doing this!" It had been over thirty hours since my water broke, with many hours of intense labor pains, and I was only three to four centimeters dilated?

Mary grabbed my face. "I don't want to hear you say that about yourself again."

Julian and I had a choice to make. We could continue laboring at home, and Mary could wait to check me again, or we could go to the hospital for assistance. I knew that assistance meant Pitocin and an epidural. We were left alone to talk it over. My water had broken a long while ago. There was the potential for infection. Waiting might mean an emergency transfer. I could ride the waves at home, try to contain the fury in my own space, or I could get assistance in the form of my worst fears. Julian held me through several contractions as we talked. I kept my eyes closed, falling asleep in between the periods of pain. He stayed calm and comforting the whole time. Held me tightly, wrapped his fingers around mine like an anchor. We were looking the storm in the eye.

My friends hugged me and told me I was making the best decision. "This has been going on for too long," they said. "It's okay to get some help," they said. I wanted to scream, "I'm doing this for the baby not for me!" I felt guilty that I was grateful for some relief and that I was starting to accept the epidural more and more. I was letting go of my fear of being numb. I didn't want anyone to tell me I was making the right decision. It wasn't making me feel any better.

I'd never packed a bag. And here I was, packing. Not kicking, not screaming.

*****

From 3:45 to 4:10 p.m. I had what felt like one continuous contraction. They must have been like this at home. But now I had a clock to watch, staring at me from the wall, mocking me. The nurses kept saying the anesthesiologist would be there in five minutes. I watched five minutes come and go for an hour. No one could fool me into riding the contractions now. I knew exactly how long they were lasting, exactly how often they were coming.

I grabbed my midwife. "I will do anything to avoid a C-section."

"Okay, that's what we'll do, but there are no guarantees."

I couldn't afford to be afraid. I had to find surrender without defeat.

*****

Julian came in with a gift from my father—a white beaded necklace for Obatala, the Orisha of peace and tranquility. My eyes welled. At that moment, I knew that everything was going to be fine. I had Nana's rosary beads adorned with shells from the slave ports in Ghana. I had Obatala with me. Deities from both sides of the Atlantic and from all bloodlines surrounded me. I couldn't bring the altar with me, but I held divine energy close.

I dozed off for a bit. When I opened my eyes, my Auntie Donna, Mom, and Auntie Mal were sitting in a semicircle at the foot of the bed. Legs crossed.

Pocket books on their laps. Eyes wide open. Holding vigil. I burst out laughing. They laughed too. "Now listen here, missy," Auntie Donna said, "I know you left your candles and your friends and your warm environment and now you're stuck with the three Sicilians, but that's what you have!"

They left, and I tried to sleep and got an hour here, an hour there. Mary checked me at some point. I was up to five centimeters dilated. The Pitocin was working. She told me I looked like someone just starting her labor.

How nice.

*****

Around 11 p.m. I started feeling contractions again. They intensified and ran down my legs. I was unable to get to my feet because of the epidural. Jen helped me breathe through the most intense, continuous pain of my labor. Being unable to move during contractions was excruciating and frustrating. The anesthesiologist arrived after an hour and a half. The catheter had slipped out. Epidural number two.

*****

Around 3 a.m. Mary woke me and asked if I wanted to start pushing.

The last thing I wanted was to be on my back. I asked to be on hands and knees, and they helped me get into position. We tried to sit-squat at the edge of the bed. I felt like the baby was coming through my tailbone. The best position, the one that moved the baby through the pelvis, ended up being on my back. Go figure. My midwife looked at the monitor and told me when I was having a contraction, and then I put my chin to my chest, bared down, and pushed. I couldn't feel the intensity of my pushes because of the epidural. After a while, Jen pulled a rebozo from her bag and told me to hold one end. Mary held the other and told me to play tug of war with her as I pushed.

I found out later that Mary is a volunteer fire fighter—she pulled that rebozo like nothing I've ever felt. I screamed, "I hate this thing! I'm going to let this go, and everyone at that end is going to go flying!"

"You let go, and I'm walking out of this room!" she yelled back at me.

That's when I got pissed. At everyone. At Jen for that goddamn rebozo. At the nurses who kept leaving the door open. "I can't do this!" I kept yelling. "Get me off my back!" And Mary finally looked up at me and said, "Gina, you are not a victim! Push!"

So I did. Screaming. Swearing. Crying with no tears. Julian at my right leg. Jen at my left. I kept telling Mary to give me her fingers. They stretched me. Gave me direction to push.

The baby started to crown. I reached down and felt the baby's head. Such soft hair. I kept pushing. Every time I screamed, "Get me off my back!" my baby came down a little more. Once Julian told me that, I let myself lose control. It felt so good to scream!

I felt a little burning and stretching. "Is the head out?" I asked Julian. His eyes were bright. "Yes!" I heard her cry. She was so pink! Her eyes were wide open, looking at Julian.

"Reach down and grab your baby," Mary told me.

I pulled my baby out of me.

From one world into the next.

After fifty-two hours since my water broke, my baby girl had arrived.

I couldn't bring her to my chest. The cord was too short. They brought her back down in between my legs, and Mary warmed her with towels as Julian stared at her face. The cord went white and stopped pulsing. I watched Julian cut the cord. He looked so proud. We fell in love with our baby instantly.

*****

Years later, I continue to reflect on my daughter's birth. Sometimes I struggle to remember labor before the hospital, and I feel like I failed because I agreed to an epidural. Yet I have also learned from this struggle. I now realize that I wanted a home birth because I was afraid of the hospital. I am no longer afraid. If I am blessed with a second child, I will choose home birth not out of fear but to affirm life. Because birth is an act of self-determination. We named our baby Xiomara Mia, which together means, "Ready for Battle, My Wished for Child." She teaches me how to be courageous.

CHAPTER 13

Sister Midwife

Nurturing and Reflecting Black Womanhood in an Urban Hospital

Stephanie Etienne

For many, the mere mention of the South Bronx conjures up not-so-distant memories of burned-out tenements and intractable poverty. Yes, this is the poorest congressional district in the country. Yes, folks here suffer the highest rates of asthma and obesity. However, those statistics don't tell the whole story. They never have. As midwives at an urban nonprofit hospital, serving women from the Dominican Republic, Jamaica, Ghana, Togo, Honduras, Mexico, and the United States, we sit at the feet of resourceful and resilient women. As we bear witness to their struggles and triumphs, we mirror each other, reflecting fears and hopes. We echo that inner voice urging a woman to engage with and sometimes confront a cold, faceless institution. Modern American midwifery is often depicted in terms of white women supporting other white women. Through documenting everyday stories in our clinic offices and labor rooms, this chapter resists this narrative by exploring the unique relationships forged between black midwives and women in the South Bronx.

I've been a midwife for over two years. After I completed midwifery school, I came to work at a nonprofit hospital that serves the South and Central Bronx. Hospital-based women's health centers serving high volumes of patients are complicated and chaotic spaces. In order to provide care to hundreds of women per month, a considerable degree of distancing occurs between the staff and the patients. Productivity necessitates a degree of desensitization from and dehumanization of the patients. In such a fast-paced environment, there is hardly time to even recognize a woman's wisdom and expertise, let alone incorporate them into her care. Staff members often become so overwhelmed by the relentless nature of the work that we resort to shorthand in the way we address and treat women. This, coupled with closely held yet unspoken racism and class biases, creates a distance between representatives of the institution and the presumed beneficiaries of its services. Moreover, a fear of litigation that often borders on paranoia permeates the workplace and promotes a highly routinized and impersonal provider-patient relationship. Once she enters this space, a woman with a whole and valued life outside the hospital's walls is reduced to a medical record number or high-risk diagnosis. She is identified by her immigration status, drug use, age, weight, or psychiatric condition. She becomes a body to be managed and moved from one space to another.

Every day at work, I notice how it becomes easier to refer to a Latina woman as "Mami" whether we are familiar with her or not. A West African woman becomes the "Fatoumata" in bed number three, whether that is her name or not. Most insidious about this shorthand are the inherent assumptions that go along with calling a woman out of her name. She becomes anonymous—a mere stereotype. The anonymity is a cruel buffer. It facilitates the disconnection that allows us to coast through the busy day without considering each woman individually. Yet, day after day, it becomes increasingly apparent that if we can't take the time to call a woman by her given name, we cannot hope to connect with her in any substantial way.

This chapter aims to illustrate the challenges that women face when seeking health care and to document the overwhelming circumstances under which hospital-based midwives work. As hospital employees, we often represent a stark contradiction. While midwives have historically facilitated self-determination and empowerment, we work in an environment that compromises our vision for midwifery care. Despite the challenges posed by the workplace, midwives subvert the "us versus them" dynamic that typifies the biomedical model by forging deep and long-lasting relationships with the women we serve.

THE CONTEXT: WOMEN IN THE SOUTH BRONX AND THEIR LOCAL HOSPITAL

The South Bronx has long held the dubious reputation of being the poorest congressional district in the United States. Its residents struggle with diabetes, asthma, drug addiction, and mental illness at higher rates than residents in other parts of the Bronx and New York City at large. Rates of teen pregnancy are among the highest in the city, with 131 teen pregnancies in every one thousand births in the Highbridge and Morrisania sections, compared to 75 in every one thousand births in New York City overall.[1] While the overwhelming majority of the women seeking prenatal care are healthy, social conditions like poverty, institutional racism, and stress, as well as preexisting health conditions, oftentimes put women in the South Bronx at a disadvantage from the moment of conception.

The hospital's main women's health center rivals some of the busiest medical clinics in the city. On any given day, the waiting room is packed with at least fifty people, including patients, family members, and children. They endure perpetually long lines and longer waits. Women can easily wait for longer than two hours for their scheduled appointments. Once they are in the exam room with a provider, their appointment may be at most forty-five minutes for a first prenatal visit, thirty minutes for a first gynecological or specialty visit, and fifteen minutes for any subsequent visit. Appointments are truncated by the process of collecting vital signs and urine dips, navigating our complicated electronic medical records system, and connecting with a telephone interpreter. On a good day, a provider can hope to spend no more than 75 percent of an allotted appointment actually talking to and examining a woman.

The women who attend this hospital's women's health clinic are mostly Latina, African, and African American. The large new immigrant population hails primarily from the Dominican Republic, Mexico, Honduras, Puerto Rico, Jamaica, Senegal, Mali, Ghana, Nigeria, Togo, Guinea, and Burkina Faso. Our conversations are intricately woven dances of English, Spanish, Arabic, and French with Mandinka, Wolof, and patois accents. The women are high school and college students. Some have only a grade school education. They are heads of household, living alone or with multigenerational extended families. Some are unemployed; others work in the home and as street vendors, home health aides, child-care providers, restaurant servers, retail store employees, and domestics. Women attending the clinic live in rented apartments, public housing, communal housing, family shelters, and drug rehabilitation programs. Many find their way to the Bronx, and this particular hospital, because of transient and insecure housing. Most are in stable, loving relationships, while others have survived or are currently struggling with intimate partner violence. Many are uninsured until pregnancy, when they become eligible for Medicaid. Others are covered under Medicare or one of a number of New York State health insurance programs for low-income earners who are ineligible for Medicaid. They generally range in age from twelve to eighty years old. They seek services for gynecologic care, contraception, abortion care, pregnancy, reproductive endocrinology and infertility, gynecological oncology, urogynecology, and HIV treatment.

As is true in most hospital systems, this hospital's profitability depends on the productivity and efficiency of its staff and health-care providers. The midwives do not labor under the illusion that this hospital holds a deep respect for the midwifery model of care. In the labor rooms, our commitment to supporting low-intervention births is tolerated to a certain extent. Our occasional use of the spa tubs (when they are functioning), birthing bars, and "alternative" birthing positions (as long as patients can be continuously monitored) is considered charming and anecdotally useful at best but in no way impacts the overarching medicalized culture of the obstetrics department. In the clinics, we are valued insomuch as we are able to see a high volume of patients at a fraction of what it would cost to pay a physician or physician assistant for the same work. As is not uncommon with other staff midwives around the city and country, we are not unionized and can make relatively few demands in terms of benefits and salaries. We are ultimately a cost-effective means to an end.

SMALL ACTS OF TRANSFORMATION: FORGING SISTERHOOD AMID THE CONTRADICTIONS OF THE EVERYDAY

By the time a woman gets to my office, she is already frustrated, tired, and suspicious of the institution. She has waited in long lines, been put on hold, and witnessed how chaotic the clinic can be. She has heard about this hospital's reputation—the good and the bad. She may be expecting to receive subpar care compared to other hospitals in the city. She can intuit that her race, class, immigrant status, lack of private insurance, or limited English may relegate her to being treated like a "Mami" or a "Fatoumata." Usually, I am one of many providers she will see throughout her pregnancy. She may have already learned that she cannot reasonably expect to be seen by one consistent provider and that the provider at this visit will almost certainly not be the person at her side when she gives birth. At first, this woman might doubt my intentions. She may, in all fairness, assume that I am merely a representative of yet another institution that attempts to exercise control over her life. I must earn her trust if I hope to mean anything more to her. My demeanor, language, and actions are critical to our ability to establish a relationship.

When trust is established, the time that I spend with a woman on a monthly or weekly basis becomes a truly sacred space. Each woman who enters my office could very likely be my sister, friend, mother, auntie, or grandmother. I grew up in New York City in a matriarchal immigrant family from Haiti. Her life mirrors my own in so many obvious and subtle ways that I am keenly aware of the responsibility that I have to her. As I honor her wisdom and experience, the countless structural divisions that exist between provider and patient start to crumble. We confide our heartaches and joys. We share our hopes and fears. I learn about the rich life she led in her home country. I learn about the circumstances of her pregnancy. She may share heart-wrenching, enraging accounts of sexual abuse, pregnancy loss, and bearing a child with severe disabilities. We are partners in her health care. I can offer choices and make recommendations, but I try to encourage her to identify her own solutions. She eventually begins to trust that I will tell her the truth no matter how difficult.

As staff midwives, we are constantly attempting to balance the hospital's expectations, our patients' needs and expectations, and our own training and midwifery wisdom. We are not there to convince women that they should not have epidurals or to push epidurals to calm "unruly" patients and facilitate the work of other providers and staff. In an environment where women have experienced grave indignities and often have very little choice about how their pregnancy or labor is "managed," our primary role is to create space for choice and agency. We struggle daily not to pathologize women or to categorize them as difficult, high risk, or noncompliant. These labels run rampant throughout the institution. They reflect an inherent distrust of the patient and imply that "doctor knows best." But how can I view my own sister with the eyes of someone who doesn't trust her or believe in her ability to make sound decisions relating to her own body and her unborn child?

Within this space where "black woman" is code for poverty, lack of education, drug addiction, and a barrage of other degrading labels, the relationships black midwives are able to forge with other black women through reproductive health care contribute to curbing this pervasive and negative mentality. Despite facing challenging financial and political barriers, we continue to function in the interstices of a very broken health-care system. We demand very little of a system that uses our labor to maximize profits rather than as a means to promote a progressive and empowering set of values around reproductive health. Yet, like our foremothers, we manage to create sacred spaces in even the most inhospitable environments. In order to maintain a sense of honor and respect for ourselves and our work, we must see every exchange as potentially meaningful and impactful to ourselves and to the women we serve. We sit at the feet of resourceful and resilient women leading lives complicated by seemingly insurmountable socioeconomic challenges. With our very touch, we hope that we are conveying to a woman that we recognize her and understand her struggles. That touch attempts to communicate that she has allies within this cold and faceless institution.

People who are unfamiliar with public and nonprofit hospital systems are often surprised and impressed that this hospital employs midwives. Perhaps they mistakenly believe that the presence of midwives will ensure a women-centered environment that is supportive of natural birth. They think that being attended by a midwife means that they will experience soothing candlelit rooms and give birth in Jacuzzi tubs. The truth is that while some women come to this hospital specifically seeking midwifery care, many are unaware of the difference between the midwives and physicians. At first glance, we are all authority figures in white coats. This is why I try not to take offense when a woman addresses me as "doctor." No matter how many times I correct her and ask her to call me by my first name, she may never stop calling me "doctor." I recognize that this is sometimes a sign of respect. Other times, women do not have a frame of reference that allows for the presence of midwives in hospitals. However, what is truly amazing is the clarity that comes when a woman has experienced prenatal care and birth with a midwife after previous experiences with physicians. She can tell the difference because she has experienced it. She will say with pride, "I love my midwife. I will always have my babies with midwives." Similarly, the teens from our prenatal class insist on only being cared for by midwives when they arrive at the triage room in our labor unit. In those miraculous moments, we know that we have earned the title midwife.

Holding On to a Vision for Midwifery

The profession of midwifery did not enter my consciousness until I was already in my mid-twenties. I was a graduate student in public health, living in Chapel Hill, North Carolina, when I first learned about birth centers and doulas. I was aware of the politics of race and class in health care and had always envisioned myself working to improve health-care access for poor and disenfranchised people of color. At that time, this did not involve a focus on women.

Upon reflection, I had my first inkling that I would someday become more consciously involved in reproductive justice the summer I worked with community health educators in a rural migrant farmworker community in eastern North Carolina. The most awe-inspiring part of the work was entering the humble, ramshackle homes of migrant families. We drove down dusty country roads to find hot, dilapidated, company-issued trailers on the edges of the fields. There we found the women pregnant and caring for their bright-eyed children. Their lives were complicated, and forces beyond their control dictated where they ate, slept, and gave birth. We played games with the children and helped their mothers access prenatal care and social services. We helped them map out a very tenuous future. It was difficult not to feel a deep connection in so intimate a setting.

Years later, providence led me to meet other like-minded women from various social justice movements who were all interested in bearing witness to women's reproductive struggles and triumphs. We were guided by the core belief that the circumstances under which we usher new life into the world are intrinsically powerful and transformative. We understood that the process of choosing whether or not to be pregnant, nurturing that pregnancy, engaging with a hypermedicalized health system, and birthing a baby in a way that is empowering to both mother and baby regardless of socioeconomic status could only further a woman's sense of her own power and agency. I was captivated. The idea of melding my political beliefs with my love of caregiving was radical. We formed a collective, raised funds, and organized a doula training program.[2] We started providing prenatal, labor, and postpartum support to New York City women and families who might not otherwise be able to afford doula services. The first birth I supported is forever etched in my mind. It was at the home of a friend and was everything I imagined an empowered birth could be. It changed me. That birth cemented my belief that every woman, no matter her life circumstances, is entitled to a miraculous birth experience of her choosing. In a world where having a doula is as much a status symbol as a valuable resource, we envisioned bringing doula care to women who do not have the privilege and resources to take expensive birthing classes and purchase the top-of-the-line baby accoutrements. These experiences as a health educator and doula put me on the long path toward midwifery.

Once I decided to become a midwife, I knew that I wanted to work with and for women who look like me. Midwifery, for me, has always been a matter of social justice and self-determination in the most disempowered communities. Still, nothing can prepare you for the challenges of working in a large urban hospital serving thousands of women annually. I am perpetually on guard for signs that I am becoming disillusioned or jaded. There are admittedly days when I fail miserably. There are days when I confuse my frustration with the work and the institution with frustration with the patients. I have to remind myself of who I am and what my purpose is. I am here to bear witness. I am here to usher in. I am an outstretched hand. I am not here to judge, criminalize, or blame. My discernment, compassion, and relentless commitment to women and their families are my armament. As we create a level playing field that prioritizes sisterhood over coercion, we conspire in small, if not unrecognizable, acts of resistance.

Everything I have experienced during these past seven years as a birth worker and reproductive justice advocate confirms that midwifery is a powerful tool for poor women of color who seek to free themselves of centuries of medical abuse. Hospital-based midwifery, however imperfect and limited, can only benefit by employing more midwives of color from the very communities we hope to serve.

As I write this chapter, I am embarking upon my own new journey to motherhood. Day after day I become more acutely aware of the vulnerabilities, fears, hopes, and challenges that come with pregnancy. I now savor each visit with another pregnant women even more than before. I welcome the lessons of women who have traveled this road before me and share their hard-won words of wisdom. I feel myself being initiated and anointed by this circle of mothers. I am filled with gratitude to be able to do this work with and for my sisters.

CHAPTER 14

A Love Letter to My Daughter

Love as a Political Act

Haile Eshe Cole

To my darling daughter ... here is a lesson in love.[1]

It was April 15, 2009, around 3 a.m., if I remember correctly. I rolled around uncomfortably in the bed, tossing and turning underneath the cool cotton quilt sewn by your great-great-aunt Lucille. Normally this patchwork quilt was a comfort during a sleepless night. I would imagine that each patch represented the hand of a woman in my (your) bloodline coming together as a field of lineage, legacy, and memory and enveloping me with love and support. Each patch burst with colors of red and blue plaid, orange and yellow flowers, and other mismatched fragments of history sewn together. Even with the now fraying pieces and occasional rip in the fabric, the blanket still provided warmth. But this April 15 was different. Every little rip and hole seemed to let a little warmth escape.

I stared up at the dark, high-vaulted ceiling of my mother's (your grand-mother's) house. I tried to resituate my aching body and heavy legs into a more comfortable position. Maybe walking three miles in the Texas April heat was not the best idea for a woman nine months pregnant, but I was determined to have you my way and on my own terms. I had hoped that waddling three miles in one-hundred-plus-degree heat would somehow jump-start my labor and sabotage the induction scheduled for the following day. Staring at the ceiling, I began to imagine what labor would be like. How long would it last?

Would I scream and ignite the firmament with a string of profanities like they do in the movies while slinging sweat and wishing death on the person nearest to me? How painful would labor be?

I thought back to the many conversations I'd had with my doctor over the nine months prior. In particular, I remember the conversation around pain medications and labor. Sitting on the exam table with my legs dangling over the side, I remember her asking, "Do you have a birth plan?" Birth plan? I barely understood the question. I was being asked if I had formulated a blueprint for what I wanted the birth to look like. Up until that point, I had thought very little about it. I knew that I wanted a healthy baby, and I had always thought that I would have a "natural birth." So I probed the doctor about her knowledge around natural birth and what the risks were, if any, of an epidural. She gave me a 100 percent assurance that epidurals were safe and would carry minimal risk for my baby and me. I wasn't sure how I felt about this. Her response was, of course, accompanied by a look that suggested that I was out of my mind for even considering a natural birth in this day and age. *What was that about?*

I was well aware of the growing trend toward natural birth, water birth, and home birth. Was it that this type of request was often associated with the practice of midwifery? Given the unacknowledged and suppressed history of black midwives in this country, was there a disjuncture for her in seeing a young, black pregnant woman seeking a midwife-assisted birth, something commonly assumed to be a white, middle-class luxury? Or was it the fact that my desire for a natural birth disrupted the routine in this country whereby a body—not to mention a black female body—functioning without intervention is obsolete? Thinking back on this reminds me of a conversation between a local physician and friend of mine who also worked in that clinic. On the topic of natural birth as an option for his pregnant patients, he expressed something to the effect of, *These* women are not capable of giving birth in that way. Whatever the hell that meant. Most of the women were poor, black, or Latina and on Medicaid. The mere knowledge about these explicit—and sometimes implicit—biases from medical staff had huge impacts on my own perspectives and experiences during prenatal care.

While I considered myself to be a well-educated, intelligent, and competent young woman, I often left my appointments feeling uncertain and like an ignorant, young, unmarried, baby-out-of-wedlock-having black girl. I often tried to remedy these feelings of inadequacy with random commentary about my law school classes to the doctor and the nurses, hoping that this would lift me out of whatever stereotypical depiction I assumed they had relegated me to. This feeling was not foreign to me. It was akin to the way I felt a few years prior when a university physician—without asking about my insurance status—informed me that I should take advantage of the free birth-control pills available to low-income women at a local grocery store chain. I remember cringing as images of Tuskegee, Norplant, and sterilized women waltzed across my brain.[2] Nah, I'm good, I thought. Despite this more blatant example, I was never quite sure whether my feelings actually emanated from the looks, comments, and interactions with my provider or my insecurities were the internalization and acknowledgment of some of the Moynihan-esque[3] assumptions placed on my body, or both.

As my thoughts wandered that night, I thought about your father as I did most nights. I wondered what he was doing in that moment. I thought about the few interactions we'd had over the months. They were always bittersweet, shrouded by the icy gray awkwardness of two people frozen in fear or unfamiliar silence, yet marked by moments of thawing potentiality and canary yellow gleams of fleeting joy. I settled on an image of his face and wondered whom you would take after. I imagined how your chubby little café au lait face would look or how your cry and baby babble would sound. What would your first toothless smile look like, and what would your first words be?

Then it happened. I felt a strong wrapping tension as if someone was tightening and squeezing a thick belt around my belly from the center of my back around both sides of my body with the sensation meeting and subsiding right around my belly button. *What was that?* About twenty-four hours later, you were here.

These experiences are part of a larger narrative. It is a narrative of love and self-discovery. Yet this is not the Disney princess story that many a young girl is familiar with. It is a progressive, winding, and dusty dirt road more than it is a short, one-way direct flight to love, as many may think. You see, while many a fairy tale will have you think that love is something that you stumble and fall into, a very significant, often neglected aspect of love is its conceptualization as a choice. In particular, for a young, black pregnant woman, the decision to love is a choice riddled with political implications and tangled in history. You see, we were used as capital during slavery. Even after Emancipation, we were mammies and workers who provided care and sustenance from our very breasts to the children and families of this country, a country intent on our exploitation. Is this depiction still relevant today? Pundits celebrating the supposed end of racism refer to our first black president and First Lady, but black women are still fighting. We struggle against ideologies that pigeonhole us with various stereotypes and deny our womanhood, dignity, and the legitimacy of our motherhood. We struggle for recognition of our humanity in a nation founded on the cement walls and cold metal bars of incarceration, governed by the machinery of subjugation, and covered with the leaking roof of systematic disparity. All the while this damaged apparatus is ignored under the false veil of a postracial society or explained away underneath the obscuring rhetoric of black pathology.

So what does all of this have to do with love? What happens when love finds a way to exist where it was never meant to be? What happens when love blossoms where life is not meant to be or where you are not meant to survive?[4] What happens when choosing to love is in actuality an act of agency and resistance? What happens when we love ourselves enough to live?

Amid oppressive interactions with medical professionals and alongside the evocation of a painful, forgotten history, I attempt to create a gentle and loving environment in a world that responds violently to my existence. Taking long walks in the Texas heat to hasten labor or assertively questioning dominant practices are attempts at self-protection and autonomy over my body, and the decision to love and care for myself informs these actions. In a world set up to maintain a particular racialized, gendered, and hierarchical order that brings black women face to face with violence and death, choosing to love and care for oneself despite these things is undoubtedly a radical—and ultimately political—act of survival.[5] What I find most profound is that my intentional choice to love myself manifested in episodes interrelated with reproduction and my body. It was most pronounced around my experience of pregnancy and birth. Although there were other critical moments in my life, one of my most powerful sites of self-realization and politicization was the historical and contemporary site of subjugation for black women—my body and reproductive capacity. For me, it seemed that everything had built up to that point. Pregnancy and birth highlighted how self-love and care contribute to my own preservation and the preservation of my child, my family, and others. During this time the fatal repercussions of not loving, caring, and advocating for myself had never been clearer. That was the beginning.

I have found that this practice creates the ability for me to live and to give love as well. Choosing to find the strength to actively love and to advocate and care for yourself is the beginning of a process of struggle and resistance. What hopefully follows is sharing that love and your experiences and supporting and empowering others to do the same. I am sure that you remember the countless Saturdays in which you would ask me, "Mama, are we going to the 'Mamas' meeting today?" What you remember as play time, fun, and snacks was in actuality a group of women building community. As members of Mamas of Color Rising,[6] we put our time, hearts, sweat, and tears into lobbying to open access for poor women of color to receive adequate, just, and loving care, creating support networks and culturally appropriate alternatives around birthing and maternal health, and challenging birth disparities. At the root of this work was/is love. It was an attempt to create the just and loving world that we imagined, centered on self-care, healthy communities, self-determination, agency, empowerment, and autonomy. We acknowledged the significance and power of self-love and care. Our work centered on giving care, love, and support to one another while encouraging other women, a community of women, to empower themselves to do the same.

So, my darling daughter, I ask what should this mean to you? My hope is that as you grow and live your life, you will find various levels of meaning in these words. While this message emphasizes pregnancy and birth, these do not make up the only medium through which to understand and experience the politics of love. Instead, I hope that you will discern from my words that, given the history that is forever written in your skin, love will always be something more than a sweet embrace or an affectionate kiss. How you love and whom you love are choices that will always have far-reaching implications that are inseparable from the political topography that is black life. My life. Your life. Yet, if you do find yourself as a burgeoning expectant mother, I hope that you will remember these words. Recall the history that precedes you, and let its memory and lessons cover you like Aunt Lucille's quilt. Let it serve as a source of strength rather than sorrow so that you never forget the indispensable role of love and self-care—however you define, practice, or experience them—in your survival and the survival of those who come after you. I hope that you uncover the power that you possess to take control of your experience. Despite the weight of this decision, I hope that you choose to love yourself radically, to share your love against the odds, and to share your story in order to empower others to do the same. Engage in active resistance. Choose life, and always struggle to live and love your way and on your own terms.

Always in infinite love,
Mommy

CHAPTER 15

New Visions in Birth, Intimacy, Kinship, and Sisterly Partnerships

Shannon Gibney and Valerie Deus

SHANNON

We are told so many things about becoming mothers, about where and with whom we should birth our babies, and about who should have the right, the privilege, and the responsibility of walking through the experience with us. Most of us imagine a partner—the baby's parent by biology or kinship—as the primary source of support during the long pregnancy and intense birth. For my part, I envisioned my male partner feeding me all manner of proteins throughout my pregnancy, helping me put my feet up on the couch after a long day, and putting in extra time around the house to make up for my exhaustion borne of cooking a person in my belly.

Many of us become fearful when we think of the actual process of birthing a baby. I know I envisioned plenty of screaming and pain and a complete lack of control. The information that we receive does little to allay our fears. As black women, we are caught between the predominantly white, middle-class natural birth movement and the patriarchal medical industry. Advocates within the natural birth movement, unaware of the unstated privilege of their ideas about childbirth, often tell us that if we set foot in a hospital or fail to embrace strict nutritional and behavioral guidelines, we are endangering not only our own health but that of our unborn baby. At a pregnancy and birth preparation class, for example, a well-meaning white female instructor told me that since I had not kept a viable food diary over the previous week and had consumed sixty grams of protein (instead of the prescribed eighty), I could well be jeopardizing my son's future. I remember sitting in her suburban house, mouth agape, trying to tell her that since I worked eighty hours per week, and my partner, who had been denied access by the US Immigration Service, was on the other side of the world, I had limited resources to complete her rigid prescriptions.

On the other hand, we are told by the mainstream medical establishment that pregnancy and birth are "medical conditions" that need to be "managed" by doctors and health-care professionals, and if we refuse this "care," we risk our own health and that of our children. I remember telling my mother, after weighing all the options and doing my research, that I had decided to have a home birth. Having worked for over thirty years in the University of Michigan's Neonatal Intensive Care Unit, my mother was utterly terrified by my choice.

Against the backdrop of all this noise, there are the stark, hard facts of birth injustice: It is more dangerous to give birth in the United States than in forty-nine other countries, black women are almost four times more likely to die of pregnancy-related complications than white women, and women of color continue to receive inadequate maternal health-care services. These data put black feminist poet Audre Lorde's observation from over thirty years ago into startling contemporary context: "For to survive in the mouth of this dragon we call America, we have had to learn this first and most vital lesson—that we were never meant to survive. Not as human beings."[1]

Indeed.

So then, what are we to do, given all of these multiple, difficult, and sobering realities?

My answer is that we must fight back by telling our own stories. By doing so, we open up new narrative space and upend dominant narratives about us that make us feel less human and less able to make choices. This, in turn, opens up more imaginative space for us to envision new modes of partnership and intimacy, new models of kinship, and ultimately new ways to give and sustain life itself.

*****

When I first learned I was pregnant, I was equal parts excited and terrified: excited because my Liberian husband and I had wanted this to happen during my recent monthlong visit to Ghana, terrified because we were right in the middle of the endless and dehumanizing process of convincing the US Citizenship and Immigration Services (USCIS) that we were in fact married (and then that the child I was growing actually was his) and that he would be able to sustain himself financially once he was here. In the end, I learned firsthand that USCIS is just another system—not unlike the child welfare system, the welfare state, or the criminal justice system—that, intentionally or unintentionally, fractures black families. So I knew that my husband would not be here for the birth; yet I also intuitively knew that I could not go through pregnancy and birth alone. I have never been particularly good at asking for help, but even I could see that I was in over my head. So I turned to my friend and colleague, Val, who had been with me, emotionally and psychologically, through all the joys and barriers of my relationship with my husband and who I knew, without a doubt, wanted the very best for us.

When I asked Val to be my birth partner, she was delighted. I was concerned that it would take up too much of her time and might be completely exhausting, especially given the demands of our teaching loads at the local community college where we both work. But she assured me on many occasions that this was not so. She and her husband had been mulling over the decision of whether or not to have children, and she thought that the experience of supporting me in my pregnancy and birth would help better inform their discussions. I could not have been more relieved.

*****

Looking through my files yesterday, I came across the narrative of my birth story. It details the central role that Val played, even though she was not my romantic partner and did not inhabit anything vaguely resembling the traditional Western model of "partner." She was and is simply my sister, my colleague, my deep-down friend, my strength during my pregnancy and birth, my child's godmother, and the reason why I made it through what was probably the most difficult, profound, and rewarding experience of my life: giving birth to my son.

VAL

"Do you have any children?" is a question I've been asked repeatedly. Society expects women to have children eventually. When I tell people that I may not want to have children, I am often treated as if I am suddenly unable to make decisions for myself. There's the dismissive "No, you must want children," the accusatory "How could you not want children?" and, my favorite, the disapproving "If your parents didn't have children, then you wouldn't be here."

People I encounter seldom know what to say to me as a woman who is ambivalent about being a parent. I believe that raising and caring for a human being is an important, rewarding job, and I salute those who make that choice. However, true reproductive freedom means that I should also be able to choose not to parent.

I knew it would take a miracle to get Shannon's husband here in time for his son's birth. As a first-generation Haitian American, I knew that trying to get someone into the United States could take years. When I was twelve, I wrote a letter to my local representative asking for assistance in applying for my uncle to come over from Haiti. I was a freshman in college when my seventy-year-old uncle was finally allowed into the country.

So when Shannon asked me to be her birth partner, I said sure. I mean, that's what friends are for, right? Your friends are the family you get to pick, and if you aren't willing to be there for each other, then what's the point? I was happy to help out, and I also had my own motives. I had recently grown out of my "Eww, babies" stage, and I was interested in exploring the possibilities of having and/or raising children. My fears about giving birth and being a parent helped me to say yes. I figured this was great research, and if I was ever ready, I would be very well informed.

Being a support for my friend was an honor. Watching Shannon's belly grow and learning about how the body shifts and changes to accommodate the growing baby helped me appreciate the capabilities of the human body and the sacrifices women make to be mothers. Birthing is not easy. The role of a birth partner is multifaceted. You are a comforter, supporter, coach, and cheerleader all at the same time, all the time. The one role I found difficult, and ultimately among the most important, is that of advocate. You are the person who advocates for the pregnant woman, so it is important to be very clear about what to do if the plan changes and to maintain clear communications with the midwife.

Shannon wanted a home birth in a birthing tub. We ended up not using the tub, and at some point an ambulance was called. Shannon was adamant; she didn't want to go to the hospital, but if she did go, she wanted to remain drug free. It was my job to make sure she got what she wanted. She was young, healthy, and without any real risk factors, so it wasn't hard to stick with her plan. But I have to admit that I was afraid. I was afraid that something would go wrong or that I would say the wrong thing or not enough of the right thing or simply that I wouldn't be enough.

Labor started in the early morning hours, and I came to her house at around 6 a.m. She experienced mild labor pains in the morning hours, but things didn't really get moving until the afternoon. I made a playlist of soothing music, which included Sade, Corinne Bailey Rae, and Billie Holiday. I drew the blinds and moved the furniture out of the way so that Shannon could walk around. We circled the room many times, all the while chatting, breathing, and laughing. When she got hot, she threw off the blanket she had wrapped around her body, and when she got cold, I put it back on. I did four loads of baby laundry while she labored. I washed receiving blankets, onesies, and hats. In between walking and laundry, I practiced swaddling. Ultimately, I did all the things I would want done for me if I was laboring for twelve hours.

The moment of truth arrived when she transitioned to full labor. All morning the mood was fun and upbeat, and we even joked about going to a department store for a while and walking around. But things got really intense during the transition. At some point Shannon looked at me and said, "I don't think I can do this," and I said, "You're doing great. You can do this." But I was scared, and I could hear it in my voice. The fear and doubt in her voice had me shook, despite the classes, the reading, and the breathing techniques.

When Shannon's son Boisey finally arrived, I felt everything at the same time. My eyes tear up just thinking about it. There was all the joy and relief and love and hope and fear of that moment all in one room. It was truly incredible.

Going through this process and being able to reflect on it helped me to sort through some of my feelings about the identity of mother and parent. Do I want to have children after that experience? I still don't know. But I have been thinking about becoming a midwife or a doula. Ultimately the identity of mother is still not a role that fits me, but I have found that there are other roles, such as Tati and god-mama, that allow me to experience the joy and intense love of nurturing a child. Many of my most treasured childhood memories were with the Tatis who loved and helped raise me when I was a child in Brooklyn.

Brooklyn, New York, has a large Haitian population. When I was growing up in the 1970s and 1980s, I had a large network of family friends, Tatis and Tontons, who were available and a big part of my life. They were part parent, part mentor, and part friend to me. There was Tati Edith, who brought me to the park on weekdays, Tati Micheline, who sewed my prettiest dresses, and Tati Magella, who always knew about children's events around town—all these people, along with my parents, played a part in my growth. My parents made sure that they themselves weren't the only grown-ups in my life. They made sure I had other trusted adults I could talk to or ask questions. Having that support system was important to my parents, and I take their example and try to support my friends when they need me.

*****

My whole body felt rubbery and loose, as if my joints were coming apart. When each contraction came, I felt like I was on fire, and when each left, I felt like I was freezing. Eventually the contractions became so strong that I could not talk at all. All I could do was walk around the house, breathe, and vocalize when a contraction came. Val was with me the whole time, watching me carefully, and engaging me when and where she could. But as time went by, I became increasingly inaccessible, as my vocalizations got stronger and I was in more pain.

I got so hot during the contractions that I threw off my clothes in my bedroom, where the shades were drawn. I asked Val to draw the shades in the front room so that I could walk around naked there too. She did that and also rearranged the furniture so that there was a large space to walk in. I started pacing immediately after she was finished, wrapping a blanket around me between contractions and throwing it off when they came.

All I could sense was my body moving in a finite space and my voice striking the walls, then holding in the sound. I started talking about the pain and how bad it was and told Val that I didn't know if I could do this. She told me that I absolutely could do it and that I was doing great. All I wanted at that moment, and really for the rest of the birth, was for someone or something—I didn't care who or what—to take the pain away. But at the same time, there was a deeper awareness in me that something would have to break, or at least come to its logical end or beginning, before the pain would subside. And I think that awareness kept me walking and kept me wholly in the space.

*****

We do nothing that is worth doing in the world alone. Giving birth to my son could have gone in so many different directions, with so many different outcomes, but knowing that I was held during the whole experience—through both the difficult and the transformative parts—allowed me and my son to make it through with some modicum of grace. Val and I both remember those first moments when his little yellow face peered into the world, taking it all in. I like to think that he knew, as we did throughout it all, that there was no place for all-too-narrow traditional models of kinship, care, and family. He might have known, even then, that his daddy was coming from halfway around the world to kiss him in a few months, that his Liberian grandparents were singing his praises throughout the Monrovian night, that his white American grandparents already held his weight in their arms, and that his mommy and her not-by-blood sister had forged an intimate partnership that made it all possible.

CHAPTER 16

I Am My *Hermana*'s Keeper

Reclaiming Afro-Indigenous Ancestral Wisdom as a Doula

Griselda Rodriguez

Reproductive liberty is vital to our human dignity.[1]

A white female nurse walks into the delivery room, without knocking, and tells me that the doctor would like to speak to me. As I walk to the phone, my heart beating in my throat, I know exactly what this is about. "If you continue to challenge my staff, I will have you kicked out of that room faster than you can imagine!" threatened the Cuban male doctor—the same doctor who, throughout the thirteen hours that my cousin Alana was in labor, stopped by infrequently and ultimately missed the baby's arrival. Apparently, he called because he was angry that someone would dare ask questions or suggest that the family should have a few minutes to discuss the options presented by the medical staff. These included administering labor-inducing drugs, such as Pitocin, and rupturing her membranes to break her water—procedures that have been noted to increase a woman's chances of delivering via cesarean section and to cause other severe side effects.[2]

Alana's was the first birth I witnessed as a doula-in-training. My training with Ancient Song Doula Services, a Brooklyn-based social justice organization, exposed me to the fact that Alana's chances of having a C-section would skyrocket if I reacted to the doctor's threat and was forced to leave the room. So rather than challenge the doctor, I politely excused myself and agreed to his terms—in theory. In practice, the two *abuelas* and I did all we could to open up my cousin's pelvis and help her dilate. We used a rebozo, or scarf, to gently rock her pelvis back and forth; we also helped her squat on the bed, ensuring that nurses didn't see us doing this. Because although this was my cousin's birth and it was her body, it felt as if the nurses were controlling her movements through the use of an IV and fetal monitor. Finally, when the doctor casually suggested that if Alana did not continue to dilate by 2 p.m., she would have to undergo a C-section because he had to be at his private practice by 3 p.m., the *abuelas* and I held hands and prayed—hard!

Ironically, at one point, the medical staff seemed to be rushing Alana's labor, and at another point, they actively tried to stall baby Amaya's arrival. As the baby crowned, one nurse literally used her thumb to hold the baby's head back because the doctor was nowhere to be found. Thankfully, a resident obstetrician rushed in and helped deliver the baby. Despite the poor care that her mother received, baby Amaya was delivered vaginally and is now healthy and strong. In hindsight, I ask how is it that in the twenty-first century, this process seemed to be more about a power struggle than about allowing a woman to come into her own power naturally? Unraveling these and other lifesaving questions has shaped my mission as a doula-in-training.

BEING A DOULA

Being a doula feels right. It's as if I am doing exactly what I promised myself I would do in life: heal myself and, in turn, help women heal themselves. Unfortunately, birthing in the United States has been transformed into a lucrative business venture in which women's and children's lives often appear to be disregarded. Marginalized communities, such as working-class women of African and Indigenous descent in the United States, often bear the heaviest burdens of this dehumanizing machine. Our bodies are treated as expendable commodities, just as our enslaved ancestors' bodies were treated as breeding machines for violent slave economies throughout the Americas. Fortunately, the story of my journey toward doulaship and that of other doulas of color is one of empowerment, self-actualization, and commitment to birthing justice among women of African descent and all women. Most importantly, the journey is about a collective reclamation of the ancestral knowledge that runs through our veins.

Being a doula is a labor of love. It requires immense trust in the Divine. Being a doula of color, an Afro-Latina doula in the twenty-first century, is revolutionary. At a time when women of color, particularly working-class, immigrant, and queer sisters of color, are often treated like second-class citizens within the medical establishment, it is imperative that support and resistance networks be created and sustained. In its report on the maternal health crisis in the United States, Amnesty International concluded, "Women of color are more likely to die in pregnancy or childbirth than women from other sections of the population. . . . The intersection of discrimination on the basis of gender, race, Indigenous status, immigration status, language and poverty may create a climate where women's needs and rights are routinely discouraged."[3] In addition to receiving care within a modern health-care system built on the suppression of women health workers,[4] women of color are within a white supremacist system that places less value on our healthy bodies and profits from our disempowerment. Although many health professionals are truly committed to the health and wellness of all their patients, their intentions are caught within a web that values profits over lives.[5]

DOULASHIP WITHIN A WESTERN MEDICAL ESTABLISHMENT

Even the best-intentioned maternal health professionals operate within a system of patriarchal medicine whose origins date back to Renaissance Europe, when physicians took control of women's ability to bear children. As Silvia Federici explains, "In the 'transition from feudalism to capitalism' women suffered a unique process of social degradation that was fundamental to the accumulation of capital and has remained so ever since. . . . While in the Middle Ages women had been able to use various forms of contraceptives, and had exercised an undisputed control over the birthing process, from now on their wombs became public territory, controlled by men and the state, and procreation was directly placed at the service of capitalist accumulation."[6] Many of these same ideas about the body are still alive in the United States, and they are also laced with racist stereotypes about women of color. Stereotypes about African and Indigenous people's supposed innate inferiority, laziness, and promiscuity were initially used to justify the brutal systems of enslavement and genocide that cemented the foundation of the Americas.[7] As a result, the wombs of our enslaved ancestors were a major layer in the foundation of the "New World."

Without the bodies of Indigenous and African women, particularly their wombs, there would have been no bodies to mine the caves for gold, cut the cane for sugar, or pick the cotton. Dorothy Roberts further explains that "the brutal domination of slave women's procreation laid the foundation for centuries of reproductive regulation that continues today."[8] The colonization of the Americas thus facilitated the perfection of technologies of control that were first tested on European women.[9] "New World" technologies of control were initially used when European colonizers raped and mutilated the Indigenous women they first encountered when invading Caribbean shores.[10] The violations continued into the sixteenth century as millions of Africans were forcibly transported to the Western Hemisphere. The profitability of slave-based economies and the need to increase enslaved labor soon spread like a tidal wave, making women the anchor for this system. An African woman's womb, like her European sister's centuries before, was eventually transformed into a profitable baby-making machine.

The extreme dependence on enslaved women's procreative capabilities, and those women's simultaneous dehumanization, led to a paradox that continues today. On one hand, women of color were vital to the survival of slave-based economies, which included most of the economies of the Western Hemisphere; on the other hand, Europeans had internalized dehumanizing ideas about African women, which were often used to justify their exploitation. As a doula, I've often witnessed this paradox in action throughout hospital rooms in New York City. The racist social structure that compromises the safety and well-being of women of color also needs the very bodies that are neglected and mistreated. This paradox leads to a contradictory health-care system that simultaneously creates initiatives to improve access and quality of health care within marginalized communities while providing substandard care for most working-class women of color in the United States.

In their analysis of racial disparities in childbirth in the United States, Louise Marie Roth and Megan M. Henley note, "African American women, U.S.-born Hispanic women, low income women who receive Medicaid, and less educated women are more likely to have pregnancy-associated or pregnancy-related mortality."[11] I have witnessed how birthing in a public hospital, with Medicaid, often leads to neglect, disrespect, and a lack of compassion for mother and baby. Though treatment in private hospitals, with private health insurance, does allow for a nicer environment, the dynamics are often similar because regardless of the specific facility, women birth in a health-care system that is built on the disempowerment of all women, particularly women of color.[12] Health professionals rarely communicate directly with the mother and family. Medical interventions are often the only options presented to women, and little to no information about the potential side effects of such procedures is provided. I have witnessed nurses discussing a baby's potential to go into distress because it had passed meconium in the womb without once speaking directly to the birthing mother. In instances like these, I will step in and request that the medical staff communicate directly with the laboring woman. This is a deed often and erroneously read as a challenge to the medical staff's authority.

MORE THAN A DOULA

My role as a doula is to advocate for the health and stability of birthing mothers and their babies. I have mostly worked with Latinas who may not have mastered the English language and who come from cultures where a lot of their power is given to males. This is why my cousin Alana handed a lot of her power over to her male doctor and did not question the options presented to her during labor. Doulas of color thus help women navigate a health-care system that can disempower them if they are not prepared to stand up for their rights. It is a system that, as noted earlier, was founded on patriarchal and racist doctrines that deemed non-European, nonmale, nonelite bodies impure and pathological. Women of color are therefore readily marginalized within this paradigm and must be diligent so as not to become dehumanized.

Training with Ancient Song Doula Services helped me understand that, as a doula of color, my role goes beyond serving as an emotional companion. I am often a cultural broker, a translator, and a buffer against the forms of neglect that often lead to unnecessary medical interventions and traumatic birth experiences for women. C-section rates skyrocketed from 4.5 percent of US births in 1965 to 32.8 percent in 2012.[13] Between 1996 and 2009, the US C-section rate rose 60 percent from the most recent low of 20.7 percent, reaching a high of 32.9 percent of all births.[14] As a result of a broken maternal-health-care system, the United States ranks fiftieth among fifty-nine developed countries for maternal mortality, and maternal mortality rates have actually increased since the mid-1980s.[15] Sadly, but not surprisingly, things are worse for working-class women of color: "African American women die from pregnancy-related causes more often than other racial-ethnic groups, and have a fourfold greater risk of maternal death than non-Hispanic white women. . . . Latinas and non-Hispanic white and Asian women all share similar rates of maternal mortality, although rates appear to be rising among U.S.-born Hispanics. . . . Negative maternal outcomes are also concentrated among low-income women, who tend to have less prenatal care, more discontinuity of care, and more risk factors."[16]

As a doula I am part of a growing movement to reclaim the bodies of women of color by transforming their experiences of birth. The major goals for this growing movement include promoting vaginal birth, minimizing medical interventions during labor and delivery, and empowering women to make decisions for themselves by providing them with ample exposure to pertinent information. The desire to reclaim ancient wisdom, passed down to us through spiritual practices, is another major driving force within this growing movement. We realize that, in addition to educating ourselves on the different aspects of pregnancy, birth, and the postpartum period, we also need to equip ourselves with a deep level of spiritual awareness. This awareness helps us navigate spaces, such as hospitals, that can often be debilitating; it also strengthens us to deal with depressing encounters with a medical establishment that fails to honor what can be the most amazing moment(s) of a woman's life: birth.

ANCIENT WISDOM

My first exposure to birth was in 1990, as an eight-year-old interpreter for my godmother's laboring daughter, as neither of them spoke English. I remember how intense the room felt as I tried to follow my godmother's guidance on what to say to the 911 operator while witnessing a woman in extreme pain. My godmother saw nothing wrong with including an eight-year-old girl in this process, as labor in the Dominican Republic is a communal and family-oriented event. Sixteen years later, I met a midwife and fellow graduate student whose doctoral research attempted to explain why midwives were continuously being pushed out of hospitals while C-section rates were steadily increasing. Born of a C-section, along with my twin sister, I felt intimately connected to this issue. In 2009, watching the film *The Business of Being Born* further sparked my interests in the birthing world. Something that stood out to me about the film was the fact that, except as birthing mothers, women of color were rarely present as actors within the birthing world. In January 2012, when I started my doula training with Ancient Song Doula Services, I learned about the web of oppression that has often kept women of color in the birthing world from having our voices heard. Moreover, the intersection of racial, gender, sexuality, and class oppressions profoundly affects our ability to carry and birth healthy babies in the United States and globally.

On a deeper level, my interest in becoming a doula is otherworldly. My work as a doula reaches beyond the material plane and stems from a deeply spiritual plane. Doulaship carries the energies of the spirits who have always resisted various forms of dehumanization. The forces I invoke to assist me as a doula stem from the energies of women and men who are united in courage to establish healthy communities despite violent opposition. Within these realms, a pregnant woman is venerated for embodying the circle of life. She is respected for her ability to demonstrate that, despite all of the madness in the world, there is hope for new life. It is from within this realm that my maternal grandmother carried my mother and in which I was able to birth a healthy baby boy at home on August 29, 2014.

My maternal grandmother birthed twelve children, at home, in the Dominican Republic. My grandmother and her foremothers emerged in environments where the local *comadrona,* or lay midwife, was the village healer and seer. The women in my lineage, both paternal and maternal, birthed in a world where a forty-day postpartum repose, with a community of support, was the order of the day. Most women of my generation find this unimaginable and ancient; I find it fascinating and vital. A woman was encouraged to remain indoors, resting, while a community of women cooked, cleaned, and tended to her and her baby's needs so that the energy she expended when birthing human life could be restored. I have also embraced this tradition. After giving birth to my son Talib, the forty-day postpartum repose allowed my body to heal while I bonded more deeply with our baby.

Robin Lim, world-renowned midwife and activist, recognizes the value of this forty-day postpartum repose and encourages women in the United States and around the world to reclaim these practices as a way to preserve human life and avoid postpartum depression.[17] She and others are currently involved in influencing health-care policies that would provide some of these postpartum services to women in the United States.

Another example of how ancient wisdom can truly regenerate life regards the treatment of the umbilical cord after birth. In hospitals, the umbilical cord is typically clamped and cut prematurely because this is believed to reduce the risk of maternal hemorrhaging. The mother-child bond that is established via the pulsing cord, as the baby is slowly weaned off the mother's womb, is imperative to the emotional and physiological well-being of both mother and child.[18] Skin-to-skin contact, with the umbilical cord attached, also increases the mother's ability to breastfeed successfully, and newborns receive invaluable iron during these final moments.[19] Midwives and alternative birth workers have long believed that it is ideal to cut an umbilical cord once it has stopped pumping blood from the placenta into the baby's system, which can often take several minutes. Recent scientific support for this practice is another indication of the value of ancient wisdom.[20] The fact that, as a doula, I can expose the expectant mother to this important information is a small victory that can significantly benefit the health of mother and newborn.

CONCLUSION: THE BENEFITS OF BEING AND HAVING A DOULA

Research shows that women with more information and support, which often means women with a college education and middle-class income, are less likely to experience major complications at birth.[21] Increasingly, these same healthy birth outcomes are being noted among working-class women who are slowly gaining access to doulas paid for by Medicaid.[22] A doula provides information not only about anatomy and the various stages of fetal development but also about a woman's rights during labor and delivery. Beyond birth, doulas inform expectant mothers and their loved ones about the human right to adequate health care.

Ironically, witnessing the miracle of life in action has at times been disheartening. As a doula, I get to see how the Divine Feminine is dishonored and exploited during the process of childbirth. The process of bringing life into this world—a sacred act—is commodified and transformed into something that looks more like an assembly line. It often brings me to tears. But then I remember that this is a task I chose to walk into consciously. I am reminded that, as a doula, my presence in a delivery room matters.

When I see a woman in active labor, electric and alive in her power, I am reminded that birthing itself is an act of resistance to dehumanization. Seeing a woman in full power, as she prepares to birth her child, is indescribable. It reminds you of the power of women, despite what patriarchy would have us believe. Mothers who eventually deliver via C-section also demonstrate their power. A woman's relinquishing control of her life to a surgeon, as a means to ensure life for her child, is a courageous act. *Gracias, Mami!* Those of us who are involved in the birth justice movement are attempting to minimize the number of women who have to risk their lives in order to give life. This is why I am my *hermana*'s keeper. If my presence as a doula can prevent one woman from experiencing a C-section, birth-related complications, or death, then I am confident that my work as a doula is vital. It is in honor of maternal energies, of the Divine Feminine, that I commit to this labor of love.

Ashe Oshun.

Hotep Renenet.

CHAPTER 17

The First Cut Is the Deepest

A Mother-Daughter Conversation about Birth, Justice, Healing, and Love

*Pauline Ann McKenzie-Day and
Alexis Pauline Gumbs*

Where does a mother-daughter relationship start? At the moment of birth? Even earlier, at the moment of choice? Before that, somewhere in a deep forgotten daydream?

In this mutual interview, mother-daughter doula team Pauline McKenzie-Day and Alexis Pauline Gumbs navigate the impact of a crucial shared moment that was interrupted by an unnecessary and unwanted C-section— Pauline's first experience of giving birth and Alexis's first breath. We discuss the experience of birth, our visions of justice, and how our relationship continues to teach us the depth of love necessary to achieve the world we all deserve.

Being born and giving birth are important moments of our liberation. In a Western society that does not yet respect and honor the full brilliance, self-determination, and spiritual power of black women, the oppressive tendencies of the medical-industrial complex violate the sacredness of birth. Women of color and oppressed people have supported each other through birth for centuries, but the medical establishment has criminalized that support in contemporary times. We have decided to become part of a movement of women of color reclaiming the power to protect and honor sacred birth experiences.

A full-circle doula, as defined by the International Center for Traditional Childbearing, a black midwives' organization, supports the birthing person before, during, and after birth, with attention to the bonding between the parent and the new child. We would have loved to have doula support at our first meeting as mother and daughter thirty years ago. Instead, we are both trained as full-circle doulas, and we are collaborating in a mother-daughter doula practice that allows us to return powerfully to the scene of birth and to support other families in having self-determined birth experiences. This conversation offers some ideas as to the origins of our relationship and how we hope the impact of our healing will empower generations to come.

ON PREGNANCY

Alexis: What was your first thought when you found out you were pregnant with me?

Pauline: Joy comes to mind. I was very happy for many reasons. One of which was because I've wanted to be a parent since I was a little girl. One of my dreams was to be a mom. So being pregnant was so exciting. Your dad was happy and proud. I loved being pregnant. I never got morning sickness with any of you.

The first thought I had was that this was the beginning of a new phase in my journey, which was to become a parent, and I was very excited. It was anticipation, it was excitement, and it was definitely joy. And then I was honored to be nurturing you. I was also very proud that as you grew, I stayed the same size, and it was just you in my belly growing. You weren't a little baby—you were almost nine pounds at birth—so I had some backaches, but still it was a joy.

Alexis: Did you talk to me when you were pregnant? What did you say?

Pauline: I would talk to you as if you were already here and a part of my life. So I talked to you about everything I was doing, everything I was eating, everything I wanted to buy, and even about what life would be when you were born. It was an ongoing conversation about life and having you in it and the possibilities. Now, I didn't know you were a girl because I didn't find out your sex before you were born, but you were going to be amazing, I knew that. I had the feeling that you would be great and special. That was my sense. You could be anything. I talked to you about anything being possible for you and even the hopes and dreams of how happy you would be.

Alexis: Did you have other friends who were pregnant or having babies at the same time that you were?

Pauline: Not really. I seemed to be the forerunner. I got married first of all my friends, I started a family first of all my close friends, so I didn't really have anyone around me that was having babies too. I think that contributed to the connection between us because it was just you and me. It was not like there were other people around experiencing the same thing.

Alexis: What was disempowering or empowering for you at times when you were pregnant or giving birth?

Pauline: You don't know what you don't know. My focus was on you being healthy. There was a sense of trust with my doctor, so even when he said to your dad and me that you were too big for me to deliver vaginally and that you had to be born by cesarean section—which was not true—I just trusted that, and the bottom line was I just wanted a healthy baby. It was disappointing because I had wanted to experience vaginal birth, but it mattered more that you were healthy.

I wasn't under full anesthesia, only half my body. And the moment that they took you out, your dad looked at you, and we had decided on a middle name for you, Nicole, and your dad looked at you, and he looked at me, and he said, "She should have your name." So you are Alexis Pauline because of that.

Having you as a cesarean section was the impetus for me to learn how to do something different with your sister and brother. After you were born, I looked into the possibility of having a vaginal birth and what my options were. I got pregnant again two years after you were born, but I miscarried beyond my first trimester. That was a huge disappointment. Two years after that, I was pregnant again, this time with Ariana. I read more and went to support groups, and I came back with a birthing plan to my doctor, asking him to support me in having the kind of birth that I wanted this time. He was very patronizing to me and wanted to take the whole birth process out of my hands, as if it were his. He said, "Well, you can try, but you will probably have to have another C-section." And I wasn't havin' it! I don't remember how far along I was in my pregnancy with Ariana, but I switched doctors. It was difficult for some family members to understand why I wanted to do it my way. I think the older generation thought, What difference does your experience giving birth make? Just have a healthy baby.

So my advocacy for how I wanted things done meant deciding to get a labor coach. I never heard the word "doula" until much later, but I knew that having someone who could support me in the process would make it more likely that I would have the type of birth that I wanted. I was told that if you have one C-section, they all have to be C-sections, which is not true and wasn't what I had read. I wanted to be sure that I wasn't going to jeopardize the baby. I did give birth to Ariana vaginally, and she was even bigger than you were! Then Jared was even bigger than she was! So the story that I was told, that my pelvis was too small to give birth to you, wasn't the truth. So I became an advocate for women's birthing rights and being able to have the birth you choose. I tell women that you can be critical of what the doctor says, because the hospital protocol is not always the best way to provide the type of special bonding between a mother and child that is so important. But, mind you, I was in the hospital for a week, and you were with me in my room the entire time, so I made sure that there was bonding and that they didn't give you a bottle. Even if there is an intervention, it can still be a positive birth experience. I want to support all women in having positive birth experiences.

Alexis: How did having a labor coach help you?

Pauline: She was a sweet spirit. She was a labor coach, not a midwife, and she would come and talk with me about things that I could do for a healthy pregnancy and things that I should eat. She also helped me to create the birthing plan. I had a midwife working with her later in my pregnancy who was also a labor coach. The midwife could physically check how dilated I was and do those kinds of things, so I could labor longer at home, which would give the hospital less of a chance to force me to have a C-section.

I had two people supporting me, and their energies were different but both great. That was when I decided that providing support to laboring people was something I wanted to do. It was so important to have that emotional and spiritual support. I don't mean to take anything away from your dad, but he wasn't able to support me in that kind of way. Also, having someone knowledgeable about the birthing process was important to me. She was willing to be there, and I could call any time, even if something happened in the middle of the night.

I didn't learn what a doula was until years after. It wasn't until I had all three of you that I learned that a doula was synonymous with a labor coach. I knew I wanted to provide labor support. I never wanted to be a nurse, but I did want to help women with the birthing process.

One of the visions I had was to provide a center for women, particularly for women who couldn't afford it. I focused not on women of color but on women who couldn't afford it. Your dad paid for my labor coach, and it wasn't cheap. It was well worth it, but I wanted to provide that gift for women. My vision was an all-inclusive center not just focusing on birthing but providing resources for teen awareness about pregnancy and birth and relationships. And that was when it became part of my life plan; that was my desire. Maybe that was when you started to hear me talk about it concretely as something I wanted to do.

ON BIRTH INTERRUPTED

Pauline: Do you remember your first thought after being born?

Alexis: I remember the stories. I remember that you were giving birth for thirty-six hours and that after you first went into labor, they told you to walk around the mall. I remember that you labored right through Daddy's birthday, and he drank terrible hospital coffee to stay awake and then never drank coffee again.

Pauline: Right. I was in labor, and I went to the hospital, and they sent me back home. They said, "You are not dilated enough, so go back home, go shopping, walk around." And so we did that, and then we went back to the hospital, and I apparently tend to labor for a long time. So the doctor said, "It looks like the baby may be too big for you to deliver." And this after they had given me an epidural, and they said, "Okay, I think you should have a C-section." And your dad and I agreed, but what did we know? As new parents, we didn't know any better, so we said okay.

Alexis: I remember the legend that I was born so late that there must have been something I was doing. There wasn't a book in your womb, but there must have been something because I see it in my life now. I am usually late because I am finishing something, whether it is the conversation or the chapter; that's how I live now. It is important for me to finish what I am doing before I move on to the next thing, which also results in my being late.

Pauline: I can't be born yet. I'm working!

Alexis: Right! I don't know if there is trauma there. I remember you saying that your long labors with all of us were seen as an inconvenience to the medical staff instead of just your own process, our processes as babies being born. I imagine that there may be trauma there. What does it look like from the perspective of someone who is in the womb when the womb is opened? I don't remember that, and I don't know. I don't know if there is consciousness at that moment or not. I imagine that there is some ability to be present because you were present to my energy when you were pregnant, and I'm sure I was present to whatever energy was moving through the words that you said.

I do know that to this day I feel very disturbed if someone interrupts me in any process before I am finished. If someone wakes me up suddenly or insists that I leave the house or stop working on something before I have come to my own natural stopping point, I have very strong reactions to that, and it can feel like a violation or a violence to me even when it is just a helpful suggestion (like, Don't miss the plane!). So maybe it connects back to being born. Maybe I felt like my experience of being born was interrupted and that is why I am so sensitive to those types of interruptions. Thinking of it that way gives me some permission to let go or at least to bring some balance to what seems like a very visceral reaction to me.

(Re)Defining Birth

Alexis: What is your definition of birth?

Pauline: My definition of birth is not just conception or that type of birthing. It's whenever there is a coming together of energy and spirit, a coming forth, an awakening, a newness, coming into being. I envision a baby coming out of the birth canal, coming into the unknown, coming into a new plane. Birth means that something is different than what was. It is coming into a new existence.

Alexis: For me birth is life expressing itself. It's life loving itself, and I resonate with what you said about newness. Birth is how we remember that creation is ongoing. Creation is something that's much bigger than us as a species or as individual people, but it's also something that we can participate in as a species and as individual people. It is so powerful because it puts things in perspective. Knowing that we're all energetically connected, birth is the punctuation. What transforms? What is there that can be perceived through my bodily existence that couldn't be perceived otherwise? And for every person there is something that was not perceptible but is now because they were born and they continue to be reborn when they create.

Alexis: What are times that you have been reborn?

Pauline: Metaphorically I get reborn every time I work with other people who are having babies, because it's amazing to me. Also, when the clients whom I work with as a therapist come to awareness about something or have what Oprah calls an "aha moment." To me, that's being reborn, because I get reenergized and moved, and I want to cry. It's so moving to me when people's lives begin to transform in some way and I'm a part of it. For me, that's like being reborn again through someone else's discovery; my life gets transformed in some way. For me that is a rebirth every time. It happened Saturday, when I was working with a client and her mother and I saw myself, I saw my mother, I saw that relationship, and all of it was tied together, and so it was me learning something and also imparting something that I think gave their life some new perspective and understanding. In the work I do, in the trainings I lead that provide ways for social service agencies to support families, instead of separating poor families, I feel that same sort of energy a lot. It makes me feel like I'm providing a way, an avenue for something.

Alexis: There is something in teaching and facilitating that makes it feel like a process of giving birth. There is an openness and a receptivity and a way of being intentional about the fact that there is something coming through, whether it is the opportunity for certain folks to do this exercise or create this poem together. There is some energy that is more than me that's coming through, and it's my responsibility to be open to it in order that other people can be open to it and be transformed by it too. I see that more as a birthing experience than as an experience of being reborn.

It relates to the idea of mothering ourselves that I think about from Audre Lorde's essay "Eye to Eye."[1] I also get to participate in the process of nurturing myself, bringing birth to myself. I can also take responsibility for it in a particular way. Other people help too, of course. You also mother me, of course, and aunts and loved ones and mentors do nurturing and mothering work too, but there is something very empowering about not only honoring the relationships with other people but also honoring my relationship as a mother to myself.

DOULA DREAMS

Pauline: So describe the moment you decided you wanted to become a doula too.

Alexis: It did not occur to me to become a doula in the literal sense until I was in the rainforest, in the middle of the night, in the rain and the dark. I was there with a midwife and her daughters. And we had been talking about birth and her experiences of giving birth.

So we are just sitting there in a car, and it is super dark and raining outside, and it's thick, thick, thick rainforest, so there is so much that you can't see. Trees and then vines and then more trees and then clouds above the trees—you can't even see the stars. Super dark. Just sitting there, perhaps I did have some sort of sense or memory of being born, because it occurred to me then that there is healing for us to do around birth, around when I was born. Maybe because it didn't have to be a C-section and it was. And I knew that part of your journey of being empowered around birth had to do with becoming a doula and doing birth work and being reborn through those experiences. It occurred to me at that moment that there would be something very healing and powerful about us returning to birth together by supporting other people giving birth. I also think it would be healing for generations in our family who could have used this kind of support when they were giving birth. I describe how dark it was because I didn't necessarily have to look to see it. Your senses change when you're in deep darkness. And, of course, that same night I got on a video call with you and shared that with you, and it has been great to envision it with you. I believe that it will be a major gift to all of those ancestors in our family who have given birth and who have made it possible for us to be here.

DOULA INSIGHTS

Alexis: What did you learn from your first experience working as a doula?

Pauline: The first birth I supported was a young couple. This was their first child, and a friend of mine told me when she was in the very last stages of the pregnancy, so I didn't get a chance to develop a really strong relationship before the birth. I met her once, and within weeks of knowing her she went into labor. It was exciting. I felt honored. I was a little nervous because this was her first, and there is always that question: Do I know what I'm doing? Am I going to be able to give her the support that she needs?

She was very open, and she had already decided on a few things herself. She had a birthing plan. She knew what she wanted. She had another friend who was a counselor also supporting her. So I was really there to support her in a way that her husband couldn't because he was nervous because this was his first child and he didn't know what to do. I was there just to support their family and to be there for her and stay with her. That was the first time that I stayed at the hospital and slept there through the night. I wanted so badly for her to have the kind of birth that she wanted. What was disappointing was that she had a lot of friends who were discouraging her from having a natural birth.

During that experience, I learned that hospital staff can be deceptive when they present what is going to happen and what you need to do and why. They can give the sense of being supportive, but there is an agenda that is underneath the process that may not be in the best interest of the mom and the baby. They are more concerned about malpractice suits. It is a defensive attitude instead of affirming that it will be okay the way she wants it. It's like they want to be in charge because they know best, and it's best if they do it their way because then everything will be safe. And I was surprised at her ob-gyn, who was a black woman. I was surprised at how distant she was.

The birth was fine. She was able to have music. It was a nice room, and she was able to relax. I helped make it comfortable for her, but I think the comfort to her was just that I was there because the husband didn't know what to do. Just for him to be able to go outside and take a break knowing that his wife wasn't alone. And then I did a minitherapy session in another room with her mom and sister and tried to help them understand what the daughter was doing and why.

I have learned how to balance between being overly assertive and delicately persistent. During labor is not the best time to make demands or be insistent because the mom is just doing the best that she can do. It is important for me to be supportive whatever happens. So, if she ends up having a C-section and that's not what she wanted, it's still okay, and she is still brave and courageous and strong. It felt good that I was able to support her with that.

Alexis: What do you think would make the most difference in people's experiences of giving birth?

Pauline: To have more midwives who are more sensitive to the birthing process rather than the medical industry having ownership of the birth. The availability of more doulas would make a difference. So would a shift in the philosophy of the hospital staff, the doctors, the nurses—everyone being more respectful of the mom and whatever her process is. And a shift in thinking about whether it matters if this mom has money, is on Medicaid or is not. I have witnessed young women who may not have a voice for themselves, who are on socially funded medical service, not treated with the type of respect and honor that someone with more financial means is. We need a change in perception of the whole birthing process so that it is not treated like something that's wrong. It is a process that women have been doing for centuries, and it can be easy. We need to reinforce that we are all there to support the mom, not there to take over and do it for her.

Sometimes hospital staff are busy. They don't have the time, and they may think, Here is another one. It is almost like an assembly line, with the thought being, Let's do this the quickest way possible. Then the baby is born, and the staff wants to have him or her cleaned up and under the lamp. And there is all this procedure that takes over, when really it should just be calm and peaceful, and the procedures can wait. There is nothing wrong with the baby having stuff on them when they're born. Just give the mom that time. We need to give mom more time with her newborn rather than whisking away her baby and giving them injections and all those interventions just because we want to make sure no one gets sued.

My theory is that the more peaceful and powerful the birth experience is for the mother, the healthier the connection is with the child. You start off on the right foot, and things just get better and better. A good foundation has been formed.

Alexis: What is one thing that you would want anyone giving birth to know?

Pauline: They should have a strong sense of who they are and how powerful they are. That way, they will not allow circumstances, institutions, hospitals, or whoever to sway them from having the type of birth that they want. They should know how strong and powerful they are to be pregnant and to be bringing another life into the world. No matter what they choose, bringing a baby into the world is powerful, and I think women are the bravest creatures on the planet to be able to do that. Whatever the person chooses, it is possible to have a beautiful birth experience. Don't be afraid to ask for what you want. Even if it's not the first child, even if with the previous children they have done what somebody else said to do, they have the opportunity prior to going into labor to make some choices. We must empower them no matter what.

Alexis: I am bringing the practices that I already do—the praise poems, the rituals—to the actual moment of birth inside the full-circle doula concept. I've been working with black LGBTQ elders and with young women, and now people joke, "Alexis is gonna get them right when they are born!"

I participate in other people's rebirth through the ritual, through poetry, through teaching, through love, through creating poetry as an act of love, through art as a space for people to be profoundly loved. That's how I see my practice. It's an opportunity to circulate the energy so that people have the opportunity to know that they are profoundly loved, to love themselves, and to have the breakthroughs that come from that. Mothering ourselves is everywhere in my work, and so we can think about it in a doula way, a supportive way, a midwife way, a holistic healing way, knowing what we know.

We are helping to give birth to new possibilities, and we need to build our skills so that we can be great at supporting each other because this is a critical time for our species.

Pauline: It's so exciting to envision you helping birthing women to open a spiritual passageway. I can envision you writing a poem for everyone who is going to give birth that we are working with and having that poem resonating with them before the baby is born and during the process of birth. It will be a powerful opening for that life to come into, and that peace, serenity, and love, no matter what else is going on, would be there for the newborn and parent.

Alexis: I keep seeking to understand what it is in a poem or an activity that can really let people know how powerful they are, despite everything that might make us feel not powerful, despite what society says about women, and despite what has happened in our lives. I do believe that it is fundamentally true that we are powerful and that somehow we can know that. The right ritual—and the poem might be the ritual—can connect us back to that. And when we're connected to our power, we really can do anything.[2]

PART IV

Taking Back Our Power
Organizing for Birth Justice

CHAPTER 18

Unexpected Allies

Obstetrician Activism, VBACs, and the Birth Justice Movement

Christ-Ann Magloire and Julia Chinyere Oparah

LET'S TALK ABOUT VBACS

Christ-Ann: I studied at Howard University's medical school and was accepted for my residency at a progressive hospital in Boston, where vaginal birth after cesarean (VBAC) was practiced on a regular basis. At Boston Medical Center (BMC), I worked alongside a team of seven midwives and learned to allow laboring women to do what their bodies were designed to do. BMC was committed to a holistic, mind-body-spirit approach to birth and offered birthing women free, culturally appropriate, multilingual doula care. When I relocated to South Florida, I brought a commitment to women's reproductive rights and confidence in women's ability to birth their babies. I arrived at a time when home birth activists, mostly white, middle-class women, were pushing for midwife-assisted births to be more widely accessible. Many women believed that they would be more successful in giving birth vaginally after a cesarean section at home. While midwives could legally assist at home VBACs, Florida law requires each woman to have an informed consent—a background review signed by a physician to ensure that she is an appropriate candidate for a VBAC and fully understands the potential risks and benefits.

156

In 2004, I started working with local midwives who were having difficulty finding an obstetrician to sign off on the informed consent. Soon I was in demand in other parts of the state, and I established an underground railroad, traveling to Sarasota, Tampa, and Orlando to support home-birthing women.

Then I got pregnant. For the most part, all of the women in my family were born vaginally and gave birth to their own children vaginally. I took my innate ability to birth for granted and never imagined that I would deviate from the clear path that the women in my family had established. Unfortunately, I was in Florida, the state with the fourth-highest cesarean rate in the country. The World Health Organization considers a cesarean section rate of 10 to 15 percent adequate. In contrast, at some hospitals in Miami the rates are 60 to 70 percent. I ended up with a cesarean section and was devastated. So when I got pregnant again, I began a quest to have a VBAC. I didn't want to give birth at home, but I struggled to find another obstetrician who would support my desire to birth the way that a woman is supposed to be able to birth. Being both an obstetrician-gynecologist (ob-gyn) and a pregnant mother has given me new insights into the need for ob-gyns to come together to challenge our hospitals and medical associations and to create new policies and practices around VBACs.

Chinyere: I came to birth justice work later in life, after more than two decades working first in antiracist and women of color movements in the United Kingdom and United States, then in the global movement to end mass incarceration and the surveillance and punishment of communities of color. My entry into birth justice work was spurred by the judgment and medical coercion I experienced during my pregnancy as an "advanced maternal age" mom. I have come to realize that my commitment to birth justice also stems from my earliest body memories as an infant separated from my mother at birth and placed into foster care. Because of the trauma that this primal separation created for me, I was committed to being fully present at my daughter's birth, physically, emotionally, mentally, and spiritually, and to holding her on my body immediately after pushing her out. My own experience led me to believe that those first hours of living and breathing in the world outside the womb do count. I was also aware of how intergenerational trauma can be passed from birthing parent to child, and I wanted to break that cycle by creating a new birth story for myself and my daughter.

As I began to learn about the natural birth and birth justice movements, I noticed a tendency to create a dualistic world of male medicine versus female bodies, coercive, profit-driven medical practitioners versus exploited pregnant women and infants, oppressive hospital births versus liberating home births, and "bad" medicalized pregnancies versus "good" natural births. As someone who has spent many years working within the antiprison and community-accountability movements, this binary worldview was familiar but disturbing. Many of us in the antiprison movement have moved away from creating simple dichotomies. We have recognized that the victim, the perpetrator, and the punishing judge often live within us simultaneously. Our work is to identify and transform the ways in which we each collaborate with the logics of punishment and incarceration that undergird the prison-industrial complex. So when I encountered these dualistic tendencies in the natural birth and birth justice movements, I was drawn to consider what would happen if we were to admit that our experiences are far more messy and complex than the binaries suggest.

As a black lesbian, diagnosed with infertility, who underwent both surgery and in vitro fertilization in order to get pregnant, I know that for some of us, access to appropriate medical interventions can help cocreate or save life. As a member of Black Women Birthing Justice, I also know that many black women seek out hospital births, some have a preference for physician assistance, and a significant number prefer to use intravenous pain medications or an epidural rather than pursuing a "natural" birth experience. While education, empowerment, and expanding health-care coverage for doula care and midwifery will open up alternatives for some of these women, many will continue to birth in a hospital, with an ob-gyn and nursing staff. A birth justice movement that is relevant to all pregnant individuals must extend its reach into the hospitals and create a space for "dissident" obstetricians who are committed to the birthing person's self-determination during pregnancy and childbirth.[1] This challenge led me to seek a dialogue with Dr. Christ-Ann Magloire.

FROM VBAC BANS TO BIRTH JUSTICE

Prior to 1980, physicians in the United States believed that the only safe way for a person with a prior cesarean section to give birth was to have a cesarean delivery in all future pregnancies. In 1980, the National Institutes for Health questioned this practice and outlined situations in which women should be offered the opportunity to try to birth vaginally, otherwise known as "trial of labor." Between 1980 and 1996, the number of VBACs increased to a high of almost 30 percent of all persons with a prior cesarean. Since that time, however, VBAC rates have declined precipitously to a low of 10.2 percent in 2012. Black women in the United States are less likely to birth their first infant vaginally than both white women and Latinas.[2] The cesarean delivery rate for black women in 2013 was 35.9 compared to 32.0 for white women.[3] For black women living in certain states and territories, the likelihood of having a cesarean delivery is even greater. For example, the 2011 cesarean rate for black women in Florida was 37.8 percent; in New Jersey it was 40.5 percent; in Puerto Rico 55.6 percent of black women who gave birth had a cesarean.[4] This disproportionate cesarean delivery rate places black women at greater risk of a cesarean delivery in any subsequent pregnancy. Black women are more likely to seek a VBAC than white women but less likely to have a successful vaginal birth.[5] In some instances, women who are allowed a trial of labor may be pressured to have a cesarean if labor does not progress rapidly. In other cases, signs of fetal distress during a closely monitored labor will lead to a cesarean section.

Physicians attending persons who have had a prior cesarean delivery are often concerned about the risks associated with vaginal birth after significant abdominal surgery. Despite the consistently high success rate of trial of labor, ranging from 60 to 80 percent, obstetricians often point to the risk of uterine rupture, which is higher after an unsuccessful trial of labor than after an elective repeat cesarean delivery but nevertheless occurs in less than 1 percent of cases.[6] They also cite studies that indicate that an unsuccessful trial of labor followed by a repeat cesarean has a higher risk of complications than a VBAC or elective repeat cesarean.[7] Ob-gyns are also susceptible to fears of large liability claims or litigation should an attempted VBAC go wrong. A 2009 American College of Obstetricians and Gynecologists (ACOG) survey revealed that 30 percent of obstetricians had stopped offering trial of labor or attending VBACs for fear of liability claims or litigation.[8] In addition, insurers pressured some obstetricians to cease attending VBACs or risk losing their malpractice insurance altogether.[9] When the patient is a black woman, disproportionate rates of maternal and neonatal mortality and the additional fear that these generate may exacerbate fear of litigation. In addition, ob-gyns are sometimes concerned about the length of time that a vaginal delivery after cesarean can take and may not wish to take time away from their practice when a repeat surgery offers a more timely alternative.

In contrast to the high standard of informed consent required when pregnant individuals seek a VBAC, obstetricians seldom impress upon those birthing their first child the risks associated with a primary or subsequent cesarean section. Risks associated with a cesarean delivery include infection, blood loss, formation of blood clots, injury to the bowel or bladder, and reaction to the medication or anesthesia used.[10] In higher-order cesarean deliveries—those where the pregnant person has already had two or more cesareans—the risks are heightened. Given that the majority of people who deliver a first child are likely to have more children, physicians' reluctance to provide alternatives to a first or primary cesarean section can be considered the first moment in which birthing parents are failed by the medical system and set up for further surgeries and associated risks. The absence of comprehensive options for pregnant individuals considering a VBAC is a second major failure. US law theoretically leaves the decision about whether to give birth vaginally or by cesarean to the pregnant person, and ACOG guidelines state that a VBAC is a safe and appropriate choice for most women who have had a prior cesarean delivery, including for some who have had two previous cesareans.[11] In practice however, hospital policies known as "VBAC bans" prevent many pregnant individuals from attempting a vaginal birth after a cesarean delivery. National Advocates for Pregnant Women (NAPW) estimates that 30 percent of US hospitals have a VBAC ban in place and that only approximately 10 percent of hospitals are truly VBAC friendly.[12] In addition, a survey of ACOG fellows found that between 2003 and 2006, 26 percent stopped offering a trial of labor for women. A pregnant individual seeking a home birth faces even greater obstacles, as most states require that a physician attest that they are an appropriate candidate for a VBAC before they can attempt a midwife-assisted vaginal birth. Few obstetricians support the midwifery model in these cases, and even fewer are willing to accept this responsibility.

A woman's right to choose how she delivers her baby has been contested by the courts in numerous cases, some of which have been documented as part of National Advocates for Pregnant Women's extensive research into forced interventions on pregnant women. In Florida, Jennifer Goodall, a white woman who had had three previous cesarean sections and was pregnant with her fourth child, decided that she wished to avoid the considerable risks associated with a fourth cesarean by attempting a vaginal birth. In July 2014, she received a letter from her prenatal care providers informing her that they intended to seek a court order to perform the surgery "with or without [her] consent" and to report her to child welfare authorities for endangering her unborn child.[13] Goodall's case became the subject of a vigorous #JenniferIsNotAlone campaign on Twitter and Facebook and a lawsuit filed by NAPW. She was ultimately able to labor at home and gave her consent to a cesarean, under difficult conditions, at another hospital.[14]

While Goodall was able to mobilize national advocacy networks to secure a modicum of control over her birth experience, Laura Pemberton, who was arrested during active labor in her home because doctors believed that she was posing a risk to her unborn child, was not as fortunate. Pemberton was taken into custody, her legs were strapped together, and she was forced to a hospital "where an emergency hearing was held to determine the state's interest in protecting the fetus still inside her."[15] The presiding judge forced her to undergo surgery, which she believed was unnecessary. Pemberton later sued for violation of her civil rights, but the judge ruled that the imperative to secure the life of her infant overruled her First, Fourth, and Fifth Amendment rights. This legal assessment was, however, called into question when she subsequently gave birth vaginally to three more children. Most black women who have an unwanted second or third cesarean against their will do not have the resources to attempt a VBAC at home. Black trans/gender nonconforming birthing persons are more likely than cisgender women to seek a home birth, but they may face particular challenges in finding medical personnel who respect their identity and reproductive choices.[16] Whether they seek to birth at home or in a hospital, black women and trans/gender nonconforming people are vulnerable to coercion and emotional manipulation by medical personnel, law enforcement, and even family members.[17] A pregnant individual who seeks a VBAC may be called irresponsible or selfish, caring more about their own experience than that of their unborn child. In this way, pregnant people are separated from and pitted against the children they are carrying inside them.

Laura Pemberton's story highlights the enormous forces stacked against those who seek a VBAC. These obstacles have sparked VBAC activism, a movement within the birth justice and alternative birth movements dedicated to educating pregnant women to make informed decisions about whether to pursue a VBAC and to ensuring that they are equipped with tools and resources to obtain care that will support their choices. VBAC activism includes home birth midwives, doula advocacy, and social media activism, such as Jill Arnold's *The Unnecesarean,* which promotes VBAC awareness to a community of forty-four thousand Facebook and Twitter followers. There are also more formal organizations, such as the International Cesarean Awareness Network, which provides Web-based information on women's right to refuse a cesarean and guidelines for what a woman can do if her hospital has a VBAC ban in place,[18] and Project Motherpath, a Florida-based organization that hosts a statewide VBAC Summit.[19] While most of these organizations do not have visible black leadership, black women's organizations like Black Women DO VBAC!, a website maintained by Melek Speros, and Oakland-based Black Women Birthing Justice seek to raise awareness about VBACs in black communities and to highlight black women's VBAC activism.[20] Few ob-gyns have joined the VBAC movement, and some are vocally opposed to it.[21] In Florida, however, Christ-Ann Magloire is a vocal advocate of the VBAC movement, a regular participant in the VBAC Summit, and an activist who straddles the dual roles of VBAC mom and physician.

RECLAIMING MY BIRTH STORY: CHRIST-ANN'S VBAC JOURNEY

Christ-Ann: When I was pregnant with my first child, I envisioned having my baby naturally in a quiet, peaceful room where I would have soothing music and dimmed lighting. My baby was breach, but a local midwife managed to turn her around. I was happy that my baby was now head down, but I wanted to check on her, so I went to the hospital for a nonstress test. My daughter's heart rate dropped during the test, but then it recovered. A doctor came and broke my waters in an attempt to start my labor, but the baby's heart rate dropped in response. As a medical practitioner, I knew the risks, and so I told them, "Let's just take the baby out."

When I became pregnant again, I knew that I wanted a very different birth experience. I knew that I wanted a VBAC, but I was very ambivalent about where and with whom I should give birth. I had a midwife, but I hadn't told her that I'd had a prior cesarean. I didn't want everyone in the natural birth community to know in case I failed. I also had an obstetrician, who was initially supportive, but as the pregnancy progressed, she seemed to turn against my birth plan. First, she started making comments about my weight gain, which was not excessive overall, and hinting that my baby was going to be very big. Then she commented on my blood pressure, which was actually perfect, and asked whether I was taking medication to keep it down. Finally, she pressured me to have a second set of cultures taken to check for sexually transmitted diseases (STDs), a procedure that I would only do with a woman who'd had a previous positive result or STD symptoms. I could see from my first experience that I was not going to be supported in having a vaginal birth.

My due date was August 10, but because of my previous experience, I set my own due date of Labor Day. I finally went into labor almost two weeks after my official due date. I decided to deliver my baby at home with my midwife. I knew that if I were in the hospital, I would be screaming for something to alleviate the pain, so I chose to be in an environment that would support a natural process. When I entered into transition—the most intense phase of labor—I desperately wanted relief. My midwife had a little black bag, and I was certain that she had something in there that would help me; instead I delivered my baby shortly afterward. When they learned about my birth, my fellow physicians were horrified and thought that I had lost my mind. That reaction is precisely why I didn't trust a doctor to be at my birth. I learned firsthand that physicians are not always truthful and often place their own schedule and concerns above the needs of the pregnant woman, even if she is one of them. In contrast, the natural birth community was excited and saw my delivery as a victory. Today, I tell my clients that I had a VBAC at home in order to inspire them and show them that it is possible.

My own birth experiences and my training at Howard University and BMC have shaped my own medical practice. My practice is called Serenity Holistic Ob/Gyn. I try to create an environment where women feel serene, calm, and as safe as possible during their prenatal visits. I allow women's labor to unfold naturally, and as long as they don't have complications that put them or their babies at risk, I expect them to go into natural labor. As a result, I have a primary cesarean section rate of just 7 percent and an overall rate of 21 percent in contrast to rates of between 37.1 and 49 percent in the hospitals where I work.[22] I let women know that I believe in the birth process and in women's bodies and that I am their greatest fan and advocate. My job is to reassure a pregnant woman, especially a first-time mom, and to relieve her anxiety so that she can allow her body to do what it does naturally. Most women I work with do not receive an epidural. I let them know that it's best to push the baby out as quickly as possible and that an epidural will slow down labor and can lead to a cesarean delivery. I am also one of a handful of physicians who will deliver a breech baby—where the buttocks or feet, rather than the head, present first. This is a skill that few physicians learn, so most women carrying a breech baby are automatically scheduled for a cesarean if the baby does not turn to a head-first presentation.

Most obstetricians treat birth as a disease that requires them to intervene. Many hospitals do not understand the natural process of birth. I choose to practice in hospitals that support the birth process, where most nurses are not afraid if the baby comes out before a doctor can get there, and that allow VBACs. The attitudes and training of the nursing staff have a huge impact on whether women can birth in a calm environment. I am selective about the nurses I work with. New and inexperienced nurses may have a great deal of anxiety, and that can impact the birth experience. Some nurses believe that any form of pain is a problem and that it is their job to relieve it. Recently, a nurse told me, "I don't understand why you won't give her an epidural. She's in pain!" If a woman gives birth in an environment that does not understand and support the natural process of birth, including the role of painful contractions, she is likely to end up in an operating room.

One of the most important ways that I, as an ob-gyn, can bring about change is to model what is possible. When other physicians and nurses see my ob-gyn practice and experience a woman allowing her body to do what it knows, they are more likely to support a natural birth process. Even where induction may be medically necessary, doctors have options. At one time, I was the only doctor in my network using mechanical forms of induction, while other doctors relied on Pitocin, a drug that has the side effect of making contractions more intense and difficult to bear and can lead to a cesarean delivery. Now, most of the doctors I work with have gained experience with my approach. An important part of my advocacy is to nurture relationships and alliances with midwives and doulas within the birth movement. Whether I am walking a client through the risks and benefits of pursuing a VBAC or participating in the VBAC Summit, I seek to create opportunities for medical practitioners and alternative birth-workers to dialogue and learn from each other.

UNEXPECTED ALLIANCES: OB-GYN ADVOCACY AND THE BIRTH JUSTICE MOVEMENT

Despite recommendations by ACOG, for too many pregnant individuals the aphorism "Once a C-section, always a C-section" continues to be true. A VBAC has significant benefits, including a lower risk of infection and other complications from the surgery, less pain after delivery, a greater opportunity to bond early on with the newborn, fewer days in hospital, a shorter recovery time at home, and a greater sense of empowerment and agency in the process of birth. Regardless of these benefits, too many pregnant individuals who could safely have a trial of labor after cesarean are denied that opportunity due to outdated hospital policies; unsupportive, unskilled, and fearful medical practitioners; and inadequate advocacy for those seeking a VBAC.

If VBAC is to become a meaningful option for more pregnant people, change needs to occur at a number of levels. Locally, we need to put pressure on hospital administrators to improve their outcomes with regard to cesarean and VBAC rates. Activists and clients can demand that ob-gyns follow ACOG guidelines and allow a client a trial of labor or else refer them to another doctor, rather than pressuring them to have a cesarean delivery. Dissident ob-gyns can play a particularly powerful role in educating their peers, modeling best practices, and encouraging colleagues to unpack biases from their training and consider alternatives. We need to demand education for nurses, who are on the front line of the battle over how women and trans/gender nonconforming birthing parents deliver their babies. An emphasis should be made on the benefits of unmedicated vaginal birth and VBAC, and efforts should be made to eliminate fear of the natural process of birth among all medical staff.

At the state level, we can demand that legislators get involved in the struggle to support safe, appropriate birth environments with minimal medical intervention as a step toward improving the health of new mothers and trans/gender nonconforming parents and their infants. Legislators could introduce measures to address physician reluctance to support VBAC. For example, providing limited immunity from litigation or caps on payments in VBAC cases would remove a significant barrier to greater VBAC rates. Reversing the current payment incentive to carry out a cesarean section, so that ob-gyns would be paid more for a VBAC, which typically takes far longer, could also begin to shift the balance toward natural birth. In addition, states should ensure that doulas are covered by Medicaid and by health insurers. Laboring women who have continuous support of an independent birth assistant have shorter labors and fewer cesareans and are less likely to be induced with Pitocin or to use pain medication including an epidural.[23] Women and trans/gender nonconforming individuals seeking a VBAC are likely to experience greater anxiety and doubt about their ability to birth vaginally, and the additional emotional and practical support provided by a culturally competent doula can increase the odds of a successful VBAC.

Nationally, we need to reconsider the role of dissident physicians in relation to the birth justice and natural birth movements. As a physician within natural birth settings, Christ-Ann has often been subjected to comments that imply that all ob-gyns are misogynist, make their decisions for financial reasons alone, do not base their practice on evidence, and spend most of their time on the beach or golfing. These stereotypes are far removed from the lived experience of many overworked and committed medical practitioners, especially women of color, and can be alienating and insulting. Alliances between nurses, physicians, and alternative birth workers and activists, based on mutual respect and learning, create more fertile ground for change for women who choose to give birth in a hospital setting. Despite real differences in philosophy and practice, our shared commitment to improving birth outcomes and experiences may provide us with common ground.

CHAPTER 19

Birthing Freedom

Black American Midwifery
and Liberation Struggles

Ruth Hays

Throughout US history, black people, especially black women, have been defined by and denigrated for their reproductive capacity. Commodified under chattel slavery and pathologized in its aftermath, black reproduction is both a principal site of racial oppression and a key area for antiracist struggle. This chapter explores how choices around childbearing[1] are an important aspect of reproductive freedom by examining the history of black midwifery and current activist efforts to revive it. I begin by tracing the history of black midwives in slavery and after Emancipation, exploring how their unique practices bound communities and families together. I then turn my attention to contemporary efforts to revive these practices as a means of improving reproductive freedom among black women as well as health outcomes for black mothers and infants. Finally, I suggest ways in which these efforts can be brought more efficiently to birthing black women who can benefit in myriad ways from community-based, culturally competent care.

BLACK MIDWIVES IN BONDAGE

In her insightful study of reproductive labor in chattel slavery, Jennifer Morgan explains that slaveholders employed both "outrageous images and callously indifferent strategies to ultimately [create an] economic and moral environment in which the appropriation of a woman's children as well as her childbearing potential become rational and, indeed, natural."[2] Chief among these strategies was the portrayal of nonwhite women as bestial and therefore enslaveable. In their visual and written descriptions, early European travelers to the African continent constructed frightful, exaggerated, and often contradictory images of the women they encountered. These depictions were informed by the image of the medieval wild woman, whose base sexuality was represented by an overly sexualized body. In travel literature from the early colonial period, African women are described as having breasts so elongated that they were able to nurse their babies over their shoulders while they worked. The image of distended breasts encapsulates many of the contradictory tropes deployed by early colonizers: these exaggerated sexual organs marked black women as, at once, hypersexual and repulsive. The image of a woman nursing over her shoulder encapsulates the European desire to exploit African women as simultaneously productive and reproductive laborers.[3]

It is important to note, however, that reproduction has also been a site of resistance to racialized oppression. Since this nation's inception, black women in the United States have found means to control and direct their fertility.[4] These means, however, are not limited to methods for preventing pregnancy and birth. Although it is seldom discussed in the literature, birthing practices have also provided rich opportunities to create community and resist dehumanization. As the system of plantation slavery developed, enslaved women combined a variety of West African ritual and medicinal traditions to form a distinctly New World healing culture. Within this culture, midwifery was not considered a trade or vocation but, rather, a calling. Enslaved midwives were often older members of communities who had already raised their own families and gained birthing experience both firsthand and through assisting friends and relatives. Their status as elders led to the title "granny midwives," which I use to refer to enslaved midwives and the women who continued their healing traditions after Emancipation. Among these wise women, supernatural manifestations were often used to identify potential midwives: babies born under a veil, as seventh children, or as one of a set of twins were said to possess especially potent spiritual powers. While these gifts could be channeled into a variety of pursuits, women who possessed them most often entered the role of midwife.[5]

Granny midwives relied almost as much on spiritual guidance as on medical knowledge and experience, and their practice reflected a holistic concern with the well-being of their charges. Among enslaved people, conjuring and other forms of magical practice were considered integral to properly maintaining one's health. In her exploration of the granny midwife as a literary and cultural figure, Valerie Lee notes that, absent the "negative associations of witchcraft, conjuring has been an empowering concept for many black women. Conjuring pays homage to an African past, while providing a present day idiom for magic, power and ancient wisdom within a pan-African cultural context."[6] Conjuring can also serve as a counterhegemonic discursive framework. Under chattel slavery, it functioned as a supernatural means of transforming an otherwise harsh reality. Such practices allowed bondwomen to claim birth as a space of care and agency for themselves, humanizing an experience that the slave economy understood as purely economic.

Because of their importance, grannies were often afforded more leeway than other enslaved people. However, their activities also tended to be closely monitored as slaveholders believed their spiritual powers could be used for evil purposes as well as good. Western societies in general, and the United States in particular, have denigrated women healers, especially in the arena of birth. Early Europeans saw birth as defilement and midwives as dishonorable women attending to an objectionable practice. Thousands of midwives and other female practitioners were burned as witches in the colonial Americas.[7] In contrast, among the various African societies that supplied the foundations of granny midwifery, these women "enjoyed their community role as facilitators of harmony, wholeness and order. As such, they continued to command respect."[8]

As they tended the sick, granny midwives also constructed a counterhegemonic system of wellness that attended to the multifaceted needs of their communities. Historians Sheila Davis and Cora Ingram argue that grannies "represented the high point of authority and control ... in plantation communities." They were seen as "models of strength, wisdom and power" who performed a variety of critical social and spiritual, as well as medical, duties.[9] One key ritual, which public health officials would later term "fussing," is especially indicative of the interwoven spiritual and medicinal aspects of granny midwifery: "Fussing involved beautifying a woman's body in preparation for the transformative event of birth. A woman's hair was braided and pomaded, her calves and legs greased, her arms and groin talcum powdered, and her person sprinkled with sweet water or perfume. . . . Strong, positive smells, provided by perfumes and lotions, [were believed to] counteract any ill will that might linger in the area, providing yet another layer of protection for the newborn child."[10] Fussing also had important, though frequently misunderstood, medicinal purposes. Massage distracts a birthing woman from labor pain, increasing her ability to cope with it, and relaxes her, which speeds up the birth process. Fussing also probably involved massage of the birthing woman's perineum.[11] Extremely effective at preventing vaginal tearing, this technique has only recently gained mainstream prominence in obstetric practice.

In the context of US slavery, fussing and other rituals surrounding childbirth pushed back against the dehumanizing tropes that slaveholders used to justify exploiting black women physically, sexually, and reproductively. Through conjuring and community building, granny midwives transformed the experience of birth into a unique space of agency, a moment in which women could care for each other, beautify each other, and celebrate the arrival of a new member of the community. In most accounts, the only forms of reproductive agency that enslaved women are said to have exercised include contraception, abortion, and, occasionally, infanticide. Historians Darlene Clark Hine and Kathleen Thompson describe this phenomenon in *A Shining Thread of Hope*: "Two ... intimately related forms of resistance peculiar to women emerge from the [slave] narratives—abortion and infanticide. The conscious decision on the part of a slave woman to terminate her pregnancy was one act that was totally beyond the control of the master of the plantation." Although infanticide was estimated as less prevalent than abortion, it also functioned as an important site of resistance. Hine and Thompson go on to note that "the relatively small number of documented cases [of infanticide] is not as significant as the fact that it occurred at all."[12] The act of bearing children, however, also functioned as a means of resistance. This was especially true when women were involved in marriages or other stable relationships. While some women certainly felt it was better not to bring children into slavery at all and acted accordingly, others built families to serve as a respite from the horrors of the institution.

Granny midwives also provided practical support to the families they served outside their healing duties. Because of their relative closeness to slaveholders, they were able to act as emissaries, carrying the concerns of the enslaved to their owners. Midwives were most able to advocate for concessions such as improved living conditions and greater stability for a new mother and her family after the birth of a child.[13] Finally, and most importantly, granny midwives played an important role in linking generations of enslaved people. Their rituals, knowledge, and support were paramount to enslaved people's collective emotional and psychological survival.

During the late antebellum period in the United States, southern elites' desire for medical attendance in birth became established among the antebellum South's planter class, and in the early nineteenth century, physicians began attending the births of both free and enslaved plantation women. When the Atlantic slave trade was officially ended in 1808, enslaved women's reproductive capacities became even more important to sustaining the slave economy. Marie Jenkins Schwartz notes, "During the antebellum era the expectation increased among members of the owning class that enslaved women would contribute to the economic success of the plantation not only through productive labor but also through procreation. . . . Slaveholders tried a variety of means to boost the number of children born to enslaved mothers, including medical treatment. As slaveholders called upon their services, doctors were increasingly drawn into the drama of slavery's perpetuation."[14]

Slaveholders' desire to increase their human property coincided with doctors' need for experience, creating an economically symbiotic relationship between the two groups. Although elite women desired medical care during birth, they did not trust inexperienced doctors, and, as noted above, most physicians completed their training with little, if any, practical knowledge of childbirth. As a result, many southern medical men attended their first births in the slave quarters. When regular physicians treated enslaved birthing women, they considered the slaveholder to be their client, often failing even to converse with the woman herself. Their lack of access to and interest in enslaved women's medical histories and needs made their treatments even less efficacious and deepened the existing tension and professional competition between medical men and granny midwives. Physicians were consistently disturbed that, in many communities, whites and blacks alike often relied heavily on enslaved healers. Despite their general antagonism, however, medical men were known to adopt enslaved midwives' herbal medicines, recognizing that they were often more effective than their own. They sometimes promoted legislation to forbid slaves from practicing medicine in an attempt to repair the "very real breach" these healers produced in "the power relations idealized by white southerners."[15] These efforts underscore the fact that, in the antebellum period, all physicians were competing for legitimacy with other types of healers. When white physicians launched their takeover of childbirth, then, slaveholders were willing to let them usurp the place of the plantation midwife as much to restore the proper balance of power as to increase fertility among their bondwomen.

Enslaved people also pushed back against physicians' burgeoning medical hegemony. They generally distrusted owner-allied physicians, and the frequently painful and ineffective treatments they employed convinced many that they were no more effective than their own healers. In an attempt to retain some control over their bodies, many disobeyed doctors' orders. Physician-attended births reinforced the desperate lack of bodily autonomy that characterized chattel slavery and, paradoxically, deepened bondwomen's reliance on granny midwives. Schwartz notes that, as white intervention in birthing and healing increased, "enslaved women were forced to keep secret certain of their own [medicinal] customs."[16] Their secrecy and mistrust was a result of black iatrophobia, a community-wide fear of physicians among black Americans as a result of the medical profession's historic neglect and abuse.[17] Midwives were and remain key figures in addressing these fears and creating more responsive and respectful models of care. Enslaved midwives in the late antebellum period were able to benefit even from cooperating with physicians, both by keeping abreast of medical trends and innovations and by making themselves appear more compliant (and therefore trustworthy) to their owners. Most importantly for the parturient woman, granny midwives worked in the same negotiating capacity with doctors as they did with masters and mistresses. Like modern-day doulas—professional birth attendants who provide nonmedical support during labor—they intervened, sometimes successfully, when doctors proposed treatments that the birthing woman objected to.[18] In doing so, they resisted the medical subjugation of black birthing bodies, even within the institution of slavery.

BLACK MIDWIVES IN FREEDOM

The wisdom, strength, and community that grannies facilitated remained valuable resources in black women's political and social struggles after slavery's end. After Emancipation, black midwives' traditional birth practices played an extremely important role in black communities, particularly in the Jim Crow South. Borrowing from Patricia Hill Collins, archaeologist Laurie Wilkie describes their vocation as "mother work,"[19] or mothering done on behalf of an entire community. Coming together to support parturient women was also an important communal event and a precious source of empowerment for poor women who controlled little in their lives. Margaret Charles Smith, an Alabama midwife who collaborated with historian Linda Janet Holmes on an enlightening autobiography, illustrates the primacy of birth work in rural black communities. She theorizes that black women "faced so much economic and political turmoil [that] passing on traditional ways became an important part of rising above subservience and establishing some cultural order."[20] The "cultural order" that was created in black birthing spaces constitutes a counter-discourse to dominant (and devaluing) ways of understanding black birthing.

After the end of slavery, black reproduction was no longer the concern of elite whites, but they continued to view it as a problem. In the early twentieth century, public health activists urged the US government to begin collecting vital statistics. Prior to this time, the US census was the primary source for population-level data, and reformers argued that introducing birth and death certificates would produce more precise and useful data. When these data revealed that the United States lagged severely behind other Western nations in infant and maternal mortality, the public health movement turned its focus to improving prenatal care. The worst birth outcomes, by far, were found among black women, who then became the focus of ameliorative interventions. These programs, however, largely ignored how factors such as poverty, over-work, and malnutrition contributed to black women's poor birth outcomes. Instead, they blamed the women themselves and the midwives who attended their births. As a result, public health reforms focused on scrutinizing and regulating granny midwives instead of improving black mothers' and infants' material conditions.[21]

The Sheppard-Towner Act of 1921 was the most significant product of these reform efforts. Under the auspices of the Federal Children's Bureau, this legislation funded health and education programs for women of childbearing age, especially the rural poor. Though certainly well intentioned, Sheppard-Towner programs were administered in a way that reinforced racialized ideas about reproduction, mothering, and the female body. Even though program administrators sometimes concluded that socioeconomic factors contributed to infant and maternal mortality in white communities, they almost always found midwives to blame for the same phenomena among black women. Consequently, public health programs in black areas were mostly directed at "reeducating" black midwives and only secondarily at providing women and children with desperately needed preventative services. In her comprehensive article chronicling midwife education programs under the Sheppard-Towner Act, historian Molly Ladd-Taylor explains that "by placing female birth attendants under state control and requiring them to yield to medical authority, midwife regulation was more acceptable to physicians than Sheppard-Towner prenatal and infant health conferences, which emphasized prevention and encouraged women to demand better care. The Children's Bureau won support for federal maternity and infancy aid in the south by focusing on the 'midwife problem' rather than on the economic and social causes of poor health."[22] Support for these programs was based on the assumption that "cultural," rather than material, deficiencies led to poor infant and maternal well-being, a misapprehension that, as Khiara M. Bridges has shown, continues to pollute medical practitioners. Bridges argues convincingly that by referring to "culture," health workers both invoke and elide race- and class-based assumptions about the populations they encounter.[23] Appealing to culture continues to be a common strategy for those dealing with racial and class-based health disparities because it both obscures the structural causes of ill health and places the onus on subordinated people to change their cultural practices to achieve better outcomes.

Public health nurses, who directly administered midwife education programs, openly displayed their distaste for nonnormative, nonwhite birth practices, perhaps most nakedly in their strict policing of grannies' supplies and persons. At a time when 90 percent of southern midwives were illiterate, reading and writing (in order to produce birth certificates) were designated necessary skills, as was adhering to a more regimented view of time that one midwife referred to as "living by the clock," that is, allowing schedules to be regulated by kept time rather than the perceived rhythms of the day. Sheppard-Towner administrators reasoned that midwives with these skills would be more amenable to medicalization. Ladd-Taylor notes that by equating literacy with "intelligence and obedience," instructors in midwife education programs "tried to replace old midwives with younger women they thought more likely to follow medical doctrine"[24] and to recognize obstetrics as the authoritative system of knowledge vis-à-vis childbirth.

As part of the newly implemented process of licensing and certification, midwives were required to submit their supplies to government inspection. Objects specifically endorsed by public health authorities were allowed, and all other items were essentially considered contraband. These included the benign implements used in fussing and other rituals.[25] Birthing stools were also commonly proscribed in an effort to force midwife-attended birthing women onto their backs.[26] Such inspections ensured that midwives practiced in a manner that nurses felt comfortable with culturally and were largely irrelevant to the safety and efficacy of their practices.

Those who continued to practice, however, did not always willingly accede to demands to conduct themselves according to dominant "cultural values." Instead, they clandestinely continued their traditions privately while publicly complying with the new standards. In the documentary *Bringin' in da Spirit,* rural black midwives and the women they attended in the early twentieth century recall that some would keep two bags of supplies: one for official inspection and one for actual use. Others even constructed false bottoms in their bags to conceal "contraband" during inspections.[27] These efforts to retain traditional practices, even when proscribed, demonstrate that midwifery was a crucial site of struggle for black women as well as a nourishing and affirming communal culture. Margaret Charles Smith, discussing the disappearance of lay midwifery in one Virginia town, noted that older women viewed the movement from home to hospital and midwife to doctor as a biological phenomenon. Older women in the community, she writes, "asserted that old medicines would not work on new, modern bodies." The continuity that granny midwives had fostered "had been fractured by medicalization." Because they now relied on doctors, rather than themselves and each other, to manage pregnancy and birth, Smith believes that "the communal body" of this town's black women "had been ruptured."[28]

In the mid-twentieth century, granny midwives increasingly disappeared due to a combination of onerous requirements for practicing and black women's newly gained access to hospital births. However, a new politics has arisen at the site of this rupture, seeking to improve birth outcomes in black communities by referencing and resurrecting traditional midwifery practices.

THE NEW POLITICS OF BLACK CHILDBEARING

One example of this new politics is the struggle to provide access to lay birth companions for low-income women. In June 2012, Oregon became the first state in the union to guarantee Medicaid reimbursement for doula services when its legislature passed HB 3311. This groundbreaking legislation means that women who rely on Medicaid now have access to the type of community-based, intensely personal care that granny midwives provided in the past. Although midwives of color do practice, they are often inaccessible to women using public aid, who are forced to use obstetricians for their prenatal care if they want the care to be reimbursed. Doulas supplement physicians' practice by providing some of the hands-on, personalized care that granny midwives once provided. They meet with women in anticipation of the birth, helping them prepare mentally and physically for the ordeal ahead; they stay with women throughout the birth process, providing continual physical and emotional support; after the birth, they visit new mothers and their babies, checking in with them and providing assistance with infant care and breastfeeding.

Although this legislation is a boon for all poor women, it is especially relevant to black women who are both disproportionately poor and more likely to have unsatisfactory encounters with health-care providers. In her fascinating book about the Black Panther Party's health campaigns, Alondra Nelson demonstrates[29] that health activism was a vital component of twentieth-century black freedom struggles. These efforts were focused on the twin goals of gaining access to quality health care and escaping the purview of dangerous, exploitative, and stigmatizing medical practices. Further, legal scholar Dorothy Roberts has shown[30] that black women's reproductive politics have not always aligned with the priorities of the mainstream reproductive rights movement. These, she argues, have tended to focus on "negative" reproductive rights, meaning the state is prohibited from barring women's access to reproductive services such as birth control and abortion care. Although these issues are certainly important for black women, "positive" protections are also necessary to fully protect their interests. Rather than restricting the actions of the state, positive liberties, Roberts explains, require state action to ensure access to a full array of reproductive choices:

> The primary concern of white, middle-class women centers on laws that restrict choices otherwise available to them, such as statutes that make it more difficult to obtain an abortion.
>
> Black women, on the other hand, especially those who are poor, must deal with a whole range of forces that impair their choices. Their reproductive freedom, for example, is limited not only by the denial of access to safe abortions, but also by the lack of resources necessary for a healthy pregnancy and parenting relationship.[31]

The Oregon bill helped remedy the lack of resources for healthy pregnancies and parenting available to many women by providing access to doula care, a positive choice that allows women greater control of their reproductive lives. The bill passed as the result of lobbying and legislative efforts by the Oregon-based International Center for Traditional Childbearing (ICTC) and the Oregon Coalition to Improve Birth Outcomes. ICTC is an important national manifestation of this new politics. It offers culturally competent doula training and annual conferences for black midwives and traditional healers, all of which promote both the tradition of granny midwives and political solutions to maternal health disparities. Shafia Monroe, a certified professional midwife, founded the organization (initially the Traditional Childbearing Group) in 1976 to serve black women interested in home birth.

Monroe had been interested in pregnancy and childbirth since she was a teenager and had been active in the (Newton, Massachusetts) Homebirth Info Movement, although, as the only black member, she felt uncomfortable in the organization. In a 1991 interview, she describes the alienation she experienced as a home birth advocate and student searching for like-minded black midwives in the early 1970s. The only black midwives she was able to get in touch with "were from the South, they were old. Unfortunately, I think the system invalidated them. They didn't want to talk: 'Oh, girl, that's an idea from a long time ago; you don't want to do that now, we got bottles, you don't have to do that now.'"[32] That older midwives were so reluctant to discuss their knowledge with her underscores the success that obstetrics has had in conquering the hearts and minds of US women. US women locate breastfeeding, as well as home birth practices, in an abandoned, unreachable—ruptured—past. Monroe goes on to describe trying to build a professional alliance with a black obstetrician who, similarly, balked at her suggestions. When asked to provide "backup" for Monroe's home birth practice, she "went off, 'Are you crazy? I'm against it. You know how long we fought to get in a hospital and now you're going to try to take us back out.'"[33]

The doctor's statement that black people in the United States had finally won the fight to birth in hospitals reflects a common conception that obstetrics necessarily represents a positive technological advance, which is not always the case. Although obstetricians are highly trained surgical specialists who, in times of crisis, can and do give lifesaving and sustaining treatment to mothers and infants, there is legitimate debate around what constitutes an obstetric emergency and who is qualified to assist parturient women in nonemergency situations. Expanding black women's access to different types of providers and modes of birthing is a crucial step toward dismantling the tangled ideologies that continue to devalue our motherhood and personhood.

From their beginnings, black midwives and traditional healers have aided women with a host of medical and social issues, chief among them being welcoming new children. During slavery, they worked as emissaries, carrying the concerns of the enslaved to masters, who were concerned only with increasing their human property. After Emancipation, they functioned as important community leaders, passing on received knowledge about childbirth and infant care. In the present moment, these traditions are being revived by a dedicated group of activists and practitioners who seek to improve health outcomes through time-honored healing methods. The Oregon bill was a good start. Ultimately, if black women are to gain access to the type of care their foremothers experienced, resources will have to be marshaled to enable women's access to midwife and doula care. Furthermore, it will require active listening on the part of practitioners and policy makers to see what works for individual women, families, and communities.

CHAPTER 20

Becoming an Outsider-Within

Jennie Joseph's Activism in Florida Midwifery

Alicia D. Bonaparte and Jennie Joseph

Using Patricia Hill Collins's conceptualization of the "outsider-within," this chapter documents the journey of midwife-activist Jennie Joseph as she successfully challenged Florida legislation outlawing midwifery. We illustrate how Jennie built alliances with other women in order to fight for marginalized women and their children in Florida. We describe how her personal and professional experiences, despite their challenges, fomented the JJ Way®[1] and reinforced her dedication to addressing the birth needs of underserved populations in Florida. We argue that Jennie's work exemplifies the role of midwife-activists who actively combat the medicalization of birth and demonstrates why midwifery care is beneficial for women of color.

African American feminist sociologist Patricia Hill Collins points to the costs and benefits of black women's positionality as "outsiders-within" when occupying predominantly white spaces. This outsider-within status provides a key benefit described by Collins as a "standpoint [that produces] distinctive analyses of race, class, and gender."[2] In particular, black women are able to view social situations and their nuances and patterns of power and privilege objectively and are privy to information or hidden confidences. We argue that, much like their academic counterparts, who have the ability to better

176

develop ways of addressing inequities in academia, black midwives also possess an outsider-within status within reproductive health care. Furthermore, black midwives can operate more effectively as reproductive justice activists for women of color thanks to their special positionality as professional birthing attendants located at the intersection of systems of dominance. Black women exist on what bell hooks refers to as the margins of society.[3] Despite the stigmatizing nature of this positionality, black midwives are able to channel their experiences of racism and sexism into creative new ways of reducing reproductive health disparities. Jennie's story highlights how an outsider-within perspective enabled her to build solidarity with other health-care practitioners and to improve black women's ability to birth safely in the state of Florida.

ENCOUNTERING RESISTANCE IN THE UNITED STATES

Jennie was born the daughter of Barbadian immigrants in England and trained to become a midwife at the Barnett College of Nursing and Midwifery in London. Jennie's background as a practicing midwife in the United Kingdom provided her with experiences that later informed her critique of the maternal-care system in the United States and shaped her as a midwife-activist. In 1989, she decided to move to Florida to be with her partner and assumed that she would continue to practice as a midwife on her arrival.

> [When I came to the United States,] foolishly, I didn't do any kind of research—after all, baby having is the same in any country, or so I thought, so I didn't see the need to "think ahead" too deeply. I was fully expecting to apply to a local hospital and resume where I had left off, delivering babies and/or supporting pregnant and postpartum moms on the maternity floor.
>
> Midwifery had been my profession and my livelihood, I certainly saw it as my vocation, but I had no idea what awaited me and was totally blindsided by what I discovered after I arrived.

Jennie's description of her arrival in the United States demonstrates how her actual experiences challenged her initial beliefs about US birthing work, which were a focus on "baby having" and "supporting pregnant and postpartum moms." The challenges she encountered as she sought to become a midwife awakened her to the struggles faced by midwives of color in the United States. First, Jennie states, "I couldn't get a job! In fact, whenever I spoke about the possibility, I received puzzled stares and vacant expressions. No one seemed to really understand what I was saying. The fact that I thought I could apply to hospitals, in my mind, [and] pick up where I left off was apparently quite laughable." Florida law at the time provided another obstacle to practicing midwifery:

At the time, 1989, the Florida Midwifery Practice Act had been sunset-ted [retired]; yet, even if I had known that, I wouldn't have been able to understand what it actually meant. In England, all midwives and nurses are registered under one national council and renew registration every five years. If a midwife is practicing in a certain area, she notifies the "Supervisor of Midwives" for that district—and that's that. If she moves, she updates the new area supervisor. It took me more than a year to figure out how to "register" as a midwife in Florida, and when it began to finally dawn on me what I was up against, I began to despair.

To provide further context regarding how birthing women in the United Kingdom utilize midwives, Jennie noted,

The midwife is standard. She is recognized, acknowledged, and supported as a professional within the maternity-care system without question. Simi-larly, you can compare her status to a registered nurse in the US. You have a midwife first always, and then if you become high risk and only then, [you have] a consultation with an obstetrician, and then you're followed by an obstetrician if you [continue to have complications]. But if you're normal, you return to a midwife [which is covered by the British National Health Service or NHS]. So, similar to the American system, women who have money or who want specialized care, more affluent women, may choose a private arrangement with a private obstetrician. What they buy with their money is that obstetrician, American style.

Jennie's comments reflect how her identity as a foreign-born midwife provided her with an understanding of her "difference" and how it would further inform and complicate her midwifery experience in Florida. We use the term "difference" to draw upon feminist literature that speaks to how women of color and other marginalized groups experience their subordinate social positions thanks to interactions with dominant members of society.[4] Comparatively, these social differences impacted US midwives of color in historical ways and, as we later discuss, in contemporary ways.

INTERLOPERS IN BIRTHING WORK

During the early twentieth century, southern lay black midwives (also known as granny midwives) in the United States fought and lost the battle to prac-tice midwifery.[5] This defeat was a consequence of the medicalization of birth (or the belief that birthing could only safely occur under the supervision of a doctor within a hospital setting). This ideology, initially put forward by the American Medical Association in the early twentieth century and later supported by the American College of Obstetricians and Gynecologists, ruled that hospital settings and medical doctors provided the best infant and maternal health outcomes.[6] This was due to the perceived unsanitary practices and poor training of black and immigrant midwives. Additionally, public health officials were concerned about white infant-mortality rates, leading to a decrease in the population. Given this anti-midwife advocacy, it is unsurprising that many states, including Florida, eventually outlawed lay midwifery practice until the early 1980s.[7] This history of anti-midwifery advocacy and legislation created the roadblocks that Jennie encountered upon her arrival in Florida. Despite these obstacles, she remained committed to working as a health-care practitioner and secured employment with an obstetrician. Working alongside this doctor also provided her with yet more evidence of her "outsider-within" status.

> [My new employer] knew enough about European midwifery training to realize he had found an asset to his practice. He hired me, although to this day I don't know in which capacity, as I was not licensed or insured; nor did I understand that I had to be. He told me in no uncertain terms that I would never be able to go to the hospital with the women or deliver any babies. I was grateful for a job and thrilled to be back to providing patient care, albeit American style, and happily accepted the terms of my position. I duly worked in his office for a year until I had to leave because I was fired!

In her new role, Jennie functioned more as a nurse or doula than as a trained midwife. The obstetrician provided "boundaries of practice" for Jennie. This boundary maintenance provides another clear example that Jennie was a "stranger" in US birthing work due to her lack of US credentials, and her "strangeness" meant she had to adhere to certain occupational restrictions. These restrictions mirror the rigid prescriptions that experienced granny midwives had to adhere to in order to continue to practice during the transition to physician-supervised childbirth.

And yet, her acknowledgment of being a "stranger" in birthing work enabled her to more fully understand another element of her early times in Florida—her status as a black health consumer. In addition to experiencing barriers as a birth practitioner, Jennie had a traumatic experience as a patient. Jennie's experience as a woman of color seeking gynecological help in the United States outlines an unfortunate but common experience: medical abuses against women of color and misplaced trust in health-care practitioners. She states,

> Having suffered from severe endometriosis my entire adult life and having undergone several attempts to resolve the condition in the UK, I was accustomed to seeking medical care when it flared up. I was provided medical insurance by my boss. So, struggling with understanding the lack of access to [quality] health care in general [in the United States], I naively thought that I

could approach my employer for medical advice. Thus began a series of events, surgeries performed by him on me—that led to the ultimate hysterectomy and removal of my ovaries, which had me in the hospital by age thirty.

Black women in predominantly white professional circles are able to see how privilege and hierarchy are maintained. Furthermore, these social spaces provide black women with a deeper insight regarding how and why race, class, and gender influence social interactions.[8] In hindsight, Jennie realizes, "obviously, you couldn't trust the same doctor you work for, the same doctor who employs you knowing that you don't have a license and knowing that he hasn't told you that you must have a license to practice, and that same doctor was also suggesting I needed these surgeries. And I was going like a sheep to the slaughter to get these surgeries." Jennie underwent a hysterectomy and an oophorectomy (removal of ovaries) "based on the fact that he essentially botched several surgeries through the year that he [assisted her with her endometriosis flare-ups]." This "botching" reflects the unfortunate and avoidable everyday experiences of many black women in the United States. Medical professionals subject African American women to an increasingly disproportionate number of unnecessary procedures, and this demographic has the highest rate of cesarean sections and the worst reproductive health outcomes, comparably.[9]

These negative experiences propelled Jennie to enter the world of US birthing work on her own terms by becoming self-employed. Jennie states, "The only way I could really work as a midwife that was not employed was as a home birth practitioner, [and by] creating linkages with the home birth community, they in turn became [my] allies." Jennie received her license as a direct-entry midwife—a category of midwives who "receive specialized training and education in the academics and skills specific to midwifery practice."[10]—and aligned herself with the home birth community. She became a member of and "created the Central Florida chapter of the Florida Friends of Midwives. [She] led that chapter and joined in the work that grassroots women were doing [statewide] as far as lobbying for the reopening of the Midwifery Practice Act in the early 1990s." Here, we note how important it is for midwives to create and work within a community of resistance that challenges power differentials between midwifery and obstetrics. Jennie had found sisters in her struggle to practice and promote midwifery. However, that sisterhood was crosscut by personal agendas, race, class, and nation, leading to further challenges in her future work.[11]

SISTERHOOD, DIFFERENCE, AND ALLIANCE BUILDING

As Crista Craven has noted, midwifery advocates are divided along racial and class lines, and Jennie noticed this disconnect in several ways.

> [I began to see] that I didn't fit, so I now understand the outsider-within [status more clearly]. I realized that I was using my profession—midwifery—as the normalizing factor. I thought that normalized me … because I was working with other midwives or women who wanted midwives or who were supporting midwives in the profession of midwifery. I didn't have a clue that I wasn't an insider. I thought I was an insider [because] maybe they weren't trying to deceive me, but they were pushing me forward as if I was an insider. In fact, much of the language was around "Oh, you will be the first one to get a license." Because I was ready to be licensed under this new practice act [I knew I could be eligible more quickly for a license] as a foreign-trained midwife. So I was pushed forward as the pioneer: "You're gonna be the first one," "We're supporting you to be the first one," "We love you," "You're doing great," "You're one of us." So that was a revelation later when I realized I wasn't really one of them.

Jennie's nationality and race interacted in complex and nuanced ways. Initially, her English accent and background facilitated her access to predominantly white midwifery circles and masked the othering that she experienced as a black woman. At the same time, the exotification of her accent positioned her as an outsider. She states, "My accent has allowed people to perhaps feel more comfortable or even less threatened about my race." This social reception of her middle-class southern British accent speaks to the fact that "a wide range of socially stratified British dialects hold considerable prestige in America. Whether it is the British of Queen Elizabeth or that of Mick Jagger, many Americans hold a British accent in higher regard than they do most American accents."[12] Jennie experienced "linguistic adoration" in a way that permitted her social acceptance by her white peers without acknowledgment of her race.

A second way Jennie experienced her outsider-within status as a black woman occurred during interactions with her only available clientele. Jennie recalled that she was able to become licensed at all only because she was charged with serving an area of "critical need"—a tricounty area of rural central Florida (Polk, Hardee, Highlands) with particularly poor birth outcomes for women of color and an ongoing shortage of health-care providers. Ironically, her service consisted solely of providing midwifery care at a birth center owned by an ally, and she was unable to actually work within the at-risk populace as a healer of social health inequities. Instead, she centered her efforts on settling in as a black practitioner and becoming accepted by the predominantly white clientele—again, an effort most definitely expedited by her British accent.

Third, while engaging in this difficult advocacy work, Jennie came to understand more firmly the connection between her experience and that of the black midwives who had practiced in the region before her. She states that she began to understand the history of persecution faced by African American midwifery and that the practice act was originally put in place to permit

African American lay midwives to practice. She reached that understanding on her own, not with the help of the allies, because although there was an element of mentioning "the grand midwives of past years," it had not been "in a connected way."

Midwifery advocates in the United States frequently refer to the historical presence of granny midwives to invoke a history and foundation for their work. Mentioning black midwives' historical presence in Florida speaks to the usage of such historical narratives to bolster midwifery activism. But omitting how social and legal persecution were prominent elements of this narrative erases significant historical events. As Jennie reflects, "I didn't connect myself. I was looking at myself as being part of [the home birth movement] group. . . . I understood the history of [granny] midwives and understood that that was thought of as quaint and very interesting but [felt] that we had moved on in midwifery and in obstetrics in general. In other words, that it was historically interesting, and of course I relate to midwives of color, but I didn't relate in a sociological way."

This experience serves as a reminder of how social institutions and social groups create invisibility around the experiences of marginalized groups—in this instance, the persecution and elimination of southern black grandmother midwives. Part of this invisibility was due to the different categorizations of midwives in the United States. Jennie notes, "When they used the term 'lay home birth midwife,' I didn't have a clue what that meant. I was a credentialed midwife in Europe, and I was planning to be a credentialed midwife [in the United States]. I didn't know there was any other type of midwife even though I'd spent a year working for an obstetrician as an uncredentialed health practitioner. So these were some dichotomies that I was dealing with."

Differentiation among midwifery types in the United States led to direct-entry midwives (which included granny midwives) receiving the lowest level of respect in the United States and then to their elimination in the early 1930s in certain areas of the US South.[13] As a result of legislative activism by Jennie and her allies, the Florida Midwifery Practice Act was reenacted and revised under the support of late governor Lawton Chiles. This act once again allowed direct-entry midwife practice in the state and led to a commitment that "Florida's maternity care goals, as identified by the Legislature and adopted by The Healthy Start Coalition (1992), intend midwives to be the care providers for 50% of all normal, healthy, pregnant women by the year 2000."[14] Interestingly, Jennie relates, "the practice act was developed off of the original 1930 act [which governed] the black grandmother midwives." Grassroots midwifery advocates made a convincing case for midwifery, both in terms of birth outcomes and in relation to fiscal realities facing the state: "In countries where midwives function as the primary care providers for normal pregnancy and birth, the perinatal morbidity and mortality rates are far lower than those we experience in the United States. [Furthermore, the] State of Florida recognized the need to utilize maternity-care funds more efficiently and to increase the limited availability of maternity care providers. It intend[ed] that the licensing, regulation, and practice of midwifery may help to reduce this shortage, thus increasing the quality of perinatal services available to pregnant women throughout the state."[15]

Jennie's role as a pioneer in the battle to bring back direct-entry midwives harkens back to Collins's and others' investigation of how black women have often labored for the benefits of whites and to their own detriment.[16] These labors are often unrewarded and come at the expense of mental and physical health.[17] Jennie recalled that during this period of midwifery advocacy, she was tired and experienced enormous stress as a forerunner for midwifery practice. Despite this, she continued both her advocacy and midwifery work and began to work on ways to expand her clientele beyond the relatively privileged patrons of the birthing center, while also learning more about the complicated nature of birthing work in Florida.

DEVELOPING THE JJ WAY

Black women's limited participation in birthing work today as practitioners and consumers is colored by the history of the home birth movement. The home birth movement that emerged in the United States in the 1960s and 1970s largely comprised white and economically privileged women seeking access to midwifery and birth outside the patriarchal medical model.[18] These trends persist today, given the fact that many health insurance companies limit the amount of coverage provided to women who choose midwives due to the supposed risks associated with midwife-assisted births.[19] Jennie was concerned about this trend: "I provided home birth services for basically white, middle-class women for many years. But then I began to realize there were not enough women of color coming into the practice."

This absence of women of color in the practice ignited Jennie's advocacy. She achieved fuller participation from women of color in midwifery using two strategies: "[One,] I began to practice and engage more marginalized women into the practice. Two, I sort of talk[ed] them into my practice." Initially, "they weren't coming. I did not get why they weren't coming. I didn't connect the history and the oppression and the ... generational thinking that was behind why they weren't coming, did not understand why." This "generational thinking" included fears black women clients had about the safety of US health care—justified fears reflective of "the killing of the black body" since the United States possesses a negative history of medical treatment of black women.[20] Such abuses include unethical medical experimentation to develop treatment for gynecological disorders and forced sterilizations.[21]

Learning about this history and its connection to black women's fears of reproductive health care spurred Jennie to develop the JJ Way. The JJ Way consists of four key components that specifically address racial disparities in health. First, women need *access* to care, practitioners, support, education, and whatever else they "need to reach full term and have enough support," health, education, and empowerment "to enjoy and fulfill a healthy pregnancy," bond with their babies, and successfully breastfeed their babies by choice. The second tenet involves *connections* to the baby, family, community, provider, and practitioner, between agencies, and to resources "with that ultimate goal of a full-term healthy baby" and a bonded, connected, and breastfeeding mother. The third tenet involves practitioners sharing information with and *educating* the patient, as well as her supporters, family members, and community, and also sharing information among themselves. Jennie notes, "Practitioners also don't know enough about [or cannot negotiate the systems] for themselves and their patients also need educating." The "final tenet is *empowerment* for the mother," the family, the community, and practitioners.

The JJ Way aims not only to diminish and ultimately eradicate health disparities but also to create a community of support for the black birthing woman and all disenfranchised women. Jennie's goal is to create an "overall culture of full-term healthy babies, bonded and connected families, breast-feeding [mothers] and health going forward and . . . to reduce poor outcomes for mother and baby and to reduce infant and maternal mortality." Jennie's experiences of marginalization and medical abuse enabled her to recognize the dearth of reproductive health care and develop programs geared toward addressing the needs of women and children of color.

Her perspective also enables her to analyze critically the medical-industrial complex. The term "medical-industrial complex" refers to a symbiotic relationship between health practitioners and corporations (e.g., insurance and pharmaceutical companies) that puts control of how medicine is provided into the hands of those who profit from it.[22] As a health-care practitioner, Jennie had several pointed observations regarding the current state of medicine:

> I see this medical-industrial complex as a capitalist endeavor [embedded with] institutionalized racism. . . . My biggest critique is that there's no humanity inside of that complex and that midwifery provides humanity in whichever way it is delivered inside of the perinatal care system. Whether . . . the midwife herself is delivering the care or whether another practitioner employs the midwifery model of care. Basically, the midwifery model of care is patient centered, is culturally competent, is humanistic, is supportive, is all of the things that will allow that the patient is working for her own best interest in an empowered way with knowledge, informed consent, informed decision-making, and respectful care.

Jennie's embrace of the midwifery model of care and the JJ Way together function as what Cheryl Gilkes calls black women's resistance to the multifaceted oppression that they face from the status quo—in this case, the medical-industrial complex.[23]

Creating community around the birthing experience functions as a form of resistance to the constraints of the medical-industrial complex for two distinct reasons. One, this community building generates agency for women of color; two, it provides women with the ability to choose a vetted practitioner geared toward patient-centered care. Jennie argues that finding practitioners with these characteristics is even more important when some "women are uninsured, or low income or on Medicaid, [because] those options are really rare to find ... within the actual provider or the practitioner pool." Maternal health outcomes provide a sense of a nation's well-being,[24] so addressing inequities using "sisterhood" not only provides social support for black women but also protects their well-being in an oppressive society. Jennie states, "This sisterhood must exist outside the practitioner pool and can come in the form of more organized support groups like MOCR [Mamas of Color Rising]."

In addition, locating doulas of color in their communities can assist women in learning about "childbirth education courses and where they can get [classes] that [are] supportive in a cultural way." Locating support in the nexus of cultural sensitivity and patient-centered care creates a birthing experience where women of color can enjoy the process of birth in a safe and comfortable environment. Jennie states that these sisterhood circles can occur in a variety of social locales, like "within their churches and their day-care centers, anywhere women of color congregate and are connected to share what they know about reproductive health care and options." So these women are supporting not only one another but also practitioners who provide comprehensive care.

Working within a system rooted in social inequity to reform it is the work of an activist working as an outsider-within.

> Reading about the outsider-within status, I understand now more about why I'm an activist. I'm an activist because I'm a black woman in America. I'm an activist because I'm a black employer. I'm an activist because I'm self-employed. I'm an activist because I am a medical professional [operating] outside of the usual way of practicing. I'm an activist because I'm fighting for change in the [negative perinatal] outcomes. I'm fighting for the removal and elimination of the disparities. . . . I understand [that] we are not poised to make any real impact on these issues [unless we can create change by engaging with other allies]. I'm an activist inside of the midwives of color movement in that the midwives of color are fighting desperately to impact these outcomes. [We] are falling by the wayside and struggling to hold our heads up. And then I'm an activist inside of the public health community because I'm saying that the midwifery model is a model that can impact these outcomes, but midwives themselves can't [do it] necessarily without help.

Jennie's work as a midwife-activist demonstrates that birthing work continues to be transformative, especially when this activism involves building communities of support for black women in public health. To this end, Jennie developed the perinatal "community health worker [CHW] model, with education, and certification that might support this new way of being inside of public health [as part of the JJ Way. With this work, she sees herself as] really revitalizing the midwives of old, the grandmother midwives and the work they did on their own inside of their communities, but bringing it forward as a midwifery model that any willing practitioner can provide rather than [as] a midwifery practitioner-led movement." Because CHWs work alongside and become doulas, childbirth educators, and lactation specialists, they work as mentors and friends within the community, while also creating pipelines for career development and diversification in medicine. Jennie argues, "[These] relationships of support [are vital] in improving and impacting the intractable and poor birth outcomes that we suffer."

CONCLUSION

Jennie's position as an outsider-within—as an immigrant, a black woman, and a foreign-born and -educated midwife—provided her with unique insight into social injustices associated with US health care. Rather than passively accepting marginalization, Jennie used the obstacles she encountered to fuel her commitment to revitalizing midwifery in her new home. Despite barriers related to race and class differences within the home birth movement, Jennie built sisterhood with other midwives and successfully lobbied to change legislation limiting midwifery practice in Florida. Her activism and midwifery practice compelled her to develop the JJ Way, a model of care that supportively meets the varied needs of women of color, who have historically been underserved by both mainstream and alternative health-care providers. As an outsider-within, Jennie created an accessible, relevant midwifery model for women of color on their journey to motherhood.[25] Her work as a midwife-activist combats the medical-industrial complex by providing a viable and important template for grassroots perinatal care for marginalized women.

CHAPTER 21

Beyond Shackling

Prisons, Pregnancy, and the
Struggle for Birth Justice

Priscilla A. Ocen and Julia Chinyere Oparah

INTRODUCTION

In 2006, Shawanna Nelson sued the Arkansas Department of Corrections for violation of her Eighth Amendment right to be free from cruel and unusual punishment, after she was forced to go through the final stages of labor with her legs shackled to the sides of her hospital bed. Shawanna, an African American woman, was sent to prison for survival crimes involving credit card and check fraud when she was six months pregnant. When she went into labor, she was shackled to a wheelchair and taken to a civilian hospital. There she suffered an agonizing labor, resulting in permanent injury.[1]

According to the Department of Justice, every year up to eighteen thousand prisoners like Shawanna undergo pregnancy and potentially deliver their babies during their incarceration.[2] This chapter explores the treatment of pregnant individuals in US prisons, jails, and juvenile detention facilities and examines the failure of the legal system to protect their interests. The chapter also examines the scope and impact of activism on behalf of and by pregnant and parenting individuals in prisons, jails, and detention centers and places this activism within an abolitionist context. Our analysis is informed by the testimonies of formerly incarcerated people who have documented their stories, including those collected by Birthing Behind Bars, a national campaign by Women on the Rise Telling HerStory to address reproductive justice issues in prison. Excerpts from these stories open each section of our discussion.

BETWEEN MOVEMENTS: REPRODUCTIVE JUSTICE, NATURAL BIRTH, AND PRISON-INDUSTRIAL-COMPLEX ABOLITION

It was a long drive from Purdy [correctional center] to the hospital. By the time we got there I'm in full-blown labor. I'm in so much pain, Oh my God, and I was like, "Help me, give me something for the pain." And as soon as I got there, [the guard] was trying to interview me and ask me my name. . . . I'm trying to answer her questions, but in between I'm saying, "Oh my God, I'm in pain, can you wait for this [contraction]?" No . . . I never did get any medicine. . . . She started getting louder and louder. "Shut up, you've got to be quiet, you can't be loud in here." Her face was getting angry and menacing, and then she took both her hands, crisscrossed them, bent over, and smashed my face and my nose . . . in a very hard pressing way pushing me into the gurney. . . . She held it there, and I couldn't even breathe because she had my nose closed. My eyes were darting back and forth looking for some face with some compassion to get the crazy lady off me, because I couldn't breathe. And they were looking at me and her like, "Yeah, shut that crazy animal up." —Kimberly Mays[3]

While the crisis of hyperincarceration[4] in the United States has become a commonplace topic in political debate and media representation, it is too often depicted as a crisis affecting men of color, thus rendering experiences like Kimberly Mays's invisible.[5] In 2012, a total of 207,372 people categorized as women and girls were in prisons and jails, and approximately 2,800 were in immigration detention.[6] Although this is less than 10 percent of the overall incarcerated population, the number of people in women's prisons and jails in the United States is more than the entire prison population of numerous countries, from the United Kingdom to South Africa, suggesting that incarcerated women are no longer "too few to count."

Since the late 1990s, a vibrant mass movement has emerged in the United States and internationally with the goal of abolishing the prison-industrial complex, an interlocking system of private and public prisons and jails, politicians, mass media, and corporations. These activists point out deep-seated racial and economic inequities in patterns of incarceration and seek to redirect the multi-billion-dollar corrections budget toward solutions to deep-rooted social problems—including drug addiction, poverty, violence, and mental illness—that are currently warehoused in the nation's prisons and jails.[7] Simultaneously, numerous nonprofit organizations and policy think tanks work to reform harsh sentencing rules, particularly in relation to the war on drugs, and to promote alternatives to incarceration. These efforts sometimes overlook the experiences and concerns of women, girls, and trans/gender nonconforming people; however, feminist and trans activists and intellectuals inside and outside prison have raised the profile of issues affecting incarcerated people who are marginalized on the basis of gender.[8] Alongside issues affecting all people in detention, such as appalling prison conditions, overcrowding, prison expansion, inadequate health care, lack of religious freedom, and institutional violence, these organizations and scholar-activists call our attention to the experiences of pregnant and parenting prisoners. These concerns for the reproductive health and rights of imprisoned women, girls, and trans/gender nonconforming individuals create fertile ground for coalition building between the antiprison, reproductive justice, and alternative birth movements.

Age, race, class, and gender identity are all determinants of who serves time. Women and trans/gender nonconforming people between the ages of twenty-five and thirty-nine are most likely to be incarcerated. Consequently, hyperincarceration disproportionately impacts their childbearing years and affects their ability to get pregnant, keep their pregnancies, birth safely and with dignity, and raise their children. The impact of incarceration on an individual's ability to have and raise a family falls within the remit of the reproductive justice movement. The term "reproductive justice," coined by black women activists in 1994, is defined by SisterSong, a national women of color collective, as "the right to have children, not have children, and to parent the children we have in safe and healthy environments." According to the collective, this framework "represents a shift for women advocating for control of their bodies, from a narrower focus on legal access and individual choice (the focus of mainstream organizations) to a broader analysis of racial, economic, cultural, and structural constraints on [their] power."[9]

The term "reproductive justice" was coined in part in response to the failure of mainstream reproductive rights organizations such as NARAL Pro-Choice America, Planned Parenthood, and the National Organization for Women to address the concerns of women of color. Rooted in legal and social battles over abortion, the mainstream reproductive rights movement identifies the locus of women's rights in their ability to choose. In this sense, the mainstream pro-choice lobby takes a consumerist, individualist position that benefits only those women who have the social and economic resources to choose from a wide range of legally available options.[10] This narrow conceptualization of reproductive rights ultimately sells women of color and low-income women short by failing to demand the full spectrum of economic and political rights that are necessary to truly achieve reproductive freedom. Incarcerated women and trans/gender nonconforming people in particular are failed by the pro-choice framework, because lack of choice about pregnancy, perinatal care, and parenting is intrinsic to the condition of confinement. Stigmatized as irresponsible or bad mothers, they are simply expected to experience a range of infringements on their reproductive self-determination as part of the penalty for their "crimes."

The reproductive justice movement, in contrast, pursues a multifaceted approach that moves beyond choice to explore what would have to change for marginalized individuals to achieve reproductive self-determination. In theory, this framework allows for a radical rethinking of reproductive rights in relation to incarcerated individuals. Because reproductive freedom—including the right to decide when to pursue pregnancy, the right to a nurturing and safe environment for the pregnant person, and individuals' right to parent their children—is incompatible with warehousing women, girls, and trans/gender nonconforming people behind bars, the reproductive justice movement might be expected to become a vocal advocate for prison-industrial-complex abolition. In reality, the reproductive justice movement has not taken this bold stance and has instead pursued legislative reforms. While these campaigns do not fundamentally challenge the belief that imprisoning people makes the rest of us safer, they do make visible the inhumane treatment of women in prison and therefore lay important groundwork for more expansive campaigns on behalf of incarcerated women and trans/gender nonconforming people.

Finally, the alternative birth movement is a site where we might expect to see considerable advocacy for and involvement of people in women's prisons, since this movement is committed to empowering women in childbirth and liberating them from medical coercion. Like the mainstream reproductive rights movement, the mainstream alternative birth movement draws on an individualist, choice-based framework that is largely irrelevant to women who experience the complete loss of autonomy and resources associated with imprisonment. For example, home birth activists seek to make home birth a legal and viable "choice," but they do not demand that incarcerated pregnant women be returned home to birth and parent their children. The lives and experiences of incarcerated women challenge some of the foundational principles of the alternative birth movement. Most birth activists promote natural birth, without narcotics or epidurals, in response to the pressure to accept such interventions. Yet incarcerated women like Kimberly—denied basic medical attention, including medication for labor pain during an emotionally traumatic and isolated labor—need support in their fight for access to medical care rather than protection from overzealous doctors. Supporting Kimberly's right to access pain medications and to labor in an environment that supports the natural process of birth requires a more complex politics that simultaneously challenges unwanted medical intervention, medical neglect, and state violence in the lives of incarcerated women.

The next section provides an overview of the conditions facing people who find themselves pregnant behind bars and surveys the legal context for challenges to the violation of incarcerated women's reproductive rights.

PREGNANCY, IMPRISONMENT, AND CONDITIONS OF CONFINEMENT

I've had ten children, a lot of them I've had while I was incarcerated due to my disease, which is addiction. . . . I've been out in the community when I've been pregnant, and I've been treated with dignity and respect. But whenever I was shackled and went to a doctor's appointment, even to the same clinic, I was treated short, rude, they didn't make sure I was comfortable, it was a total disregard of my needs as a mother and a patient. I was talked down to, left in the corridor, it was really demoralizing and demeaning. —Kimberly Mays

Pregnancy often represents an occasion for the imposition of unique and gendered forms of punishment. Motherhood may be used to justify a longer sentence for a woman convicted of a drug crime. For example, during Tammy Johnson's sentencing hearing, the judge condemned her because she was a mother: "You are nothing but a drug addict, a dressed-up drug addict . . . and a terrible mother who does not care about her son or herself."[11] In another case, a judge imposed a sentencing enhancement because the defendant manufactured methamphetamine while pregnant. The sentencing enhancement roughly doubled the woman's sentence.[12]

Once incarcerated, pregnant and parenting prisoners are stigmatized because of their perceived failure as mothers. One Cook County guard stated, "I'm a mother of two, and I know what that impulse, that instinct, that mothering instinct feels like. It just takes over. You would never put your kids in harm's way. . . . Women in here lack that. Something in their nature is not right, you know? They run out and leave their kids alone, babies, while they score drugs or go over [to] their boyfriend's house, you know? . . . That's a sign that something is wrong, some kind of psychological problem or something."[13] Incarcerated women perceive this stigmatized status as well: "I felt that my son was only taken into account as a reason to despise me for not adhering to an expected stereotypical female role, and to justify giving me a longer sentence. There was no consideration given to my personal circumstances or thought given to whether prison was an appropriate response to my individual situation or to the 12-year-old who would become the ultimate victim of my incarceration."[14]

Pregnancy as a stigmatized status is enforced through formal and informal policies and practices in jails and prisons across the country. During pregnancy, prisoners are often unable to access adequate medical care. In a landmark lawsuit, *Shumate v. Wilson,* people in California women's prisons alleged that they could not access doctors for annual examinations, and when they were seen, the care fell well below established medical standards.[15] Inadequate medical care in prison extends to prenatal care as well. Several studies found that pregnant women often cannot meet their basic needs through nutritional supplements such as prenatal vitamins and are treated in substandard medical facilities on those occasions when they are able to obtain medical care.[16] Similar dynamics occur in the context of juvenile detention facilities. In one study, pregnant girls reported "ha[ving] a difficult time getting enough food and not being able to rest properly."[17]

When removed from the custodial setting for medical appointments, pregnant individuals are often subject to degrading practices such as strip searches and shackling. Many pregnant individuals are shackled not only when taken to and from medical visits but also during labor and delivery.[18] In at least thirty-four states, this practice is permitted without justification of a security threat to prison staff or the public. Although no statistics exist regarding the use of shackles, testimonies from incarcerated women and lawsuits challenging the practice demonstrate that it is often conducted as a matter of routine procedure. This practice continues despite opposition from medical professionals and associations such as the American College of Obstetricians and Gynecologists (ACOG). According to ACOG, shackling can "interfere with the ability of health care providers to safely practice medicine by reducing their ability to assess and evaluate the mother and the fetus and making labor and delivery more difficult. Shackling may put the health of the woman and fetus at risk."[19] Moreover, the United Nations condemns shackling as a form of "cruel and unusual punishment."[20]

Additionally, during the birthing process, treatment condemned by international human rights law and organizations is routinely practiced in the United States. For example, pregnant prisoners are often unable to determine how they will deliver their children. Rather, many are scheduled for cesarean surgery without notice and over their objections or desire for a natural childbirth.[21] Family members are not informed of the scheduled surgery, and women go through the birthing process alone, except for the watchful eyes of guards and medical staff.

In some cases, pregnant prisoners are inhumanely denied medical care during labor and delivery. For example, in *Doe v. Gustavus,* a woman brought suit against a Wisconsin prison for failure to render aid during her labor and delivery. After the plaintiff's water broke, guards and nurses refused to summon additional help or to transfer the plaintiff to a hospital. Instead, she was placed in a segregated unit. Despite repeated calls for help, the plaintiff was given no assistance or medication, was called a "dumb bitch," and was told that she "would have to clean up her own vomit if she got sick again."[22] Eventually, the plaintiff was forced to deliver her baby without medical assistance in an isolation cell. Later, guards accused her of "push[ing] that baby out on purpose, just to get out of segregation."[23] Failure to render aid to pregnant prisoners and the notion that women use pregnancies to manipulate their surroundings reflect the profound devaluation of the bodies of incarcerated individuals and their children.

Indeed, this devaluation often means that people in prison who give birth and those parenting from the inside find it difficult to maintain connections with their children. In many prisons, women are separated from their newborn infants within twenty-four to forty-eight hours after giving birth. This woman's experience exemplifies this dynamic:

> After seventy-two hours of hard labor, I gave birth to a healthy baby girl. She was perfect from head to toe. Looking at her, I forgot about the pain and only wanted to hold my baby. But thirty minutes after giving birth, I was once again handcuffed and chained and wheeled to another floor. My daughter was allowed to stay in the room with me, instead of the nursery. MDOC [Michigan Department of Corrections] policy states that a woman can only spend twenty-four hours with her child before she is brought back to prison. I had to figure out a way to spend more time with her: I refused to eat.[24]

Moreover, women who parent from prison are at significant risk of permanently losing their parental rights or of their children being placed in foster care.

Incarcerated individuals' reproductive capacities are further compromised by policies and practices that often prevent women from procreating after their release. For example, many women prisoners have been subject to sterilization while incarcerated. The United States has a long and troubled history of targeting institutionalized persons for sterilization. In 1927, in *Buck v. Bell*, the Supreme Court upheld policies authorizing the sterilization of individuals institutionalized in mental hospitals for "feeblemindedness" based on the fear that undesirable traits such as criminality would be passed from one generation to the next.[25] Although eugenics has been formally repudiated in public policy, recent investigative reports have confirmed that sterilization continues to be practiced inside California's prisons. According to the Center for Investigative Reporting, California prison authorities sterilized over 150 individuals between 2006 and 2010.[26] These sterilizations were done without required state approval and often after medical staff coerced individuals into signing consent forms.

Overincarcerated and Underprotected: The Failure of Law to Protect the Rights of Pregnant Prisoners

I had my baby in the delivery room and the officer was really nice to me. After I gave birth she shackled me, she put the chain irons on my legs. They took me to a room, and they brought my baby up, and my baby stayed with me. My problem was ... how am I supposed to get my baby, shackled? Walking with leg irons is very hard. Now the officer who was nice was gone, and [the new officer] was really nasty. She told me I had to learn to walk holding my baby, and I said if I trip and I drop my baby, I'm suing. The pain that you're in after you've had your baby, and to walk with the baby and the leg irons, it's really hard. . . . Every officer was a little different. The next officer took everything off. She said, "Where you going? You're not going to leave your baby." She took the leg irons off, and she took the cuffs off, and she said to me only when her captain was in the area she would put the leg irons on. —Mercedes Smith

The Supreme Court of the United States has affirmed the notion that "prison walls do not form a barrier separating prison inmates from the protections of the Constitution."[27] Nevertheless, legal protections in the penal context are often weak and insufficient to protect the interests of pregnant and parenting individuals. For example, although individuals possess the fundamental right to procreate, this interest is often regarded as subordinate to the administrative and security interests of the state in the operation of jails and prisons. As the Supreme Court noted in *Turner v. Safley,* a landmark conditions-of-confinement case, "When a prison regulation impinges on inmates' constitutional rights, the regulation is valid if it is reasonably related to legitimate penological interests."[28] The prioritizing of the state interest in administrative efficiency and security often comes at a significant cost to the safety and autonomy of pregnant women.

In addition, federal law makes it difficult for incarcerated women to vindicate their rights through litigation. The Prison Litigation Reform Act (PLRA) requires prisoners to exhaust administrative remedies prior to filing suit.[29] Typically, this means that an incarcerated individual must file a complaint with prison administrators. If an incarcerated individual is unaware of the grievance process or fails to submit a complaint, a federal court will dismiss the lawsuit.[30] For many people in prison, the PLRA's exhaustion requirement functionally operates as a bar to challenging prison practices.

Notwithstanding these significant barriers, people in prison use litigation to challenge inhumane practices that burden their reproductive autonomy. The results, however, have been mixed. In *Nelson v. Correctional Medical Services,* Shawanna Nelson, supported by a coalition of thirty-five advocacy organizations, challenged the Arkansas Department of Correction's use of shackles during her labor and pregnancy. Nelson alleged that the use of shackles violated the Eighth Amendment's ban on cruel and unusual punishment. Nelson was required to demonstrate that in utilizing the shackles, prison officials were deliberately indifferent to her serious medical needs. In evaluating her claim, the Eighth Circuit Court of Appeals found that the use of shackles was wholly unnecessary to meet the security needs of prison, as Nelson posed no threat to herself or others. Moreover, the court found that the use of shackles posed an unjustified risk of harm to both Nelson and her unborn child. Consequently, the court found that the use of shackles was inconsistent with Eighth Amendment values and principles.

Although this was a significant victory for pregnant and parenting individuals, the reasoning of the *Nelson* court has not been widely adopted by other jurisdictions. In *Mendiola-Martinez v. Arpaio,* an undocumented Latina held in an Arizona detention center filed suit against Sheriff Joe Arpaio and Mariposa County jail officials after she was shackled en route to the hospital during labor and following delivery of her child.[31] Miriam Martinez argued that the use of shackles violated her clearly established right to be free from cruel and unusual punishment under the Eighth Amendment. The court hearing Martinez's claim, however, disagreed and dismissed the suit. Thus, notwithstanding the result in *Nelson,* pregnant prisoners in Arizona and elsewhere continue to be vulnerable to practices such as shackling. In many states, such as Illinois and Pennsylvania, where shackling has been prohibited, numerous instances of the use of shackles on pregnant prisoners have been documented.

In sum, *Nelson* and *Martinez* demonstrate that, for incarcerated people, legal protection operates as a limitation, but one that is often inadequate to truly protect them against inhumane treatment, particularly while they are pregnant.

FIGHTING BACK

Seventeen years ago, I had my child in prison—my last son—and I was shackled and handcuffed while I gave birth to him. I thought that was the most egregious, dehumanizing, oppressive practice that I'd ever experienced within my experience of going to prison. And these stories have not been told, these stories have not been shared. These stories will help and assist in our national effort to end shackling in our fifty states. . . . There are fifteen states that will no longer shackle pregnant women, but it's taking too long. We feel that gathering the stories of women who've had this experience, sharing these stories amongst our allies and the general public, will push this initiative forward. —Tina Reynolds

These egregious violations of incarcerated women's reproductive rights have led to campaigns by grassroots and nonprofit organizations to challenge the conditions under which criminalized women carry their pregnancies and experience labor and childbirth. Formerly incarcerated women at the forefront of these efforts use storytelling as one of their most powerful tools. When these women tell their stories, they risk further stigmatization and labeling as "criminals" or "bad mothers." But they also challenge the dehumanization of people in prison, put a human face on the caging of pregnant women, and galvanize public opinion. Birthing Behind Bars provides an online forum where formerly incarcerated women can share their stories through blogs, video recordings, and audio journals. Online readers are encouraged to sign a pledge to help mobilize public support for local and statewide legislative initiatives to support pregnant women in prisons, jails, and detention centers.

Justice Now, an abolitionist organization led by women prisoners, also uses stories to bring about social change. Its human rights documentation program collaborates with people in women's prisons to produce human rights reports on abusive prison conditions. Because people in prison are empowered to document what is important to them, this project has the capacity to bring to the surface human rights violations that were previously invisible. When Justice Now realized that several women in California state prisons were telling stories of being coerced into sterilization, the group worked with people in prison to research the practice. This work led to an exposé of the illegal sterilizations, a state audit of the practice, and passage of a bill to outlaw sterilization for the purpose of birth control of anyone under the control of the California Department of Corrections and Rehabilitation.[32]

In the past decade, the fight to end the shackling of pregnant and laboring women has been at the forefront of activism to challenge the treatment of pregnant incarcerated women. A combination of research documentation and legislative activism has been particularly successful in capturing the attention of legislators and the general public. For example, Legal Prisoners for Prisoners with Children published a report exposing the impact of the practice and worked with supportive California Assembly members to enact legislation in 2005, making the state one of the first to prohibit shackling of prisoners in labor.[33] In 2010, a coalition of reproductive justice, criminal justice, and civil liberties organizers in California came together to build a legislative campaign to prohibit shackling of prisoners in the state throughout pregnancy. After two years of lobbying, tweeting and blogging, sharing incarcerated women's stories, and producing supporting expert opinions, the coalition overcame law enforcement opposition and saw the bill pass the legislature with bipartisan support.[34] The struggle to ban the shackling of pregnant prisoners is a model for coalition building and involves activists and advocates from the prison abolition, human rights, reproductive justice, and birth justice movements. By working together, organizations and individuals from a range of social justice orientations learn about each other's struggles and lend greater support to issues that may not be on the immediate agenda of each organization.

While antishackling successes are important, they do little more than scratch the surface of the inadequate care and support received by pregnant incarcerated individuals. In response to these conditions, a number of social justice–oriented doula associations are working in solidarity with women inside to provide prenatal care, childbirth education, birth attendance, and breastfeeding support. Organizations like the Prison Birth Project (Massachusetts), the Birth Attendants (Washington State), the Birth Justice Project (California), and Isis Rising (Minneapolis) bring experienced doulas into jails, prisons, recovery centers, and county hospitals to empower women within the constraints of the carceral environment, to improve birth experiences, and to support mother-infant bonding.[35] By bringing doula principles into prisons and jails, these doulas challenge powerful dehumanizing and punitive penal cultures.

Doula training, however, can be expensive, and many women of color and formerly incarcerated people are not able to volunteer their time in a local prison or jail. As a result, prison doula programs sometimes struggle to involve people who have been in prison or jail and people of color as volunteer doulas or organizational leaders. Therefore, they risk perpetuating the race and class hierarchies that structure penal regimes. This in turn makes their services more palatable to prison authorities and can lead to these programs becoming incorporated as an extension of the prison-industrial complex rather than a challenge to it. The Prison Birth Project addresses this concern by working to mentor formerly incarcerated women to take leadership positions. Similarly, the Birth Justice Project addressed this problem by cofounding the East Bay Community Birth Support Project with Black Women Birthing Justice. The project provides doula training, mentorship, and work experience for formerly incarcerated women and women of color. By involving formerly incarcerated women as leaders and doulas in this work, these projects help to break the cycle of incarceration and build the capacity of women who have survived a pregnancy in detention as leaders and agents of change.

CONCLUSION

Advocacy efforts led by formerly incarcerated people challenge prevailing social and reproductive justice movements by centering the needs of the most vulnerable pregnant and parenting women. In raising their collective voices to call attention to the dehumanizing conditions within women's prisons, they break down the walls between the reproductive justice, natural birth, and prison abolition movements. Yet, despite the successes and reforms achieved by these movements, the fact of incarceration remains the critical impediment to reproductive autonomy. No pregnant or parenting person should be subjected to the violence of incarceration, and no child should suffer separation from his or her birth parent because of a bloated and unjust criminal punishment system. Only by placing an abolitionist politics at the center of our reproductive justice and birth activism can we create a world in which poor pregnant and parenting individuals are treated with compassion and support rather than criminalization and incarceration.

Notes

INTRODUCTION

1. "Teen Pregnancy and Child-Bearing among Non-Hispanic Black Teens," National Campaign to Prevent Teen and Unplanned Pregnancy, accessed July 29, 2013, www.thenationalcampaign.org/resources/pdf/FastFacts_TPChildbearing_Blacks.pdf; "About Teen Pregnancy," Centers for Disease Control, accessed July 29, 2013, www.cdc.gov/TeenPregnancy/AboutTeenPreg.htm#b.

2. Kristin Luker, *Dubious Conceptions* (Cambridge, MA: Harvard University Press, 1996), 81–108.

3. Maternal, Child, and Adolescent Health Program, *The California Pregnancy-Associated Mortality Review,* California Department of Public Health, April 2013, accessed July 28, 2013, www.cdph.ca.gov/data/statistics/Documents/MO-CA-PAMR-Maternal DeathReview-2002-04.pdf; "California's Infant Mortality Rate Reaches Historic Low," California Department of Public Health, accessed July 29, 2013, www.cdph.ca.gov/Pages/NR12-020.aspx.

4. Committee to Study Medical Professional Liability and the Delivery of Obstetrical Care, Institute of Medicine, *Medical Professional Liability and the Delivery of Obstetrical Care* (Washington, DC: National Academies Press, 1989), 1:90.

5. Briggett C. Ford et al., "Racial Disparities in Birth Outcomes: Poverty, Discrimination and the Life Course of African American Women," Institute for Social Research, accessed October 10, 2014, www.rcgd.isr.umich.edu/prba/perspectives/fall2005/ford.pdf.

6. Patricia Hill Collins, "Learning from the Outsider-Within: The Sociological Significance of Black Feminist Thought," *Social Problems* 33, no. 6 (1999): S14–S32.

7. Michael C. Lu et al., "Closing the Black-White Gap in Birth Outcomes: A Life-Course Approach," *Ethnicity and Disease* 20 (2010): 52.

8. Barbara and John Ehrenreich introduced the term "medical-industrial complex" to describe the commodification of health care and the accompanying rise in influence of the medical industry in US health-care policy. Barbara Ehrenreich and John Ehrenreich, *The American Health Empire: Power, Profit and Politics* (New York: Random House, 1971).

9. Zakiya Luna, "From Rights to Justice: Women of Color Changing the Face of US Reproductive Rights Organizing," *Societies without Borders* 4 (2009): 343–365. Although the term "reproductive justice" was coined in the mid-1990s, women of color have formed autonomous reproductive rights organizations since the 1980s, a history documented by Jael Silliman et al. in *Undivided Rights: Women of Color Organize for Reproductive Justice* (Cambridge, MA: South End Press, 2004). This work also has antecedents in the activism

of women of color who sought to put reproductive rights on the agendas of civil rights and nationalist movements and to resist nationalist tendencies to police women's reproductive choices. See Jennifer Nelson, *Women of Color and the Reproductive Rights Movement* (New York: New York University Press, 2003).

10. Kimala Price, "What Is Reproductive Justice? How Women of Color Activists Are Redefining the Pro-Choice Paradigm," *Meridians* 10, no. 2 (2010): 42–65.

11. "Why Is Reproductive Justice Important for Women of Color?," SisterSong, accessed July 29, 2013, www.sistersong.net/index.php?option=com_content&view=article&id =141&Itemid=81.

12. Laura Nixon, "The Right to (Trans) Parent: A Reproductive Justice Approach to Reproductive Rights, Fertility and Family-Building Issues Facing Transgender People," *William and Mary Journal of Women and the Law* 20, no. 1 (2013): 73–103. Available at http://scholarship.law.wm.edu/wmjowl/vol20/iss1/5.

13. Andrew Smith, "Beyond Pro-Choice versus Pro-Life: Women of Color and Reproductive Justice," *NWSA Journal* 17, no. 1 (spring 2005): 119–140, 127.

14. Nelson, *Women of Color and the Reproductive Rights Movement.*

15. "NAPW Working Paper: Birth Justice as Reproductive Justice," National Advocates for Pregnant Women, January 2010, accessed July 29, 2013, http://advocatesforpregnant women.org/BirthJusticeasReproRights.pdf, 2.

16. Christa Craven, *Pushing for Midwives: Homebirth Mothers and the Reproductive Rights Movement* (Philadelphia: Temple University Press, 2010), 44.

17. Ina May Gaskin, *Birth Matters: A Midwife's Manifesta* (New York: Seven Stories Press, 2011), 20.

18. Ina May Gaskin, *Spiritual Midwifery,* 4th ed. (Summertown, TN: Book Publishing Company, 2002).

19. Deborah Gray White, *Telling Histories: Black Women Historians in the Ivory Tower* (Chapel Hill: University of North Carolina Press, 2008).

20. Latin American and Caribbean Network for the Humanization of Childbirth, "The Traditional Midwife in Our Region," Partera.com, March 2007, accessed July 29, 2013, http://partera.com/pages_en/tpe.html.

21. The Sheppard-Towner Act of 1921, the first federal initiative to improve standards of maternity care, was a coup for the recently enfranchised white, middle-class, northern women who campaigned for it. However, for African American and immigrant women, it meant greater surveillance and regulation of their midwifery and birthing practices, ultimately leading to the near elimination of lay midwifery in these communities. Craven, *Pushing for Midwives,* 34–36.

22. Shafia Monroe quoted in Gloria Waite, "Childbirth, Lay Institution Building and Health Policy: The Traditional Childbearing Group, Inc., of Boston in a Historical Context," in *Wings of Gauze: Women of Color and the Experience of Health and Illness,* ed. Barbara Bair and Susan E. Cayleff (Detroit, MI: Wayne State University Press, 1993), 203.

23. Craven, *Pushing for Midwives,* 7–8.

24. Harriet Washington, *Medical Apartheid* (New York: Doubleday, 2006), 63–65.

25. Ibid., 106.

26. John Duffy, *From Humors to Medical Science: A History of American Medicine* (Chicago: University of Illinois Press, 1993), 106.

27. Margarete Sandelowski, *Pain, Pleasure and American Childbirth: From the Twilight Sleep to the Read Method, 1914–1960* (Westport, CT: Greenwood Press, 1984).

28. Craven, *Pushing for Midwives,* 33.

29. Barbara Lee, *Renegade for Peace and Justice: A Memoir of Political and Personal Courage* (Lanham, MD: Rowman and Littlefield, 2011).

30. David Barton Smith, "Eliminating Disparities in Treatment and the Struggle to End Segregation," The Commonwealth Fund, August 1, 2005, accessed December 9, 2014, www.commonwealthfund.org/publications/fund-reports/2005/aug/eliminating -disparities-in-treatment-and-the-struggle-to-end-segregation.

31. Alondra Nelson, *Body and Soul: The Black Panther Party and the Fight against Medical Discrimination* (Minneapolis: Minnesota University Press, 2013).

32. Washington, *Medical Apartheid,* 21.

33. Darlene Clark Hine, "Rape and the Inner Lives of African American Women: Thoughts on the Culture of Dissemblance," in *Hine Sight: Black Women and the Reconstruction of American History* (Bloomington: Indiana University Press, 1997).

34. Valerie Lee, *Granny Midwives and Black Women Writers* (New York: Routledge, 1996), 43–46.

35. Katherine Beckett and Bruce Hoffman, "Challenging Medicine: Law, Resistance, and the Cultural Politics of Childbirth," *Law and Society Review* 39, no. 1 (2005): 125–169.

36. Ibid., 143.

37. Ibid., 132–135; see also Alicia Bonaparte in Chapter 2 of this volume.

38. Carol Mueller, "Ella Baker and the Origins of Participatory Democracy," in *Women in the Civil Rights Movement: Trailblazers and Torchbearers, 1941–1965,* ed. Vicki Crawford, Jacqueline Rouse, and Barbara Woods (Bloomington: Indiana University Press, 1990).

39. Letter to MANA Board from Darynée Blount et al., Midwives Alliance North America, accessed July 29, 2013, http://mana.org/pdfs/MOCLetter.pdf.

40. Craven, *Pushing for Midwives,* 40–60.

41. Mariko Chang, "Lifting as We Climb: Women of Color, Wealth and America's Future," Insight Center for Community Economic Development, 2010, accessed July 29, 2013, www.insightcced.org/uploads/CRWG/LiftingAsWeClimb-WomenWealth -Report-InsightCenter-Spring2010.pdf.

42. Barton Smith, "Eliminating Disparities," 17.

43. Organizations at the forefront of this movement include the International Center for Traditional Childbearing, Black Women Birthing Justice, Mamas of Color Rising, National Advocates for Pregnant Women, Mobile Midwife, Black Women Birthing Resistance, Women on the Rise Telling HerStory, and the Birthing Project, USA.

CHAPTER 1

1. The author would like to thank the following family members for providing interviews, letters, photographs, and other information about Grandma Elizabeth's life: Arleemah Shakoor (born Novella Turner), last living child of Queen Elizabeth Perry Turner; Evelyn Turner, granddaughter; Leahnora Hill, granddaughter; Ozella Evans, granddaughter; Shannon Porter, granddaughter; Thomas A. Turner, grandson; and Michelle Mitchell, great granddaughter.

2. Archival resources for this essay are located in the Warren County Court House, Office of Records; Warren County Health Department; and Warren County Memorial Library.

3. James Drife, "The Start of Life: The History of Obstetrics," *Postgraduate Medical Journal* 78 (2002): 311–315.

4. P. S. Summey and M. Hurst, "Ob/Gyn on the Rise: The Evolution of Professional Ideology in the Twentieth Century—Part I," *Women and Health* 11, no. 1 (1986): 133–145; P. S. Summey and M. Hurst, "Ob/Gyn on the Rise: The Evolution of Professional Ideology in the Twentieth Century—Part II," *Women and Health* 11, no. 2 (1986): 103–122; Alicia D. Bonaparte, "The Persecution and Prosecution of Granny Midwives in South Carolina, 1900–1940" (PhD diss., Vanderbilt University, 2007).

5. Phyllis L. Brodsky, "Where Have All the Midwives Gone?," *Journal of Perinatal Education* 17, no. 4 (2008): 48–51.

CHAPTER 2

1. Jessica Mitford, *The American Way of Birth* (New York: Dutton/Penguin Books, 1992), 173.

2. Margaret Charles Smith and Linda Janet Holmes, *Listen to Me Good: The Life Story of an Alabama Midwife* (Columbus: Ohio State University Press, 1996); Debra Anne Susie, *In the Way of Our Grandmothers: A Cultural View of Twentieth-Century Midwifery in Florida* (Athens: University of Georgia Press, 1988).

3. Alicia D. Bonaparte, "The Persecution and Prosecution of Granny Midwives in South Carolina, 1900–1940" (PhD diss., Vanderbilt University, 2007).

4. Linda Janet Holmes, "Midwives, Southern Black," in *Encyclopedia of Childbearing: Critical Perspectives,* ed. Barbara Katz Rothman (Phoenix: Oryx Press, 1992), 258–260.

5. Gertrude Jacinta Fraser, *African American Midwifery in the South: Dialogues of Birth, Race, and Memory* (Cambridge, MA: Harvard University Press, 1998); Marie Campbell, *Folks Do Get Born* (New York: Rinehart and Company, 1946).

6. Bonaparte, "The Persecution and Prosecution of Granny Midwives."

7. Judith Pence Rooks, *Midwifery and Childbirth in America* (Philadelphia: Temple University Press, 1985).

8. Ronald L. Numbers, "The Fall and Rise of the American Medical Profession," in *The Professions in American History,* ed. Nathan O. Hatch (Notre Dame, IN: University of Notre Dame Press, 1988), 51.

9. Alyson Reed and Joyce E. Roberts, "State Regulation of Midwives: Issues and Options," *Journal of Midwifery and Women's Health* 45, no. 2 (2000): 130–149.

10. Barbara Katz Rothman, *In Labor: Women and Power in the Birthplace* (New York: W. W. Norton and Company, 1991).

11. Sheila P. Davis and Cora A. Ingram, "Empowered Caretakers: A Historical Perspective on the Roles of Granny Midwives in Rural Alabama," in *Wings of Gauze,* ed. Barbara Bair and Susan E. Cayleff (Detroit, MI: Wayne State University Press, 1993), 191–201.

12. Ibid.

13. Judith Walzer Leavitt, "Science Enters the Birthing Room: Obstetrics in America since the Eighteenth Century," *Journal of American History* 70, no. 2 (1983): 298.

14. Barbara Ehrenreich and Deirdre English, *Witches, Midwives and Nurses: A History of Women Healers,* 2nd ed. (New York: Feminist Press, City University of New York, 2010).

15. Holmes, "Midwives, Southern Black," 258.

16. Ibid.

17. Holly F. Mathews, "Killing the Medical Self-Help Tradition among African Americans: The Case of Lay Midwifery in North Carolina, 1912–1983," in *African Americans in the South: Issues of Race, Class, and Gender,* ed. Hans A. Baer and Yvonne Jones (Athens: University of Georgia Press, 1992); Molly C. Dougherty, "Southern Lay Midwives as

Ritual Specialists," in *Women in Ritual and Symbolic Roles,* ed. Judith Hoch-Smith and Anita Spring (New York: Plenum Press, 1977), 151–164.

18. Susie, *In the Way of Our Grandmothers.*

19. Valerie Lee, *Granny Midwives and Black Women Writers* (New York: Routledge, 1996), 39.

20. Holmes, "Midwives, Southern Black," 258–259.

21. Bonaparte, "The Persecution and Prosecution of Granny Midwives."

22. Rose Weitz and Deborah Sullivan, "Midwife Licensing," in *Encyclopedia of Childbearing: Critical Perspectives,* ed. Barbara Katz Rothman (Phoenix: Oryx Press, 1992), 246.

23. Mathews, "Killing the Medical Self-Help Tradition among African Americans."

24. Rooks, *Midwifery and Childbirth in America.*

25. Patricia Hill Collins, *Black Feminist Thought: Knowledge, Consciousness, and the Politics of Empowerment* (New York: Routledge, 2000), 5.

26. Edwin M. Schur, *Labeling Women Deviant: Gender, Stigma, and Social Control* (Philadelphia: Temple University Press, 1983).

27. Collins, *Black Feminist Thought,* 5.

28. Mary M. Lay, *The Rhetoric of Lay Midwifery: Gender, Knowledge, and Power* (New Brunswick, NJ: Rutgers University Press, 2000), refers to this process as the creation of authoritative knowledge, which functioned as a component of the professionalization of medicine.

29. Judy Barrett Litoff, "An Historical Overview of Midwifery in the United States," *Pre- and Peri-Natal Psychology* 5, no. 1 (1990): 12.

30. I examined selected issues of the *Journal of the American Medical Association* (*JAMA*) and the *Journal of the South Carolina Medical Association* (*JSCMA*) for the period 1900 through 1940. *JAMA,* the official journal of the American Medical Association, influenced the beliefs and attitudes of physicians nationwide due to its large readership. *JSCMA,* published by the South Carolina Medical Association, was the major source of medical information for medical societies in South Carolina. For a more detailed discussion of my methodology, see Bonaparte, "The Persecution and Prosecution of Granny Midwives."

31. W. P. Manton, "The Role of Obstetrics," *JAMA* 55, no. 6 (1910): 463.

32. James A. Haynes, "Annual Report of the State Health Officer," *JSCMA* 15, no. 1 (1919): 340. Emphasis mine.

33. "Old Dipper" is another moniker given to granny midwives, and physicians used the term when discussing them. The origins of the term may be linked to the use of a "dipper" water-collecting tool during birthing.

34. D. H. Smith, "A Consideration of the Proper Management of Obstetrical Engagements in Sparsely Settled Districts," *JSCMA* 14, no. 5 (1918): 128.

35. "South Carolina Medical Association: What Has Been Done for the Prevention of the Increase of Blindness, and What Can Be Done," *JAMA* 54, no. 22 (1910): 1816.

36. Ibid.

37. Angela Y. Davis, *The Meaning of Freedom: And Other Difficult* Dialogues (San Francisco: City Lights, 2012), identifies terms such as "gang member" and "criminal" to demonstrate how politicians use them to discuss black deviance without specifically naming black people.

38. "Better Obstetrics in South Carolina," *JSCMA* 16, no. 1 (1920): 4. Emphasis mine.

39. Bonaparte, "The Persecution and Prosecution of Granny Midwives."

40. "Medical News: Report on Midwifery," *JAMA* 67, no. 23 (1916): 1786.

41. Manton, "The Role of Obstetrics," 462.

42. John Lunney, "A Case of Caesearean Section Not Hitherto Reported," *JSCMA* 11, no. 1 (1915): 6.

43. Oliver C. Cox, *Caste, Class, and Race: A Study in Social Dynamics* (New York: Monthly Review Press, 1949).

44. Ibid.

45. T. H. Dreher, "Birth Control among the Poor," *JSCMA* 27, no. 1 (1931): 329–332. Emphasis mine.

46. Werner Sollars, "The Curse of Ham; or 'Race' and Biblical Exegesis Lecture," University of Missouri–St. Louis, accessed May 5, 2005, www.umsl.edu/~cfh/abstracts /ham.html; David M. Goldenberg, *The Curse of Ham: Race and Slavery in Early Judaism, Christianity, Islam.* Jews, Christians, and Muslims from the Ancient to the Modern World (Princeton, NJ: Princeton University Press, 2005).

47. R. B. Furman, "Ignorance, Superstition, Quackery," *JSCMA* 12, no. 4 (1916): 113–115.

48. W. E. Simpson, "Infant Mortality in South Carolina," *JSCMA* 24, no. 2 (1928): 27–32.

49. Dreher, "Birth Control among the Poor," 329–332.

50. Fraser, *African American Midwifery in the South*; Lee, *Granny Midwives and Black Women Writers.*

51. Fraser, *African American Midwifery in the South.*

CHAPTER 3

1. Central Statistical Office (CSO) Zimbabwe and Macro International Inc., *Zimbabwe Demographic and Health Survey, 2010–2011* (Calverton, MD: CSO and Macro International Inc., 2012).

2. Ian Douglas Smith, *The Great Betrayal* (London: Blake Publishing Ltd., 1997), 331–360.

3. Brian Raftopoulos and Alois Mlambo, *Becoming Zimbabwe: A History from the Pre-colonial Period to 2008* (Harare: Weaver Press, 2009).

4. Jane Mutambirwa, "Pregnancy, Childbirth, Mother and Child Care among the Indigenous People of Zimbabwe," *International Journal of Gynecology and Obstetrics* 23 (1985): 275–285.

5. Ministry of Health and Child Welfare, *National Health Strategy for Zimbabwe, 1997–2000: Working for Quality and Equity in Health* (Harare: Ministry of Health and Child Welfare, 1999).

6. World Health Organization (WHO), UNICEF, UNFPA, World Bank, and United Nations, *Trends in Maternal Mortality, 1990–2014* (Geneva: WHO, 2014), 43.

7. Zimbabwe National Statistics Agency (ZIMSTAT) and ICF International, *The Zimbabwe Demographic Health Survey 2010–2011 Report* (Calverton, MD: ZIMSTAT and ICF International, Inc., 2012), 15.

8. Ibid.

9. UNICEF, *Guidelines for Monitoring the Availability and Use of Obstetric Services* (New York: UNICEF/WHO/UNFPA, 1997).

10. K. Peltzer, N. Phaswana-Mafuya, and L. Treger, "Use of Traditional and Complementary Health Practices in Prenatal, Delivery and Postnatal Care in the Context of HIV Transmission from Mother to Child (PMTCT) in the Eastern Cape, South Africa," *African Journal of Traditional, Complementary and Alternative Medicines* 6 (2009): 155–162.

11. S. Ngomane and F. M. Mulaudzi, "Indigenous Beliefs and Practices That Influence the Delayed Attendance of Antenatal Clinics by Women in the Bohlabelo District in Limpopo, South Africa," *Midwifery* 28, no. 1 (2012): 30–38.

12. Royal College of Midwives, *Woman-Centered Care,* Position Paper No. 4a (London: Royal College of Midwives, 2008). Available from www.rcm.org.

CHAPTER 4

1. Afua Cooper, *The Hanging of Angelique: The Untold Story of Canadian Slavery and the Burning of Old Montreal* (Athens: University of Georgia Press, 2007).

2. Viviane Saleh-Hanna and Ashanti Omowali Alston, "Introduction: Responding to Centuries of Violence, Imprisonment and Oppression," *Journal of Prisoners on Prisons* 15–16 (2007): 1–9.

3. Julia Sudbury, *Global Lockdown: Race, Gender and the Prison-Industrial Complex* (New York: Routledge, 2005).

4. Viviane Saleh-Hanna, *Colonial-Systems of Control: Criminal Justice in Nigeria* (Ottawa: University of Ottawa Press, 2008).

5. Viviane Saleh-Hanna and Ashanti Omowali Alston, "Taking Too Much for Granted: Studying the Movement and Re-assessing the Terms," in *The Case for Penal Abolition,* ed. Ruth Morris and W. Gord West (Toronto: Canadian Scholars Press, 2000).

6. Saleh-Hanna and Alston, "Introduction."

7. dead prez, "I'm a African," on *Lets Get Free* (Relativity, 2000).

8. Peter Tosh, "Arise Black Man," on *Honorary Citizen* (Columbia/Sony, 1999, 1972).

9. Nina Simone, "Young, Gifted and Black," on *Black Gold* (Bmg Int'l, 2004, 1970).

10. Harriet A. Washington, *Medical Apartheid: The Dark History of Medical Experimentation on Black Americans from Colonial Times to the Present* (New York: Doubleday, 2007); Andrea Smith, *Conquest: Sexual Violence and American Indian Genocide* (Cambridge, MA: South End Press, 2005).

11. Spiritchild, "Cry for Peace," on *Creative Politics Chapter 1—Reports from the Rhythmic Poet* (Baby.com/Indys [CDBY], 2006).

12. Leonard Cohen, "The Great Event," on *More Best of Leonard Cohen* (Sony, 1997).

13. Faith Nolan, "We Got a Right," on *Mannish Gal, Queering the Blues* (faithnfaith, 2008).

14. Peter Tosh, "Get Up Stand Up (Acoustic)," on *Honorary Citizen* (Columbia/Sony, 1999, 1977).

15. Toni Morrison, *Beloved* (New York: Alfred A. Knopf, 1987).

16. Octavia Butler, *Kindred* (Boston: Beacon Press, 1975).

17. Sonya McCoy-Wilson, "In 'Rememory': Beloved and Transgenerational Ghosting in Black Female Bodies" (paper presented at the Graduate English Association New Voices Conference, 2007); Samira Kawash, "Haunted House, Sinking Ships: Race, Architecture, and Identity in Beloved and Middle Passage," *New Centennial Review* 1, no. 3 (Winter 2001): 67–86.

18. Washington, *Medical Apartheid*; Susan Reverby, "Inclusion and Exclusion: The Politics of History, Difference, and Medical Research," *Journal of the History of Medicine and Allied Sciences* 63, no. 1 (January 2008): 103–113.

19. Dennis Childs, "'You Ain't Seen Nothin' Yet': Beloved, the American Chain Gang, and the Middle Passage Remix," *American Quarterly* 61, no. 2 (2009): 271–297.

20. Sweet Honey in the Rock, "Wade in the Water," on *Selections* (Rounder, 1997, 1988).

CHAPTER 5

1. Luz Gibbons et al., *The Global Numbers and Costs of Additionally Needed and Unnecessary Caesarean Sections Performed per Year: Overuse as a Barrier to Universal Coverage,* World Health Report, Background Paper 30, World Health Organization, 2010, accessed September 22, 2014, www.who.int/healthsystems/topics/financing/healthreport/30C-sectioncosts.pdf.

2. US Department of Health and Human Services, Health Resources and Services Administration, *Child Health USA 2013,* Maternal and Child Health Bureau, October 2013, accessed September 22, 2014, http://mchb.hrsa.gov/chusa13/dl/pdf/chusa13.pdf.

3. M. J. K. Osterman and J. A. Martin, "Changes in Cesarean Delivery Rates by Gestational Age: United States, 1996–2011," National Center for Health Statistics, Data Brief no. 124, accessed September 22, 2014, www.cdc.gov/nchs/data/databriefs/db124.htm.

4. Truven Health Analytics, "The Cost of Having a Baby in the United States," Childbirth Connection, 2013, accessed September 22, 2014, http://transform.childbirthconnection.org/wp-content/uploads/2013/01/Cost-of-Having-a-Baby1.pdf.

5. Shankar Vedantam, "Money May Be Motivating Doctors to Do More C-Sections," NPR, August 30, 2013, accessed September 2014, www.npr.org/blogs/health/2013/08/30/216479305/money-may-be-motivating-doctors-to-do-more-c-sections.

CHAPTER 6

1. Syrus Marcus Ware, "Going Boldly Where Few Men Have Gone Before: One Trans Man's Experience of Fertility Clinics," in *Who's Your Daddy and Other Writings on Queer Parenting,* ed. Rachel Epstein (Toronto: Sumach Press, 2009).

2. Karlene Pendleton Jiménez, *How to Get a Girl Pregnant* (Toronto: Tightrope Books, 2011); Maura Ryan, "Beyond Thomas Beatie: Trans Men and the New Parenthood," in Epstein, *Who's Your Daddy*; Thomas Beatie, *Labor of Love: The Story of One Man's Extraordinary Pregnancy* (Berkeley: Seal Press, 2008).

3. Susan Goldberg and Chloe Brushwood, eds., *And Baby Makes More: Known Donors, Queer Parents, and Our Unexpected Families* (London, ON: Insomniac Press, 2009); Remy Huberdeau, *Transforming Families* (Toronto: LGBTQ Parenting Network, 2012).

4. Beatie, *Labor of Love.*

5. Ibid., 20–22.

6. Mitsuru Mitsuru, "Thomas Beatie Is Asian! Reclaiming Trans Histories of Colour," Racialicious, accessed July 30, 2009, www.racialicious.com/2009/07/30/thomas-beatie-is-asian-reclaiming-trans-histories-of-colour.

CHAPTER 7

1. James Baldwin, "As Much Truth as One Can Bear," in *The Cross of Redemption: Uncollected Writings,* ed. Randall Kenan (New York: Pantheon Books, 2010).

2. Population and Development Program, *Population in Perspective: A Curriculum Resource* (CreateSpace Independent Publishing Platform, 2013), vii.

3. Betsy Hartmann, *Reproductive Rights and Wrongs: The Global Politics of Population Control* (Boston: South End Press, 1995).

4. Brian Tashman, "Perkins Warns of Government Promotion of Same-Sex Relations for Population Control," Right-Wing Watch, accessed October 13, 2011, www .rightwingwatch.org/content/perkins-warns-government-promotion-same-sex-relations -population-control.

5. In the "Hobby Lobby decision," named for the chain of craft stores that brought the case, the Supreme Court ruled that religious business owners cannot be required to pay for insurance coverage of contraception. Brian Tashman, "Traditional Values Coalition Links Contraception Mandate to Islamic Shariah Law, Population Control," Right-Wing Watch, accessed March 26, 2014, www.rightwingwatch.org/category/people/andrea-lafferty.

6. Margaret Sanger, *The Pivot of Civilization* (Amherst, NY: Humanity Books, 2003), 177.

7. Aviva Galpert, "Demographic Winter: Right-Wing Prophecies of White Supremacy's Decline," Political Research Associates, accessed July 7, 2014, www.politicalresearch.org /2014/07/03/demographic-winter-right-wing-prophecies-of-white-supremacys-decline/#.

8. Kelli Goff, "Why White Supremacists Have Embraced the War on Contraception," *Huffington Post,* accessed May 22, 2012, www.huffingtonpost.com/keli-goff/are-white -supremacists-be_b_1534814.html.

9. Alexandra Minna Stern, *Eugenic Nation* (Berkeley: University of California Press, 2005), 8.

10. Andrea Smith, *Conquest: Sexual Violence and American Indian Genocide* (Boston: South End Press, 2005), 8–9.

11. Loretta J. Ross, "The Color of Choice," in *The Color of Violence: The Incite! Anthology,* ed. Incite! Color of Violence (Boston, MA: South End Press, 2006). Available at www.racialequitytools.org/resourcefiles/The-Color-of-Choice----Public-Version-with -footnotes-1.pdf (accessed October 5, 2014).

12. Rickie Solinger, *Pregnancy and Power: A Short History of Reproductive Politics in America* (New York: New York University Press, 2005), 27.

13. Associated Press, "Supreme Court Rejects Challenge to Nebraska City's Immigration Law," *Huffington Post,* May 5, 2014, accessed October 15, 2014, www.huffingtonpost .com/2014/05/05/supreme-court-immigration_n_5266776.html.

14. Stern, *Eugenic Nation,* 3.

15. Gregory H. Stanton, "8 Stages of Genocide," Genocide Watch, accessed October 6, 2014, www.genocidewatch.org/aboutgenocide/8stagesofgenocide.html.

16. Loretta J. Ross, "African American Women and Abortion, 1800–1970," in *Theorizing Black Feminisms,* ed. Stanlie James and Abena Busia (London: Routledge Press, 1993), 150.

17. Jael Silliman, Marlene Gerber Fried, Loretta Ross, and Elena Gutierrez, *Undivided Rights: Women of Color Organize for Reproductive Justice* (Boston: South End Press, 2004), 5.

18. National Advisory Commission on Civil Disorders, *Report of the National Advisory Commission on Civil Disorders* (New York: Bantam Books, 1968), 1–29.

19. Ibid., www.eisenhowerfoundation.org/docs/kerner/Kerner_C16.pdf, 216, accessed October 14, 2014.

20. National Advisory Commission on Civil Disorders, "Summary of Report of the National Advisory Commission on Civil Disorders," Eisenhower Foundation, accessed October 14, 2014, www.eisenhowerfoundation.org/docs/kerner.pdf, 16.

21. Yulanda Ward Memorial Fund, "Spatial Deconcentration," 1981, libcom.org, accessed October 5, 2012, http://libcom.org/library/spatial-deconcentration-d-c; Yulanda Ward, "Spatial Deconcentration," ABC No Rio, accessed October 5, 2012, www.abcnorio .org/about/history/spatial_d.html.

22. Yulanda Ward Memorial Fund, "Spatial Deconcentration," 1981.

23. Ibid.

24. I would particularly like to thank Shana Griffith of the Women's Health Justice Initiative for her brilliant analyses of population-control measures in New Orleans after the Katrina hurricane.

25. Rickie Solinger, *Wake Up Little Susie: Single Pregnancy and Race before Roe v. Wade* (New York: Routledge Press, 2000), 208.

26. Martha C. Ward, *Poor Women, Powerful Men: America's Great Experiment in Family Planning* (Boulder, CO: Westview Press, 1986), 68.

27. Thomas Littlewood, *The Politics of Population Control* (Notre Dame, IN: University of Notre Dame, 1977), 51.

28. Peter C. Engleman, *A History of the Birth Control Movement in America* (Santa Barbara, CA: Praeger Press, 2011), 136.

29. Loretta Ross, "What Is Reproductive Justice?," Trust Black Women, accessed October 5, 2014, http://trustblackwomen.org/our-work/what-is-reproductive-justice /9-what-is-reproductive-justice.

30. Rickie Solinger, *Reproductive Politics* (New York: Oxford University Press, 2013), 160–161.

31. Paige Lavender, "After Saying Women on Medicaid Should Be Sterilized, Russell Pearce Resigns from Arizona GOP," *Huffington Post,* accessed September 20, 2014, www .huffingtonpost.com/2014/09/15/russell-pearce-resigns_n_5822136.html.

32. Dorothy Roberts, *Fatal Invention* (New York: New Press, 2011), x.

33. John Griffith, "Fed Study Debunks Conservative Myth That Affordable Housing Policies Caused Subprime Crisis," ThinkProgress, accessed October 5, 2014, http://think progress.org/economy/2012/03/28/453978/fed-study-affordable-housing-myth; Mary Lugton and Phoebe McKinney, *Population in Perspective* (Amherst, MA: Population and Development Program, Hampshire College, 2013), 159.

34. Walter E. Williams, "Williams: U.S. Is Morally, Spiritually Poor," *Amarillo Globe News,* July 31, 2012, accessed October 14, 2014, http://amarillo.com/opinion/opinion -columnist/weekly-opinion-columnist/2012-07-31/williams-us-morally-spiritually-poor.

CHAPTER 8

1. Jacqueline Gahagan, *Women and HIV Prevention in Canada: Implications for Research, Policy, and Practice* (Toronto: Women's Press, 2013).

2. Helena Shimeles et al., *African, Caribbean and Black Communities in Canada: A Knowledge Synthesis Paper for the CIHR Social Research Centre on HIV Prevention* (Toronto: University of Toronto, Dalla Lana School of Public Health, 2010).

3. In Ontario, 16 percent of prevalent cases, meaning cases within the total population, and 26 percent of incident cases, meaning new cases, of HIV are within black communities.

4. Juan Liu and Robert S. Remis, *HIV Prevalence, Incidence, Mother-to-Child Transmission among African, Caribbean, and Black (ACB) Populations in Canada as of 2008* (Toronto: University of Toronto, Dalla Lana School of Public Health, 2008).

5. Gahagan, *Women and HIV Prevention in Canada.*

6. "At a Glance—HIV and AIDS in Canada: Surveillance Report to December 31st, 2012," Public Health Agency of Canada, modified November 29, 2013, accessed December 9, 2014, www.phac-aspc.gc.ca/aids-sida/publication/survreport/2012/dec/index-eng .php.

7. "Ontario HIV/AIDS Strategy for African, Caribbean and Black Communities 2013–2018," African and Caribbean Council on HIV/AIDS in Ontario, accessed December 9, 2014, www.accho.ca/Portals/3/documents/resources/ACB_Strategy_Web _Oct2013_En.pdf.

8. "At a Glance—HIV and AIDS in Canada."

9. "Summary Tables: Permanent and Temporary Residents 2010," Citizenship and Immigration Canada, accessed December 9, 2014, www.cic.gc.ca/english/resources /statistics/facts2010-summary/01.asp.

10. "Ontario HIV/AIDS Strategy for African, Caribbean and Black Communities 2013–2018."

11. Wangari Tharao, "The Intersection of Migration with HIV Risk in Vulnerable Populations and Their Families in Canada," August 6, 2009, accessed December 9, 2014, www.google.ca/url?sa=t&rct=j&q=&esrc=s&source=web&cd=10&ved=0CFgQFjAJ&url =http%3A%2F%2Fwww.ohtnweb.ca%2FFFCentre%2F2_THARAO_no%2520notes .ppt&ei=-ZD3U8__MsKAygTYjIKoAQ&usg=AFQjCNHSjzOcOrEnpkH192-SHh0Q 8uirLA&bvm=bv.73612305,d.aWw.

12. Laura Bisaillon, "Mandatory HIV Testing and Everyday Life: A Look inside the Canadian Immigration Medical Examination," *Aporia* 3 (2011): 5–14.

13. Laura Bisaillon, "Human Rights Consequences of Mandatory HIV Screening Policy of Newcomers to Canada," *Health and Human Rights* 12 (2010): 119–134.

14. C. Logie et al., "Associations between HIV-Related Stigma, Racial Discrimination, Gender Discrimination, and Depression among HIV-Positive African, Caribbean, and Black Women in Ontario, Canada," *AIDS Patient Care STDS* 27, no. 2 (February 2013).

15. Gahagan, *Women and HIV Prevention in Canada.*

16. N. Muturi and S. An, "HIV/AIDS Stigma and Religiosity among African American Women," *Journal of Health Communication* 15 (2010): 388–401.

17. Logie et al., "Associations between HIV-Related Stigma."

18. Anne C. Wagner et al., "Correlates of HIV Stigma in HIV-Positive Women," *Archives in Women's Mental Health* 13 (2010): 207–214.

19. Yvette P. Cuca et al., "Factors Associated with Pregnant Women's Anticipations and Experiences of HIV-Related Stigma in Rural Kenya," *AIDS Care* 24 (2010): 1173–1180.

20. "HIV/AIDS Epi Updates–July 2010. Chapter 7: Perinatal HIV Transmission in Canada," Public Health Agency of Canada, accessed December 9, 2014, www.phac-aspc .gc.ca/aids-sida/publication/epi/2010/7-eng.php.

21. Robert S. Remis et al., "High Uptake of HIV Testing in Pregnant Women in Ontario, Canada," *Plos One* 7, no. 11 (2012).

22. Robert S. Remis, Dale Guenter, and Susan King, "Testing Pregnant Women in Canada for HIV: How Are We Doing?," *Canadian Family Physician* 47 (2001): 2194–2195.

23. "HIV/AIDS Epi Updates–July 2010. Chapter 7: Perinatal HIV Transmission in Canada."

24. B. Nattabi et al., "A Systematic Review of Factors Influencing Fertility Desires and Intentions among People Living with HIV/AIDS: Implications for Policy and Service Delivery," *AIDS Behavior* 13 (2009): 949–968.

25. Vertical or perinatal HIV infections are acquired during pregnancy, at birth, or through breastfeeding. Historically this type of transmission was referred to as mother-to-child transmission. Advocates have demanded the elimination of this terminology as there is a covert direction of blame placed upon mothers. The preferred terminology depicts the direction (vertical) or timing (perinatal) of transmission but suggests no culpability.

26. Jack Forbes and the Canadian Pediatric AIDS Research Group, "A National Review of Vertical HIV Transmission," *AIDS* 26 (2012): 757–763.

27. O. Nnaemeka, *The Politics of (M)othering: Womanhood, Identity, and Resistance in African Literature* (New York: Routledge, 1997).

28. D. Cooper et al., "'Life Is Still Going On': Reproductive Intentions among HIV-Positive Women and Men in South Africa," *Social Science and Medicine* 65 (2007): 274–283.

29. S. Finocchario-Kessler et al., "Understanding High Fertility Desires and Intentions among a Sample of Urban Women Living with HIV in the United States," *AIDS and Behavior* 14 (2010): 1106–1114.

30. Sarah MacCarthy et al., "The Pregnancy Decisions of HIV-Positive Women: The State of Knowledge and Way Forward," *Reproductive Health Matters* 20 (2012): 119–140.

31. V. Logan Kennedy, "Desiring a Balanced Identity: A Heideggerian Phenomenological Inquiry into the Pregnancy Experiences of Newcomer Women to Canada with HIV," Paper 743, Theses and dissertations (2012).

32. "HIV/AIDS Epi Updates–July 2010. Chapter 7: Perinatal HIV Transmission in Canada."

33. Gahagan, *Women and HIV Prevention in Canada.*

34. Alexandra Samur, "For Moms-to-Be, It's Frightening to Be Uninsured," The Tyee, March 21, 2014, accessed December 9, 2014, http://thetyee.ca/News/2014/03/21/Uninsured-Moms.

35. Mona R. Loutfy et al., "Canadian HIV Pregnancy Planning Guidelines," *Journal of Obstetrics and Gynecology of Canada* 34, no. 6 (June 2012).

36. MacCarthy et al., "The Pregnancy Decisions of HIV-Positive Women."

37. "Towards the Development of a Coordinated National Research Agenda for Women, Transwomen, Girls, and HIV/AIDS in Canada: A Multi-stakeholder Dialogue," Event Report, Canadian AIDS Society, April 13–14, 2011, accessed December 9, 2014, www.cdnaids.ca/files.nsf/pages/womensresearchagenda-final/$file/Women's%20Research%20Agenda-Event%20Report-Final.pdf.

38. "The Forced and Coerced Sterilization of HIV Positive Women in Namibia," The International Community of Women Living with HIV, March 2009, accessed December 9, 2014, www.icw.org/files/The%20forced%20and%20coerced%20sterilization%20of%20HIV%20positive%20women%20in%20Namibia%2009.pdf.

39. Ibid.

40. "Preventing Forced Abortion and Sterilization," amFAR, June 28, 2013, accessed December 9, 2014, www.amfar.org/preventing-forced-abortion-and-sterilization.

41. Ibid.

42. Alison Duke, *The Woman I Have Become* (documentary) (Toronto: Goldelox Productions, 2008); Alison Duke, *Positive Women: Exposing Injustice* (documentary) (Toronto: Goldelox Productions, 2013); Alison Duke, *Research Shouldn't Sit on a Shelf: Stories of Strength, Action, and Resilience from Women Living with HIV and Community-Based HIV Researchers* (documentary) (Toronto: Women's Health in Women's Hands and Women's College Research Institute, 2013).

CHAPTER 9

1. The United States ranks third in the world for administering the most cesarean sections; 33 percent of all births in the United States are C-sections. Theresa Morris, *Cut It Out* (New York: New York University Press, 2013).

2. A nuchal scan is a prenatal sonographic screening of the fluid at the back of a baby's neck; it is used to screen for possible chromosomal conditions including Down syndrome.

CHAPTER 10

1. For more information, visit the Safe Motherhood Quilt Project (www.remem berthemothers.org).

CHAPTER 11

1. Warsan Shire, "Untitled Poem," accessed December 2012, www.warsanshire.tumblr .com.
2. Toni Morrison, *Love* (New York: Alfred A. Knopf/Random House, 2003).
3. Ruth King, *Healing Rage: Women Making Inner Peace Possible* (New York: Gotham Books, 2007).
4. Brené Brown, quote retrieved from her website (www.brenebrown.com) in March 2013.
5. Audre Lorde, *Sister Outsider: Essays and Speeches* (New York: Quality Paperback Book Club, 1984).
6. Eckhart Tolle, *The Power of Now: A Guide to Spiritual Enlightenment* (Vancouver, BC: Namaste Publishing, 2004).

CHAPTER 12

1. According to DONA International, a doula is "a trained and experienced professional who provides continuous physical, emotional and informational support to the mother before, during and just after birth; or who provides emotional and practical support during the postpartum period" ("What Is a Doula?," DONA International, accessed July 1, 2014, www.dona.org/mothers).
2. In 1810, twenty-one-year-old Saartjie Baartman was smuggled from South Africa to Europe by her white master and put on a touring display, where she was subjected to physical abuse by European onlookers. Scientists studied her body in life and in death, putting her skeleton, genitals, and body cast on display in France until 1974. Her remains were not given proper burial until 2002, and she has since become a symbol of anticolonial and feminist struggle. For more, see Rachel Holmes, *The Hottentot Venus: The Life and Death of Saartjie Baartman, Born 1789–Buried 2002* (London: Bloomsbury Publishing, 2007).
3. This history is discussed in detail in the introduction to this volume.

CHAPTER 13

1. New York City Department of Health and Mental Hygiene, "Community Health Profile: Highbridge and Morrisania," 2nd ed., NYC.gov, 2006, accessed February 20, 2013, www.nyc.gov/html/doh/downloads/pdf/data/2006chp-106.pdf.
2. The Community Birthing Project, a women of color collective founded in 2005, is committed to supporting positive birthing experiences among immigrant and low-income communities in New York City. The sisters from this collective continue to do radical work as doulas, midwives, and reproductive justice activists.

CHAPTER 14

1. This chapter was inspired by a conversation between me and a good friend/sister, Kellee Coleman, on the topic of love. I am always grateful for her words, support, and insight.

2. The history of medical violence and abuses against reproductive bodies in marginalized populations, particularly communities of color, has been well documented. The Tuskegee experiment was a forty-year clinical study in which African American men with syphilis were studied and denied treatment under the false pretense of receiving free medical care. James Jones, *Bad Blood: The Tuskegee Syphilis Experiment* (New York: Free Press, 1981). Dorothy Roberts documents the detrimental yet widespread use of Norplant as birth control for poor women of color, as well as histories of sterilization as a eugenicist strategy. Dorothy Roberts, *Killing the Black Body: Race, Reproduction and the Meaning of Liberty* (New York: Pantheon Books, 1997).

3. A controversial report, authored by Daniel Patrick Moynihan and released in 1965, argued that single-family and maternal-led households were responsible for the decline of black communities and placed much of the blame on black single mothers for transmitting pathological behaviors to their children and creating a cycle of poverty. Daniel Patrick Moynihan, "The Negro Family: The Case for National Action," US Department of Labor, Office of Policy Planning and Research, March 1965, accessed September 22, 2014, www .dol.gov/dol/aboutdol/history/webid-meynihan.htm.

4. This draws on Audre Lorde's popular poem "A Litany for Survival." Audre Lorde, *The Collected Poems of Audre Lorde* (New York: Norton, 1997).

5. This concept is inspired by Audre Lorde's highly quoted statement that "Caring for myself is not self-indulgence, it is self-preservation, and that is an act of political warfare." Audre Lorde, *A Burst of Light: Essays* (New York: Firebrand Books, 1988), 131.

6. Mamas of Color Rising (MOCR), a grassroots organization of mothers of color established in 2008 in Austin, Texas, organizes around the various issues, such as housing, food, child care, and health, that poor and working-class women of color face on a daily basis. In 2009, MOCR launched its reproductive and birth justice campaign to create access to just and loving maternal health care. See www.mamasofcolorrising.wordpress .com (accessed September 22, 2014).

CHAPTER 15

1. Audre Lorde, "The Transformation of Silence into Language and Action," in *Sister Outsider* (Berkeley, CA: Crossing Press, 1984), 42.

CHAPTER 16

1. Dorothy Roberts, *Killing the Black Body: Race, Reproduction and the Meaning of Liberty* (New York: Vintage Books, 1997), 55.

2. Rosalie M. Grivell et al., "Maternal and Neonatal Outcomes Following Induction of Labor: A Cohort Study," *Acta Obstetricia et Gynecologica Scandinavica* 91, no. 2 (2012): 198–203; Louise Marie Roth and Megan M. Henley, "Unequal Motherhood: Racial-Ethnic and Socioeconomic Disparities in Cesarean Sections in the United States," *Social Problems* 59, no. 2 (2012): 207–227.

3. "Deadly Delivery: The Maternal Health Care Crisis in the USA," Amnesty International, 2010, accessed September 24, 2014, www.amnestyusa.org/sites/default/files/pdfs/deadlydelivery.pdf, 19.

4. Barbara Ehrenreich and Deirdre English, *Witches, Midwives and Nurses: A History of Women Healers,* 2nd ed. (New York: Feminist Press, City University of New York, 2010), 8.

5. Stanley Wohl documented the transformation of medicine and health care into big business in *The Medical Industrial Complex* (New York: Harmony Books, 1984). The idea was further popularized by the documentary *The Business of Being Born,* directed by Abby Epstein (International Film Circuit, 2008).

6. Silvia Federici, *Caliban and the Witch: Women, the Body and Primitive Accumulation* (Brooklyn, NY: Autonomedia, 2004), 75, 89.

7. Lucille Mair, *The Rebel Woman in the British West Indies during Slavery* (Kingston: Institute of Jamaica Publications Ltd., 1995); Roberts, *Killing the Black Body.*

8. Roberts, *Killing the Black Body,* 23.

9. Federici, *Caliban and the Witch*; Jennifer Nelson, ed., *Women of Color and the Reproductive Rights Movement* (New York: New York University Press, 2003).

10. Andrea Smith, *Conquest: Sexual Violence and American Indian Genocide* (Cambridge, MA: South End Press, 2005); Nelson, *Women of Color and the Reproductive Rights Movement.* Smith quotes testimonials from US colonizers during the conquest of North America: "I heard one man say that he cut a woman's private parts out, and had them for exhibition on a stick. . . . I also heard of numerous instances in which men had cut out the private parts of females, and stretched them over their saddle-bows and some of them over their hats" (Smith, 15).

11. Roth and Henley, "Unequal Motherhood," 208.

12. Nelson, *Women of Color and the Reproductive Rights Movement.*

13. Roth and Henley, "Unequal Motherhood," 7; Joyce A. Martin et al., *Births: Final Data for 2012,* National Vital Statistics Reports 62, no. 9 (Hyattsville, MD: National Center for Health Statistics, 2013), 2.

14. Michelle J. K. Osterman and Joyce A. Martin, "Changes in Cesarean Delivery Rates by Gestational Age: United States, 1996–2011," NCHS Data Brief No. 124, National Center for Health Statistics, June 2013, accessed December 9, 2014, www.cdc.gov/nchs/data/databriefs/db124.pdf.

15. The maternal mortality rate increased from 6.6 deaths per 100,000 live births in 1987 to 13.3 deaths per 100,000 live births in 2006. "Deadly Delivery," 1.

16. Roth and Henley, "Unequal Motherhood," 208–209.

17. Robin Lim, *After the Baby's Birth . . . a Woman's Way to Wellness: A Complete Guide for Postpartum Women* (Berkeley, CA: Celestial Arts, 1991); Valeri Lynn, *The Mommy Plan: Restoring Your Post-pregnancy Body Naturally, Using Women's Traditional Wisdom* (Malaysia: Percetakan Lenang Istimewa Sdn Bhd, 2012).

18. K. J. Mikiel-Kostyra and Mazur I. Boltruszko, "Effect of Early Skin-to-Skin Contact after Delivery on Duration of Breastfeeding: A Prospective Cohort Study," *Acta Paediatrica* 91, 12 (2002): 1301–1306.

19. Susan J. McDonald et al., "Effect of Timing of Umbilical Cord Clamping of Term Infants on Maternal and Neonatal Outcomes," *Cochrane Database of Systematic Reviews* 7 (2013): doi: 10.1002/14651858.CD004074.pub3.

20. Ibid.

21. S. K. McGrath and J. H. Kennell, "A Randomized Controlled Trial of Continuous Labor Support for Middle-Class Couples: Effect on Cesarean Delivery Rates," *Birth* 35 (2008): 92–97.

22. Katy Backes Kozhimannil et al., "Doula Care, Birth Outcomes, and Costs among Medicaid Beneficiaries," *American Journal of Public Health* 103, no. 4 (2013): e113–e121.

CHAPTER 17

1. Audre Lorde, "Eye to Eye: Black Women Hatred and Anger," in *Sister Outsider* (Berkeley, CA: Crossing Press, 1984): 145–151.

2. Postscript: Months after this conversation, Alexis and Pauline collaborated as doulas for the first time to support their stepsister/stepdaughter Kyla Day-Fletcher and her husband as Kyla gave birth to her first child, Logan Fletcher. For pictures and more updates, see lexandpauline.wordpress.com.

CHAPTER 18

1. Joffe, Weitz, and Stacey document the role of "dissident" physicians in health social movements and suggest that missing out physicians as key actors limits our understanding of these movements. C. E. Joffe, T. A. Weitz, and C. L. Stacey, "Uneasy Allies: Pro-Choice Physicians, Feminist Health Activists and the Struggle for Abortion Rights," *Sociology of Health and Illness* 26, no. 6 (2004): 775–796.

2. Joyce A. Martin et al., "Births: Final Data for 2012," Centers for Disease Control, National Vital Statistics Reports, 2013, accessed August 26, 2014, www.cdc.gov/nchs /data/nvsr/nvsr62/nvsr62_09.pdf, 11. Statistics for trans/gender nonconforming birthing parents are unavailable.

3. Brady E. Hamilton et al., "Births: Preliminary Data for 2013," Centers for Disease Control, 2014, accessed August 26, 2014, www.cdc.gov/nchs/data/nvsr/nvsr63/nvsr63 _02.pdf, 4.

4. "Total Cesarean Rate by Race, All U.S. States, 2011," Cesareanrates.com, accessed October 1, 2014, www.cesareanrates.com/blog/2013/7/20/cesarean-rates-by-race-all-us -states-2011.html.

5. A. G. Cahill et al., "Racial Disparity in the Success and Complications of Vaginal Birth after Cesarean Delivery," *Obstetrics and Gynecology* 111, no. 3 (2008): 654–658.

6. National Institutes of Health, "Vaginal Birth after Cesarean: New Insights," *NIH Consensus and State-of-the-Science Statements* 27, no. 3 (March 8–10, 2010): 5, 9, available at http://consensus.nih.gov/2010/images/vbac/vbac_statement.pdf (accessed August 26, 2014).

7. Ibid., 5.

8. Ibid., 27.

9. Amy Tuteur, "NIH, VBAC and the Politics of Resentment," The Skeptical OB, March 10, 2010, accessed August 26, 2014, www.skepticalob.com/2010/03/nih-vbac -and-politics-of-resentment.html.

10. "Cesarean Birth: Frequently Asked Questions, FAQ 006," American Congress of Obstetricians and Gynecologists, May 2011, accessed July 15, 2014, www.acog.org /~/media/For%20Patients/faq006.pdf?dmc=1&ts=20120725T1708145870.

11. American Congress of Obstetricians and Gynecologists, "ACOG Practice Bulletin No. 115: Vaginal Birth after Previous Cesarean Delivery," *Obstetrics and Gynecology* 116, no. 2 pt. 1 (August 2010).

12. Farah Diaz-Tello, "VBACs and Reproductive Justice," *Black Women Birthing Justice Newsletter* 3 (October 2013): 4.

13. "Press Release: Florida Hospital Says It Will Force Pregnant Woman to Have Cesarean Surgery," National Advocates for Pregnant Women, July 2014, accessed October 1, 2014, http://advocatesforpregnantwomen.org/blog/2014/07/press_release_florida _hospital.php.

14. Kathi Valeii, "Be the Change You Want to See—an Interview with Jennifer Goodall," Birth Anarchy, August 25, 2014, accessed October 1, 2014, http://birthanarchy.com /change-interview-jennifer-goodall.

15. Lynn M. Paltrow and Jeanne Flavin, "Arrests of and Forced Interventions on Pregnant Women in the United States, 1973–2005: Implications for Women's Legal Status and Public Health," *Journal of Health Politics, Policy and Law* 38, no. 2 (April 2013): 306.

16. Alexis D. Light et al., "Transgender Men Who Experienced Pregnancy after Female-to-Male Gender Transitioning," *Obstetrics and Gynecology* 124, no. 6 (2014): 1120–1127.

17. Ibid. Paltrow and Flavin, "Arrests of and Forced Interventions on Pregnant Women," note that African American women, especially those in the South, were particularly overrepresented among the women in their study (311). Reasons given for the arrests and prosecutions included allegedly exposing the fetus to illegal drugs or alcohol, failing to attend prenatal care or follow medical advice, refusing a cesarean or blood transfusion, contracting gestational diabetes, or suffering pregnancy loss (317).

18. International Cesarean Awareness Network, "Your Right to Refuse: What to Do if Your Hospital Has 'Banned' VBAC," Feminist Women's Health Center, accessed August 26, 2014, www.fwhc.org/health/pdf_about_vbac.pdf.

19. Project Motherpath, "Who We Are," VBAC Summit, accessed July 15, 2014, www .vbacsummit.org/who.html.

20. *Black Women Birthing Justice Newsletter* 3, October 2013, accessed December 9, 2014, http://media.wix.com/ugd/be55e7_61e07c47d954419b977350d1a18e976d.pdf; Black Women Do VBAC, www.blackwomendovbac.com (accessed August 26, 2014).

21. Amy Tuteur, "VBAC Should Not Be a Woman's Right," KevinMD.com, accessed July 27, 2014, www.kevinmd.com/blog/2010/03/vbac-womans.html.

22. In 2012, cesarean rates for Miami hospitals were as follows: Jackson North Medical Center, 37.1 percent; North Shore Medical Center, 38.8 percent; Jackson Memorial Hospital, 49 percent. Jill Arnold, "Hospital-Level Cesarean Rates by State: Florida Cesarean Rates," CesareanRates.com, accessed July 15, 2014, www.cesareanrates.com /hospital-level-cesarean-rates.

23. E. D. Hodnett et al., "Continuous Support for Women during Childbirth," Childbirth Connection, 2012, accessed August 26, 2014, https://childbirthconnection .org/pdfs/CochraneDatabaseSystRev.pdf.

CHAPTER 19

1. I define "childbearing" broadly as the time, place, and community surrounding the events of conception, pregnancy (and loss/termination), childbirth, and infant care.

2. Jennifer L. Morgan, *Laboring Women: Reproduction and Gender in New World Slavery* (Philadelphia: University of Pennsylvania Press, 2004), 7.

3. Ibid., 18.

4. Marie Jenkins Schwartz, *Birthing a Slave: Motherhood and Medicine in the Antebellum South* (Cambridge, MA: Harvard University Press, 2006).

5. Ibid., 146–148.

6. Valerie Lee, *Granny Midwives and Black Women Writers: Double-Dutched Readings* (New York: Routledge, 1996), 12–13.

7. Tina Cassidy, *Birth: The Surprising History of How We Are Born* (New York: Grove Press, 2006), 32–36.

8. Ibid., 33–34.

9. Sheila P. Davis and Cora A. Ingram, "Empowered Caretakers: A Historical Perspective on the Roles of Granny Midwives in Rural Alabama," in *Wings of Gauze: Women of Color and the Experience of Health and Illness,* ed. Barbara Bair and Susan Cayleff (Detroit, MI: Wayne State University Press, 1993), 195.

10. Laurie A. Wilkie, "Granny Midwives: Gender and Generational Mediators in the African American Community," in *Engendering African American Archaeology: A Southern Perspective,* ed. Jillian Galle and Amy Young (Knoxville: University of Tennessee Press, 2004), 84–85.

11. The skin and muscle between the vagina and rectum.

12. Darlene Clark Hine and Kathleen Thompson, *A Shining Thread of Hope: The History of Black Women in America* (New York: Broadway Books, 1998), 98–99.

13. Schwartz, *Birthing a Slave,* 150.

14. Ibid., 10–11.

15. Ibid., 50–57.

16. Ibid., 3.

17. Harriet A. Washington, *Medical Apartheid: The Dark History of Medical Experimentation on Black Americans from Colonial Times to the Present* (New York: Harlem Moon, 2006), 47–51.

18. Schwartz, *Birthing a Slave,* 153–154.

19. Wilkie, "Granny Midwives," 80.

20. Margaret Charles Smith and Linda Janet Holmes, *Listen to Me Good: The Life Story of an Alabama Midwife* (Columbus: Ohio State University Press, 1996), 43–44.

21. Davis and Ingram, "Empowered Caretakers," 1993.

22. Molly Ladd-Taylor, "'Grannies' and 'Spinsters': Midwife Education under the Sheppard-Towner Act," *Journal of Social History* 22, no. 2 (winter 1988): 259–260.

23. Khiara M. Bridges, *Reproducing Race: An Ethnography of Pregnancy as a Site of Racialization* (Berkeley: University of California Press, 2011), 120–122.

24. Ladd-Taylor, "'Grannies' and 'Spinsters,'" 264.

25. Lee, *Granny Midwives,* 43–45.

26. Robbie Davis-Floyd, *Birth as an American Rite of Passage* (Berkeley: University of California Press, 1992), 86–87.

27. Rhonda L. Haynes, dir., *Bringin' in da Spirit* (New York: Third World Newsreel, 2003).

28. Smith and Holmes, *Listen to Me Good,* 89.

29. Alondra Nelson, *Body and Soul: The Black Panther Party and the Fight against Medical Discrimination* (Minneapolis: University of Minnesota Press, 2011).

30. Dorothy Roberts, *Shattered Bonds: The Color of Child Welfare* (New York: Basic Books, 2001).

31. Dorothy Roberts, *Killing the Black Body: Race, Reproduction and the Meaning of Liberty* (New York: Vintage Books, 1997), 300.

32. Evelyn C. White and Shafia Monroe, "Interview: Lay Midwifery and the Traditional Child-Bearing Group," in *It Just Ain't Fair: The Ethics of Healthcare for African Americans,* ed. Annette Dula and Sara Goering (Westport, CT: Praeger Publishers, 1994), 209.

33. Ibid., 213.

CHAPTER 20

1. The JJ Way® is a registered trademark and cannot be reproduced without permission.

2. Patricia Hill Collins, "Learning from the Outsider-Within: The Sociological Significance of Black Feminist Thought," *Social Problems* 33, no. 6 (1999): S14–S32.

3. bell hooks, *Feminist Theory: From Margin to Center* (Boston: South End Press, 2000).

4. Maxine Baca Zinn and Bonnie Thornton Dill, "Theorizing Difference from Multiracial Feminism," in *Gender through the Prism of Difference,* ed. Maxine Baca Zinn, Pierette Hondagneu-Sotelo, and Michael Messner, 3rd ed. (New York: Oxford University Press, 2005); Patricia Hill Collins, *Black Feminist Thought: Knowledge, Consciousness, and the Politics of Empowerment* (New York: Routledge, 2000).

5. Alicia D. Bonaparte, "Physicians' Discourse for Establishing Authoritative Knowledge in Birthing Work and Reducing the Presence of the Granny Midwife," *Journal of Historical Sociology* (2014), doi: 10.1111/johs.12045; Gertrude Jacinta Fraser, *African American Midwifery in the South: Dialogues of Race, Birth, and Memory* (Boston: Harvard University Press, 1998); E. Auerbach, "Black Midwives in Mississippi: The Professionalizing of a Folk Role," *Human Mosaic* 3 (1968): 125–132.

6. Mary M. Lay, *The Rhetoric of Midwifery: Gender, Knowledge, and Power* (New Brunswick, NJ: Rutgers University Press, 2000).

7. Debra Ann Susie, *In the Way of Our Grandmothers: A Cultural View of Twentieth Century Midwifery in Florida* (Athens: University of Georgia Press, 1998).

8. Collins, *Black Feminist Thought.*

9. Amani Nuru-Jeter et al., "'It's the Skin You're In': African American Women Talk about Their Experiences of Racism, an Exploratory Study to Develop Measures of Racism for Birth Outcome Studies," *Maternal and Child Health Journal* 13, no. 1 (2009): 29–39; Alicia D. Bonaparte and Christine Morton, *Sociological Perspectives on Disparities in African American Maternal and Reproductive Health* (forthcoming).

10. Yvonda L. Hedrick and Justine Clegg, "The Perfect Combination of Art and Science: Florida's Licensed Midwives," Division of Medical Quality Assurance Council of Licensed Midwifery, Florida Department of Public Health, Tallahassee, 1996.

11. Christa Craven, *Pushing for Midwives: Homebirth Mothers and the Reproductive Rights Movement* (Philadelphia: Temple University Press, 2010).

12. John Baugh, "Linguistic Profiling," in *Black Linguistics: Language, Society, and Politics in Africa and the Americas,* ed. Sinfree Makoni et al. (New York: Routledge, 2003).

13. Alicia D. Bonaparte, "The Persecution and Prosecution of Granny Midwives in South Carolina, 1900–1940" (PhD diss., Vanderbilt University, 2007).

14. Hedrick and Clegg, "The Perfect Combination of Art and Science."

15. Ibid.

16. Cheryl Townsend Gilkes, "From Slavery to Social Welfare: Racism and the Control of Black Women," in *Class, Race, and Sex: The Dynamics of Control,* ed. Amy Smerdlow and Helen Lessinger (Boston: G. K. Hall, 1981).

17. Nuru-Jeter et al., "'It's the Skin You're In.'"

18. Robbie E. Davis-Floyd, *Mainstreaming Midwives: The Politics of Change* (New York: Routledge, 2006).

19. Amy Cohen, "The Midwifery Stalemate and Childbirth Choice: Recognizing Mothers-to-Be as the Best Late Pregnancy Decisionmakers," *Indiana Law Journal* 80, no. 3 (2005): 850–880.

20. Dorothy Roberts, *Killing the Black Body: Race, Reproduction and the Meaning of Liberty* (New York: Random House, 1997).

21. Harriet Washington, *Medical Apartheid: The Dark History of Medical Experimentation on Black Americans from Colonial Times to the Present* (New York: Anchor Books, 2006).

22. Donald L. Barlett and James B. Steele, *Critical Condition: How Health Care in America Became Big Business—and Bad Medicine* (New York: Broadway, 2005).

23. Cited in Collins, *Black Feminist Thought.*

24. Gregory L. Weiss and Lynne E. Lonnquist, *Sociology of Health, Healing and Illness* (Boston: Pearson Education, 2011).

25. For further information regarding Jennie's advocacy work, please visit Commonsense Childbirth (www.commonsensechildbirth.org).

CHAPTER 21

1. "One Protection for Prisoners," *New York Times,* October 14, 2009, 30.

2. Between 6 and 9 percent of incarcerated women in the United States are pregnant, with the highest rates in local jails. Jennifer Clarke et al., "Reproductive Health Care and Family Planning Needs among Incarcerated Women," *American Journal of Public Health* 96, no. 5 (May 2006): 834–839.

3. Official statistics erase the presence of gender-fluid and transgender individuals in prisons and jails. Throughout this chapter, we recognize that not all people in women's prisons or all pregnant people identify as women. See also Syrus Marcus Ware's Chapter 6 in this volume. "Incarcerated Women" fact sheet, The Sentencing Project, accessed July 23, 2014, www.sentencingproject.org/doc/publications/cc_Incarcerated_Women_Fact sheet_Sep24sp.pdf. In 2012, there were 108,772 people in state and federal women's prisons and 98,600 in local women's jails. D. Minton, *Jail Inmates at Midyear 2012* (Washington, DC: Bureau of Justice Statistics, 2013); E. Ann Carson and Daniela Golinelli, *Prisoners in 2012* (Washington, DC: Bureau of Justice Statistics, 2013).

4. We use the term "hyperincarceration" to point to the intensive and selective targeting of low-income communities of color for surveillance and punishment. See Loic Wacquant, "Class, Race and Hyperincarceration in Revanchist America," *Daedalus* 139 (Summer 2010), no. 3: 203–221.

5. Julia Sudbury, "Unpacking the Crisis: Women of Color, Globalization and the Prison-Industrial Complex," in *Interrupted Life: Experiences of Incarcerated Women in the U.S.,* ed. Rickie Solinger, Paula C. Johnson, and Martha L. Raimon (Berkeley: University of California Press, 2010).

6. As mentioned above, in 2012, there were 108,772 women in state and federal prisons and 98,600 in local jails. Minton, *Jail Inmates at Midyear 2012*; Carson and Golinelli, *Prisoners in 2012*; Dora Schriro, *Immigration Detention Overview and Recommendations* (Washington, DC: Homeland Security, Immigration and Customs Enforcement, 2009).

7. Julia Sudbury, "A World without Prisons: Resisting Militarism, Globalized Punishment and Empire," *Social Justice* 30, no. 3 (2000): 134–141.

8. Rickie Solinger, Paula C. Johnson, and Martha L. Raimon, eds., *Interrupted Life: Experiences of Incarcerated Women in the U.S.* (Berkeley: University of California Press, 2010); Eric A. Stanley and Nat Smith, eds., *Captive Genders: Trans Embodiment and the Prison Industrial Complex* (Oakland, CA: AK Press, 2011).

9. "What Is RJ?," SisterSong, accessed October 6, 2014, http://sistersong.net/index.php?option=com_content&view=article&id=141&Itemid=8.

10. Andrea Smith, "Beyond Pro-Choice versus Pro-Life: Women of Color and Reproductive Justice," *NWSA Journal* 17, no. 1 (2005): 128.

11. Jody Raphael, *Freeing Tammy: Women, Drugs and Incarceration* (Boston: Northeastern University Press, 2007), 42.

12. Katie McDonough, "Federal Judge: Pregnancy Can Be Grounds for Enhanced Criminal Penalties," *Salon*, July 15, 2014, accessed August 1, 2014, www.salon.com/2014/07/15/tennessee_womanmay_face_a_double_prison_sentence_simply_because_she_was_pregnant.

13. Raphael, *Freeing Tammy.*

14. Ibid.

15. *Shumate v. Wilson* (E.D. Cal), CIV S-95-0619 (2000).

16. Barbara A. Hotelling, "Perinatal Needs of Incarcerated, Pregnant Women," *Journal of Perinatal Education* 17, no. 2 (spring 2008): 37–44.

17. Meda Chesney-Lind, "Jailing 'Bad' Girls," in *Fighting for Girls: New Perspectives on Gender and Violence,* ed. Nikki Jones and Meda Chesney Lind (Albany: State University of New York Press, 2010).

18. Priscilla A. Ocen, "Punishing Pregnancy: Race, Incarceration and the Shackling of Pregnant Prisoners," *California Law Review* 100, no. 5 (2012): 1239–1311.

19. "Health Care for Pregnant and Post-partum Incarcerated Women and Adolescent Females," Committee Opinion No. 511, American Congress of Obstetricians and Gynecologists, November 2011, accessed August 20, 2014, www.acog.org/~/media/Committee%20Opinions/Committee%20on%20Health%20Care%20for%20Underserved%20Women/co511.pdf?dmc=1&ts=20121228T0522022147.

20. Solinger, Johnson, and Raimon, *Interrupted Life,* 49.

21. *Doe v. Gustavus,* 294 F. Supp. 2d 1003 (E.D. Wis. 2003).

22. Ibid.

23. Ibid.

24. Solinger, Johnson, and Raimon, *Interrupted Life,* 91.

25. *Buck v. Bell,* 274 U.S. 200 (1927).

26. Corey Johnson, "Female Inmates Sterilized in California Prisons without Approval," Center for Investigative Reporting, July 7, 2013, accessed December 9, 2014, http://cironline.org/reports/female-inmates-sterilized-california-prisons-without-approval-4917.

27. *Turner v. Safley* 482 U.S. 78, 84 (1987).

28. Ibid., 89.

29. 42 U.S.C. § 1997e(a).

30. Although she may be able to refile after submitting a complaint if the statute of limitations has not yet expired.

31. *Mendiola-Martinez v. Arpaio,* 2014 WL 231962 (D. Ariz. 2013).

32. Johnson, "Female Inmates Sterilized in California Prisons without Approval"; California Legislature, Senate Bill No. 1135, Chapter 558, June 26, 2014, accessed July 23, 2014, http://leginfo.legislature.ca.gov/faces/billNavClient.xhtml?bill_id=201320140SB1135.

33. Jess Stout, *No More Shackles* (San Francisco: Legal Services for Prisoners with Children, 2014).

34. Alicia Walters, "Victory: No More Shackles on Pregnant Prisoners," ACLU of Northern California, October 5, 2012, accessed July 23, 2014, www.aclu.org/blog/reproductive-freedom-prisoners-rights-womens-rights/victory-no-more-shackles-pregnant-prisoners.

35. See the Prison Birth Project (http://theprisonbirthproject.org); Isis Rising Prison Doula Program (http://prisondoulas.blogspot.com/p/what-we-do.html); Jennifer

Sullivan, "Birth behind Bars: Doulas Offer Advice, Help to Incarcerated Mothers," *Seattle Times,* May 29, 2008, accessed July 23, 2014, http://seattletimes.com/html /localnews/2004444808_prisondoulas29m.html.

Index

abolitionism: and birth, 46–54; of prison-industrial complex, 188–191, 196

abortion: coercive, 87; enslaved women and, 169; experiences of, 90–95; mainstream movement and, 189; and social justice issues, 79

abuse: and birthing, 106–111; and postpartum recovery, 60–61

access issues, 6; granny midwives and, 22; HIV and, 82–83, 85–86; Joseph and, 183–184; paradox of, 140; in prison, 191–192; in Zimbabwe, 40–41

ACOG. See American College of Obstetricians and Gynecologists

activism: approaches to, 13; health, 174; for midwifery, 176–186; for VBAC, 161

advanced maternal age, 2, 5, 157

advocacy: for birth options, 147–148; birth partners and, 134; formerly incarcerated people and, 197; Joseph and, 183

Affordable Care Act, 73

African women, controlling images of, 32, 112, 167, 210n2

ageism: medical system and, 5; and suppression of granny midwives, 26–27, 172

agency: HIV and, 88–89; midwives and, 123

alliances: midwifery advocates and, 180–183; obstetricians and, 156–165, 213n1

alternative birth movement: and consumerism, 12–15; development of, 7–8; and granny midwives, 8, 175; issues with, 131–132, 174–175, 180–183; obstetricians and, 156–157; and prison-industrial-complex abolition, 188–191

American College of Obstetricians and Gynecologists (ACOG), 159, 179, 192

American Medical Association, 178

Amnesty International, 139

Ancient Song Doula Services, 137–144

apartheid, medical, 10

Arnold, Jill, 161

Arpaio, Joe, 195

art, doulas and, 153–154

Asian Communities for Reproductive Justice. See Forward Together

assisted reproduction: experiences of, 64–65, 158; HIV and, 86

Baartman, Saartjie, 112, 210n2

Baker, Ella, 13

Baldwin, James, 72

Batts, Lucinda, 101

Beatie, Thomas, 63–71

biomedical model of care, 35, 40–41, 120

birth: definitions of, 149–151; doulas and, 141; experiences of, 1–5, 90–95, 106–111, 126–136, 142; fear of, 131; medicalization of, 22–23, 28, 30, 89, 172–173, 176, 178; pain-free, 7–8

Birth Attendants, 197

birth control. See contraception

birth defects, 90–95

Birthing behind Bars, 188, 196

Birthing Project, USA, 200n43

birthing stools, 173

birth justice, term, 72

birth justice movement: Monroe on, v–vi; obstetricians and, 156–165; Oparah on, 1–18; and population control, 72–80; recommendations for, 152–153, 197; vision of, 15

Birth Justice Project, 197

birth oppression, 6–7

birth options: advocacy for, 147–148; economic issues and, 14–15, 173–175; Joseph and, 183; race and, 11–12

birth partners, 131–136; role of, 134

birth plan, experiences of, 70, 127, 147

birth stories, 1–5, 90–95, 131–136, 142; love and, 126–130; survivors and, 106–111

Black Panther Party, 174

Black Power movement, 12

black superwoman myth, 4

black trans people, and pregnancy, 63–71

black women: abuse and, 106–111; and alternative birth movement, 13; C-section rates, 59, 158–159; as doulas, 137–144; and HIV, 81–89; and maternal-health-care system, 1–3; maternal mortality rates, 4, 139–141; as midwives, 119–125, 166–186; and pain relief, 158; in prison, 101, 187–197; subjugated knowledge of, 8; and teen pregnancy rates, 3–4; and VBAC, 158; and wealth, 14

Black Women Birthing Justice, 1–18, 158, 161, 197, 200n43

Black Women Birthing Resistance, 200n43

Black Women DO VBAC!, 161

Black Women for Reproductive Justice, 5

Black Women for Wellness, 5

Black Women's Health Imperative, 5

bodies: abuse and, 106–111; economic use of, 75–76, 78, 138–140, 166–171, 212n10; labor and, 115; medical system and, 127; prison-industrial complex and, 192–193

Bonaparte, Alicia D., 24–33, 176–186

Boultinghouse, Hayley, 99

Branch, Cealie, 21

breastfeeding: and abortion recovery, 94; difficulties with, 2; tradition and, 175; trans people and, 71; umbilical cord treatment and, 143; in Zimbabwe, 37, 41

breech birth, 58, 162–163

Bridges, Khiara M., 172

Bringin' in da Spirit, 173

Brown, Brené, 108

Buck v. Bell, 193

Bush, George H. W., 78

The Business of Being Born, 109, 142

Butler, Octavia, 50

California Department of Corrections and Rehabilitation, 196

Canada: demographics of, 82–83; HIV and pregnancy in, 81–89

capitalism, 73, 78, 91, 139–140

certified nurse midwife (CNM), 113

certified professional midwife (CPM), 113

cesarean sections, 10; complications of, 99–100; doulas and, 137–138, 152; experiences of, 55–62, 70, 142, 145, 147–149; forced, 192; history of, 31; HIV and, 87; rates of, 7, 57, 59, 141, 157–159, 162, 209n1; risks with, 159

childbearing, 166; black, new politics of, 173–175; decision making on, 133; definition of, 214n1. *See also* birth; pregnancy

childbirth. *See* birth

children, importance of, in Zimbabwe, 36

child spacing, in Zimbabwe, 38, 42t

Chiles, Lawton, 182

choice: Joseph and, 183; and love, 128–130; mainstream movement and, 189; midwives and, 123

CHW. *See* community health worker

Citizens for Midwifery, 13

Civil Rights Act, 11–12

Civil Rights Movement, 12

class: and alternative birth movement, 8–9, 180–183; and birth outcomes, 4–5

CNM. *See* certified nurse midwife

Cohen, Leonard, 49

Cole, Haile Eshe, 126–130

Collins, Patricia Hill, 8, 28, 171, 176
colonialism, 32, 35, 40, 75, 139
colonization, 17–18, 47, 49, 113
colostrum, in Zimbabwe, 37, 41
comadrona, 142. *See also* midwives/
    midwifery
Combahee River Collective, 8
Community Birthing Project, 210n2
community building: granny midwives and,
    168; Joseph and, 185
community health worker (CHW), 186
conjuring, 167–168
Connor, Michelle, 103
consumerism, and alternative birth
    movement, 12–15
contraception: dangerous, 7, 74, 211n2;
    enslaved women and, 169; eugenics
    and, 32; history of, 139; Hobby Lobby
    decision and, 73, 206n5; issues with,
    72–80; in Zimbabwe, 41*t*–42*t*
court cases: on prison treatment of
    pregnancy, 187, 191–192; on
    sterilization, 193; on VBAC, 160–161
CPM. *See* certified professional midwife
Craven, Crista, 9, 14, 180
culture: of dissemblance, 12; of fear, 4;
    health arguments and, 172; Moynihan
    on, 211n3
Cytotec, 97

Davis, Angela Y., 30
Davis, Sheila, 168
decision making: and abortion, 94; and
    childbearing, 133; medical system and,
    52
defensive medicine. *See* litigation avoidance
DeLee, Joseph, 26
Depo-Provera, 7
Deus, Valerie, 131–136
Dick-Read, Grantley, 7
direct-entry midwives, 14, 180, 182
disablism, medical system and, 5
dissemblance, culture of, 12
Dodd, Mary Ruth, 30
Doe v. Gustavus, 192–193
doulas: advantages of, 143–144; definition
    of, 210n1; experiences of, 53, 56–57,

112–118, 138–139; Medicaid and,
    173–175; and mother-daughter
    relationship, 145–154; in prison, 197; role
    of, 140–141, 174; and traditional birth
    knowledge, 137–144; training for, 125
Dreher, T. H., 32
drug crimes, imprisoned mothers and, 191
drug-free birth, 47–49; experiences of,
    56–57, 110–111, 134
dualism, activism and, 157–158
Dube, Peggy, 34–44

Eady, Akira, 103
East Bay Community Birth Support
    Project, 197
economic issues: and birth options, 14–15,
    173–175; capitalism, 73, 78, 91, 139–140;
    and cesarean sections, 60; and population
    control, 75–76; slavery, 166–171; use
    of black bodies, 75–76, 78, 138–140,
    166–171, 212n10; and VBAC, 164
ectopic pregnancy, 101
education, Joseph and, 184
Eggelston, Mary, 22
Ehrenreich, Barbara and John, 198n8
emotional work in pregnancy, 3; and birth
    justice, 157; doulas and, 150; miscarriage
    and, 51; survivors and, 106–111
empowerment: and consumerism, 12–15;
    doulas and, 153–154; Joseph and, 184;
    labor and, 114; midwives and, 125
epidurals, 56–57; black women and, 158;
    complications of, 103; experiences of,
    116–118
equipment, of midwives, 117, 172–173
erotic, birth and, 106–111
Etienne, Stephanie, 119–125
eugenics, 6, 10–11, 32, 73, 75, 78, 193

The Farm, 8, 56
fear: of birthing, 131; culture of, 4; of
    hospitals, 55, 113–114, 118. *See also*
    iatrophobia
Federici, Silvia, 139
Felkin, Robert W., 31
fetal monitor, 1, 53, 59, 138
fistulas, 9

Flavin, Jeanne, vii–viii
Florida: birth options in, 156–157; midwifery activism in, 176–186
Florida Friends of Midwives, 180
Florida Midwifery Practice Act, 178, 180, 182
forceps, 11
Forward Together, 5–6
foster care, 157, 193
Freeman, Allen W., 29
French, Tatia Oden, 97
Furman, R. B., 32
fussing, 168

Garner, Margaret, 50
Gaskin, Ina May, 8, 56, 96–104
gender nonconforming people: and birth, 63–71; and birth options, 160–161; in prison, 189, 217n3. *See also* trans people
genocide, 75–76
gentrification, 77–78
Gibney, Shannon, 131–136
Gilkes, Cheryl, 184–185
Gilkey, Laura, 96–104
Goodall, Jennifer, 160
granny midwives, 8, 11, 178–179, 182; background of, 24; experiences of, 20–23; in freedom, 171–173; and resistance, 12; roles of, 24–25; in slavery, 167–170; suppression of, 24–33, 170–173, 182
grief, 88, 94
Griffith, Shana, 207n24
Gumbs, Alexis Pauline, 145–154
gynecologists. *See* obstetricians

Harlem Birth Action Committee, 9
Harris, Cecily, 104
Harris, Robert P., 31
Haynes, James A., 29
Hays, Ruth, 166–175
Henley, Megan M., 140
high risk pregnancies, 99; and natural birth, 46–49, 52
Hine, Darlene Clark, 12, 169
HIV: and pregnancy, 81–89; testing for, 84; transmission of, 84–85, 208n25; in Zimbabwe, 39
Hobby Lobby decision, 73, 206n5

Holmes, Linda Janet, 171
home birth: experiences of, 2, 90–91, 132, 134; Joseph and, 180; suppression of, 13; and VBAC, 160, 162
Homebirth Info Movement, 175
hooks, bell, 177
hospitals: doulas and, 112–118, 152; fear of, 55, 113–114, 118; integration of, 11–12, 175; midwives and, 119–125; recommendations for, 164; shift to, 22–23, 30; and VBAC bans, 158–161
housing issues, 77
human rights framework, 6
hyperincarceration, 188; term, 217n4

iatrophobia, black, 12, 170, 183
ICTC. *See* International Center for Traditional Childbearing
IFHP. *See* Interim Federal Health Program
immigrants: and family separation, 132–134; and HIV, 81–89; midwives, 8, 27
Indigenous birth knowledge. *See* traditional birth knowledge
Indigenous peoples: forced sterilization and, 113; HIV and, 82; population control and, 75–76
induction: experience of, 116–118; mechanical, 163. *See also* Pitocin
infanticide, enslaved women and, 169
infant mortality rates, 4
infertility, in Zimbabwe, 36
Ingram, Cora, 168
insemination. *See* assisted reproduction
insurance: and birth options, 15; and cesarean sections, 60; and VBAC, 164
Interim Federal Health Program (IFHP), 85
International Center for Traditional Childbearing (ICTC), 174–175, 200n43
International Cesarean Awareness Network, 161
intersectional approach, 6; doulas and, 139, 142; and HIV stigma, 83
Isis Rising, 197

Jacob, Iris, 90–95
JJ Way, 176, 183–186
Johnson, Corrine, 100

Johnson, Lyndon B., 78
Johnson, Tammy, 191
Joseph, Jennie, 176–186
*Journal of the American Medical Association
    (JAMA)*, 28–30, 202n30
*Journal of the South Carolina Medical
    Association (JSCMA)*, 29, 31–32, 202n30
Justice Now, 196
juvenile detention facilities, 192

Kennedy, Victoria Logan, 81–89
Kerner Commission Report, 77–78
King, Ruth, 108
Kollock, Charles W., 30

labor, trial of, 158–160, 164
labor coach, 147–148. *See also* doulas
Ladd-Taylor, Molly, 172
Lafferty, Andrea, 73
Lamaze, Ferdinand, 7
land-use policies, 73, 75, 78
Lapetino, Jan, 101
Latinas/os: C-section rates, 59, 158; as
    doulas, 137–144; hospitals and, 121,
    127; stereotypes and, 120
Law Students for Reproductive Justice, 5
Lee, Barbara, 11
Lee, Mildred, 11
Lee, Valerie, 167
legalism, 13
legal issues. *See* court cases
Legal Prisoners for Prisoners with Children,
    196
legislation: alternative birth movement and,
    13–14; and birth options, 173–175;
    and midwifery, 27, 170, 176–186; and
    shackled birth in prison, 196–197; and
    VBAC, 164
LGBTTI2QQ community: and birth
    options, 158; and HIV, 86. *See also* trans
    people
liberation: black midwifery and, 166–175.
    See also transformation
Lim, Robin, 143
litigation avoidance, medical system and, 4,
    120, 152; and VBAC bans, 159
Lorde, Audre, 107, 110, 132, 150, 211n5

love, as political, 126–130
low-birth-weight infants, 4

Magloire, Christ-Ann, 156–165
mainstream reproductive rights movement,
    issues with, 6, 174, 189
Mamas of Color Rising (MOCR), 129,
    185, 200n43, 211n6
MANA. *See* Midwives Alliance of North
    America
Martinez, Miriam, 195
Mashone people, traditional birth
    knowledge of, 34–44
maternal mortality rates, 4, 139–141; Safe
    Motherhood Quilt and, 96–104; in
    Zimbabwe, 39–40
Maxen, Elizabeth, 98
Mays, Kimberly, 188, 191
McFarquhar, Tameka, 98
McKenzie-Day, Pauline Ann, 145–154
media: and alternative birth choices, 7;
    and black women, 17; and HIV, 81; and
    hyperincarceration, 188; and population
    control, 74, 80; and trans parenthood,
    64, 66
Medicaid, 11; and birth options, 14,
    173–175; and cesarean sections, 60
medical-industrial complex: class and, 4–5;
    current status of, 184; development
    of, 7–12; distrust of, 12; and doulas,
    137, 139–140; experiences of, 1, 109,
    127; and granny midwives, 24–33; and
    midwives, 177–180; recommendations
    for, 152; reproductive justice movement
    and, 6–7; term, 184, 198n8; and
    Zimbabwe, 34–44
medicalization of birth, 22–23, 28, 30, 89,
    172–173, 176, 178
medical violence and coercion, 7; and
    cesarean sections, 55–62; experiences of,
    49, 112, 179–180; history of, 211n2
Mendiola-Martinez v. Arpaio, 195
Midwives Alliance of North America
    (MANA), 13
midwives/midwifery, 7; activism for, 176–
    186; and birth defects, 92; development
    of, 8; direct-entry, 14; experiences of,

2, 47, 110, 113–115, 117, 119–125, 148; and liberation struggles, 166–175; rates for, 15, 21, 23; regulation of, 22–23, 113, 171–173; suppression of, 13, 22–33, 182; training for, 21, 26, 30, 40; trans people and, 68, 70; vision for, 124–125; in Zimbabwe, 38–41. *See also* granny midwives
military-industrial complex, 73
Millennium Development Goals, 39–40
miscarriage: experiences of, 50–52, 147; HIV and, 86–88; in Zimbabwe, 37
Mitsuru Mitsuru, 66–67
mixed-race persons, experiences of, 63–71
Mobile Midwife, 200n43
Monroe, Shafia, v–vi, 9, 174–175
Morgan, Jennifer, 166
morphine, 10
Morrison, Toni, 50, 107
mothering: development of, 61–62; doulas and, 145–154
motherwit, 12. *See also* traditional birthing knowledge
mother work, 171
Moynihan, Daniel Patrick, 211n3
Moyo, Nester T., 34–44
Muchenje, Marvelous, 81–89
Mudokwenyu-Rawdon, Christina, 34–44
Mugabe, Robert Gabriel, 36
Munjanja, Stephen, 34–44
music: for birthing, 48–49, 53, 134; and turning breech baby, 58

National Advocates for Pregnant Women (NAPW), viii, 6–7, 160, 200n43
National Black Feminist Organization, 8
National Institutes for Health, 158
National Latina Institute for Reproductive Health, 5
natural birth, experiences of, 46–54, 90–91, 95, 109–110, 127
natural birth movement. *See* alternative birth movement
Nelson, Alondra, 174
Nelson, Shawanna, 187, 194–195
Nelson v. Correctional Medical Services, 194–195

neoliberalism, 78–79
Nixon, Richard, 78
noise, in birthing, 46–49, 117; in prison, 188
Nolan, Faith, 49
nonnormative gender. *See* trans people
Norplant, 7, 79, 211n2
North Carolina, granny midwives in, 20–23
nuchal scan, 91, 209n2
nurses: certified nurse midwife (CNM), 113; public health nurses, 30, 172; and VBAC, 163
nutrition: mothering and, 61; in Zimbabwe, 37, 41

Obama, Barack, 79, 128
obstetricians: and birth justice movement, 156–165, 213n1; experiences of, 47–48, 50; granny midwives and, 22–23, 170
obstetrics: history of, 9–11, 112–113, 139, 169–170, 178–179; in Zimbabwe, 39–41
Ocen, Priscilla A., 187–197
Old Dippers, 29–30; term, 202n33. *See also* granny midwives
Oparah, Julia Chinyere, 1–18, 156–165, 187–197
Oregon Coalition to Improve Birth Outcomes, 174
out-of-hospital births, 7–8
outsiders within: advantages of, 176; and birthing work, 28; in Florida midwifery activism, 176–186; stressors on, 4
overpopulation, myth of, 73

pain relief: black women and, 158; history of, 10–11; in prison, 188
Paltrow, Lynn, viii
parteras. See midwives/midwifery
participatory democracy, 13
patriarchy: experiences of, 50, 53–54; stresses of, 51
Patterson, Chuniece, 101
Pearce, Russell, 79
Pemberton, Laura, 160
Pérez, Biany, 106–111
perineum: definition of, 215n11; massage of, 168

Perkins, Tony, 73
physicians. *See* obstetricians
Pitocin, 163; experience of, 1, 116–118
placenta increta, 98
poetry, doulas and, 153–154
population control, 72–80; elements of,
    74–75; factors affecting, 76–79; history
    of, 74–75, 78. *See also* contraception
positions for labor, 115, 117; doulas and, 138;
    hospitals and, 122; midwives and, 173
posterior birth, 53, 115
postpartum depression, 2; in Zimbabwe, 37
postpartum recovery: abuse and, 60–61;
    forty-day, 142–143
preeclampsia, 70
pregnancy: experiences of, 146–148; HIV
    and, 81–89; in prison, 101, 187–197;
    trans men and, 63–71premature birth, 4
Prévost, François Marie, 10
Prison Birth Project, 197
prison-industrial complex: abolition
    movement, 188–191, 196; conditions
    in, 191–195; demographics of,
    188; and pregnancy, 101, 187–197;
    transformation and, 158
Prison Litigation Reform Act (PLRA), 194
Project Motherpath, 161
public health nurses, 30, 172

Quarles, Trishawna, 99

race and racial issues: and alternative birth
    movement, 8–9, 180–183; and birth
    options, 11–12; and birth weight, 4;
    current status of, 79–80, 128; and
    development of obstetrics, 9–11;
    experiences of, 53–54; medical system
    and, 5; physicians' attitudes toward, 31–
    32; and population control, 73–74; and
    reproductive politics, 74; and suppression
    of granny midwives, 26–27; and trans
    parenthood, 63–71. *See also under* black
rebozo, for labor, 117, 138
relationship model: Joseph and, 184;
    midwives and, 119–125; in Zimbabwe,
    42–43
religion. *See* spirituality

reproductive justice, 5–7; elements of, 79,
    190; term, 6, 189, 198n9; vision of, 15
reproductive justice movement, 5; history
    of, 198n9; and prison-industrial-complex
    abolition, 188–191
reproductive oppression, current status of,
    79–80
reproductive politics, racialization of, 74
reproductive rights, definition of, 6
ReproNet, 5
Resendes, Barbara, 102
resilience, HIV and, 88–89
resistance: doulas and, 143–144; granny
    midwives and, 12; infanticide and, 169;
    Joseph and, 184–186; love as, 126–130;
    and prison-industrial complex, 195–197;
    reproduction and, 167
Reynolds, Tina, 195
Rhode Island, midwifery in, 113
Roberson-Reese, Kalilah, 102
Roberts, Dorothy, 139, 174, 211n2
Rodríguez, Gina Mariela, 112–118
Rodriguez, Griselda, 137–144
Roosevelt, Teddy, 73
Ross, Loretta J., 6, 72–80
Roth, Louise Marie, 140

sacred. *See* spirituality
Safe Motherhood Quilt, 96–104
Saleh-Hanna, Viviane, 46–54
Sanger, Margaret, 78
Schwartz, Marie Jenkins, 169–170
scopolamine, 10
Section 8 housing, 77
segregation, and birth options, 11–12, 175
self-care, 211n5; doulas and, 150–151;
    experiences of, 129
self-determination, birth and, 113, 118
self-employment, 180, 185
Seminarians for Reproductive Justice, 5
sentencing reform, 189
sex education, 4, 74
sexuality: birthing and, 106–111; slavery
    and, 167
sexually transmitted diseases. *See* HIV
shackling, 192–195
Sheppard-Towner Act, 171–172, 199n21

Shire, Warsan, 106

Shumate v. Wilson, 191–192

sickle cell anemia, 99

silence: about miscarriage, 50–52; about
pregnancy, 36, 52

Simone, Nina, 48

Simpson, W. E., 32

Sims, J. Marion, 9–10

sisterhood: and birth partners, 131–136;
doulas and, 137–144; Joseph and,
180–183; midwives and, 122–124

SisterSong, 5–7, 189

slavery: and development of obstetrics,
9–10; midwifery in, 166–171; and
silence, 50

Smith, Andrea, 212n10

Smith, D. H., 29

Smith, David Barton, 14–15

Smith, Margaret Charles, 171, 173

Smith, Mercedes, 193–194

societal expectations on reproductive
choices, 51, 133

Solinger, Rickie, 74

South Bronx: demographics of, 121;
midwifery in, 119–125

South Carolina, regulation of midwives in,
24–33

spatial deconcentration, 77–78

Spencer, Lesley Ann Marshall, 104

Speros, Melek, 161

Spiritchild, 49

spirituality: and abortion, 93; and birth,
109; doulas and, 138, 142–143, 154;
and labor, 115–116; midwives in slavery
and, 167–168; physicians and, 32

stereotypes: of alternative birth choices,
7; medical system and, 120, 127, 139;
midwives and, 122–123; and physicians,
164; and slavery, 167; and suppression of
midwives, 26–27, 29–31

sterilization: coercive/forced, 7, 76, 79,
86–87, 113, 193, 196; voluntary, 60

stigma: HIV and, 81–89; imprisonment
and, 190–193, 195–196

stillbirth. *See* miscarriage

storytelling, and resistance to prison-
industrial complex, 195–197

stress, reproductive oppression and, 4, 13, 51

strip searches, 192

surrender, and birth, 110–111, 116

Sweet Honey in the Rock, 53

teen pregnancy rates, 3–4, 120–121

Thompson, Kathleen, 169

Tolle, Eckhart, 110–111

Tosh, Peter, 48–49

Townsend, Jacinda, 55–62

traditional birth knowledge, 8, 12;
advantages of, 42*t*; disadvantages of,
41*t*; doulas and, 137–144; elements
of, 36–38; granny midwives and, 167,
173; Turner and, 20–23; in Zimbabwe,
34–44, 41*t*–42*t*

Traditional Childbearing Group, 9,
174–175

transformation: birth justice movement
and, 158; doulas and, 141; Joseph and,
186

trans people: and birth, 63–71; and birth
options, 160–161; in prison, 189,
217n3; and reproductive justice, 79

trauma: and birthing, 106–111; cesarean
section and, 149; separation and, 157

trial of labor, 158–160, 164

trisomy 13, 91–93

Trust Black Women, 7

tubal ligation. *See* sterilization

Turner, Darline, 20–23

Turner, Mary Ellen, 21

Turner, Queen Elizabeth Perry, 20–23

Turner v. Safley, 194

Tuskegee syphilis experiment, 128, 211n2

twilight sleep, 10

Tyehemba, Nonkululeko, 9

ultrasound, 36, 92

umbilical cord, treatment of, 143

United Kingdom, midwifery in, 177–178

urban black women, and midwives, 12,
119–125

vaccines, 47

vaginal birth, plan for, 3

vaginal birth after cesarean (VBAC), 7; bans

on, 158–161; benefits of, 163; and birth justice movement, 156–165; experiences of, 55–62, 147, 161–163; rates of, 158–159
vesicovaginal fistulas, 9
violence. *See* abuse; medical violence
voice: and abortion, 94; and miscarriage, 51–52
vulnerability, Pérez on, 108

Ware, Syrus Marcus, 63–71
Washington, Harriet, 9–10, 12
wealth, black women and, 14
Western medicine. *See* medical-industrial complex

white supremacy. *See* race and racial issues
Wilkie, Laurie, 171
women of color. *See* black women
Women on the Rise Telling HerStory, 188, 200n43
Women's Health in Women's Hands (WHIWH), 88
Woodland, E. Jasper, 21
World Health Organization (WHO), 57

Young Women United, 5

Zimbabwe, 34–44; history of, 35–36

About the Contributors

Black Women Birthing Justice (BWBJ) is an Oakland, California–based collective of African American, African, Caribbean, and multiracial women committed to transforming birthing experiences for black women. BWBJ's vision is that every woman should have an empowering birthing experience free of unnecessary medical interventions. The collective's goals are to educate women to advocate for themselves, to document birth stories, and to raise awareness about birthing alternatives. BWBJ aims to challenge medical violence, rebuild women's confidence in giving birth naturally, and decrease disproportionate maternal mortality. For more information, visit www.bwbj.org.

Alicia D. Bonaparte is a medical sociologist and associate professor of sociology at Pitzer College, specializing in the gendered and racialized occupational hierarchy within US reproductive medicine, reproductive health disparities, and social constructions of female deviance. Her current research examines the psychosocial agency of teens of color and sociostructural factors in maternal health outcomes. She is currently working on a book addressing how racism, sexism, and interoccupational conflict impacted granny midwives in South Carolina from 1900 to 1940.

Haile Eshe Cole currently resides in Austin, Texas, and holds a PhD in anthropology and African diaspora studies from the University of Texas, Austin. She has organized with Mamas of Color Rising, a grassroots organization of mamas of color, since 2009 and is trained as a birth educator and birth companion (doula). Her dissertation, "Belly: Blackness and Reproduction in the Lone Star State," examines the intersections between blackness and reproduction in the state of Texas.

Valerie Deus is a writer, poet, and film festival programmer. Her work has been featured in the *Brooklyn Rail,* Ishmael Reed's *Konch Magazine, Apt, Midway,* and *Saint Paul Almanac.* Her work deals with women, body politics, and the African diaspora experience. In 2011, her long poem was published in *How to Write an Earthquake* by Autumn Hill Books. When not programming films for the Minneapolis Underground Film Festival, she's teaching writing at Minneapolis Community and Technical College.

Peggy Dube has been the principal tutor of the Harare Central Hospital School of Midwifery for the past twenty years. She is a master trainer and course director in emergency obstetrics and neonatal care, an international course offered by Liverpool School of Tropical Medicine in collaboration with the University of Zimbabwe Department of Obstetrics and Gynecology and Ministry of Health. She is also a researcher for the Lugina African Midwives Network.

Stephanie Etienne is a certified nurse-midwife born and raised in Queens, New York. After attending an amazing home birth in 2005, she became an adamant believer in the transformative power of birth. Stephanie worked as a doula for several years before taking a leap of faith and going into midwifery. She received her midwifery training at Columbia University and holds a master's in public health from the University of North Carolina, Chapel Hill. She currently lives in Washington, DC, with her partner and beautiful son.

Jeanne Flavin is professor of sociology at Fordham University. Her publications include the award-winning book *Our Bodies, Our Crimes: Policing Women's Reproduction in America.* She is the recipient of a 2009 Fulbright research award and the 2013 Sociologists for Women in Society's Feminist Activism Award. Currently, she serves as president of the board of directors for National Advocates for Pregnant Women. She grew up on a farm in rural Kansas but since 1995 has lived in New York City.

Ina May Gaskin, midwife at and founder and director of The Farm Midwifery Center in Tennessee, is author of *Spiritual Midwifery, Ina May's Guide to Childbirth, Ina May's Guide to Breastfeeding,* and *Birth Matters: A Midwife's Manifesta.* She has lectured at conferences and medical schools worldwide. In 2011, she received the Right Livelihood Award. She is founder of the Safe Motherhood Quilt Project, intended to raise awareness about American maternal mortality. For a complete bio, please visit www.inamay.com.

Shannon Gibney lives, writes, and teaches in Minneapolis. Her creative and critical works have been published in a variety of venues, including in the anthologies *Parenting as Adoptees* and *The Black Imagination: Science Fiction, Futurism, and the Speculative.* Her as-yet untitled young adult novel will be published by Carolrhoda/Lerner Books in fall 2015, and she is currently at work on a novel about African Americans who colonized Liberia in the nineteenth century.

Laura Gilkey is coordinator of Ina May Gaskin's Safe Motherhood Quilt Project, intended to raise awareness about maternal mortality in the United States. She is a producer and host of *Maternally Yours,* a weekly community radio program dedicated to improving the conversation about maternal health.

She serves on the board of directors for the Healthy Start Coalition of Sarasota County and authors *Mommy Magazine*'s "Off the Air" column. She enjoys practicing patience with her wildly intelligent boys, Banyan and Benjamin.

Alexis Pauline Gumbs is founder of the Eternal Summer of the Black Feminist Mind planetary community school and cocreator of the Mobile Homecoming project documenting generations of black LGBTQ experiences. She has a PhD in English, Africana studies, and women's studies from Duke University and wrote a dissertation about revolutionary practices of mothering gleaned from black feminist literature. She also has almost two decades' experience as a facilitator and activist.

Ruth Hays is a PhD candidate in the Department of African American Studies at Northwestern University. She received her BA from New York University's Gallatin School of Individualized Study. Her research focuses on black women, reproduction, and the politics of the body. She is currently completing her dissertation, titled "'So I Could Be Easeful': Black Women's Authoritative Knowledge on Childbirth."

Iris Jacob is a mother, author, sister, organizer, lover, daughter, and educator. She finds her most important work to be challenging systems of oppression through a black feminist framework. By focusing on communal healing, she consults with organizations and schools around the country to find unique ways to infuse social justice into their work, outreach, and internal practices. She holds an MEd in social justice education and currently teaches women's studies courses centered on intersectionality and radical change.

Jennie Joseph is a British-trained midwife and executive director of the Birth Place, a freestanding birthing facility in Winter Garden, Florida, as well as her own nonprofit corporation, Commonsense Childbirth. Her "Easy Access" Prenatal Care Clinics offer quality maternity care for all, regardless of choice of delivery site or ability to pay, and have successfully reduced perinatal disparities. Her school, Commonsense Childbirth School of Midwifery, trains and certifies midwives, doulas, and paraprofessionals, emphasizing culturally competent and community-focused care.

Victoria Logan Kennedy has extensive experience in pregnancy and HIV. Prior to working in research, she was a labor and delivery nurse and played a leadership role in developing equitable pregnancy care for women with HIV. She collaborates with HIV-affected communities to develop research related to pregnancy. She is an instructor at Ryerson University, focusing on the professional development of nursing students with an understanding of nursing and health in relation to the social determinants of health.

Christ-Ann Magloire, MD, is the first female board-certified Haitian American obstetrician/gynecologist to practice in North Miami. She is a vaginal birth after cesarean (VBAC) advocate who puts her words into practice with a 7 percent primary C-section rate. She is physician champion for breastfeeding promotion at Jackson North Medical Center and a member of the American Congress of Obstetrics and Gynecology, the Association of Haitian Physicians Abroad, and Delta Sigma Theta Sorority. Her proudest accomplishment is being the mother of two, the second a VBAC.

Pauline Ann McKenzie-Day, MS, LPC, CPCS, is founder of Inspired Lives Counseling and has over ten years' experience in the therapeutic community. Inspired Lives Counseling fulfills her passion to support individuals, couples, and families in their journey to wholeness. She is a training specialist at Georgia State University with Safe Care, a program to create positive bonding between parents and children ages zero to five. She completed the ICTC full-circle doula program in 2010.

Shafia Monroe is a veteran midwife, childbirth educator, doula trainer, motivational speaker, and health activist. She is founder of the International Center for Traditional Childbearing, which works to increase the number of culturally competent midwives, and created the ICTC Full Circle Doula Training Program using the traditional midwifery model of care. She founded the Oregon Coalition to Improve Birth Outcomes, which was instrumental in the inclusion of doulas for Medicaid reimbursement as a national model. She mothers seven children and nine grandchildren.

Nester T. Moyo, a midwife leader and educationalist from Zimbabwe, is the senior midwifery advisor of the International Confederation of Midwives (ICM) at its headquarters in The Hague, Netherlands. She coordinates the work of the ICM's 116 member associations in 101 countries. She has gained invaluable insights into the impact of culture on women's health through several years of experience working in all health settings in Zimbabwe and abroad, focusing on sexual and reproductive health and community development.

Marvelous Muchenje is the community health coordinator at Women's Health in Women's Hands, Community Health Centre, Toronto, Canada. With fifteen years' working experience in the HIV sector, she has developed a thorough understanding of the many issues related to the human rights dimensions, the socioeconomic impact of HIV and AIDS, and the complex dynamics of prevention and treatment policy. Diagnosed with HIV in 1995, she participates passionately in the HIV movement.

Christina Mudokwenyu-Rawdon, PhD, is a freelance research consultant in midwifery and reproductive health with vast experience in midwifery education and clinical practice, as well as a winner of the 2011 ICM Marie Goubran Award for demonstrating outstanding leadership potential and extraordinary commitment to childbearing women and their families. She is editor in chief of the *African Journal of Midwifery and Women's Health,* Zimbabwe national coordinator of the White Ribbon Alliance for Safe Motherhood, and Zimbabwe focal lead for Lugina Africa Midwives Research Network.

Stephen Munjanja is an academic and clinician who has worked in Zimbabwe for thirty-three years as an obstetrician/gynecologist. He specialized in this field while working in Scotland for three years. He lectures to undergraduate and graduate University of Zimbabwe medical students and to midwives at schools of midwifery. His main research areas are prenatal care and measurement of maternal health indicators. He has been a member of several maternal health working groups at the World Health Organization.

Priscilla A. Ocen is associate professor of law at Loyola Law School. Her work examines the relationship between race and gender identities and punishment. In particular, her scholarship explores conditions of confinement within women's prisons and the race and gender implications of the use of practices such as shackling during labor and childbirth. Her work has appeared in academic journals such as the *California Law Review,* the *UCLA Law Review,* and the *Du Bois Review,* as well as in popular media outlets such as *Ebony* and Al Jazeera.

Julia Chinyere Oparah (formerly Sudbury) is an educator, writer, and community organizer with roots in Nigeria and the United Kingdom. She is professor and chair of ethnic studies at Mills College and cofounder of Black Women Birthing Justice. She is author and editor of numerous articles and books, including *Global Lockdown: Race, Gender and the Prison-Industrial Complex*; *Activist Scholarship: Antiracism, Feminism and Social Change*; and *Outsiders Within: Writing on Transracial Adoption.* She lives in Oakland, California, with her partner and daughter.

Biany Pérez is a mother, trained birth doula, breastfeeding counselor, educator, and therapist-in-training. She is the daughter of Dominican immigrants and a proud native of the South Bronx, New York. She received a bachelor's degree in human development from Binghamton University and an MEd in urban education from Temple University. She is currently pursuing a master's in social service (social work) at Bryn Mawr College. She lives in Philadelphia with her partner, Kenneth, and son, Zen.

Gina Mariela Rodríguez is an Afro-Taino-Cuban-Sicilian writer and birth companion living in Providence, Rhode Island. Trained in birth and postpartum support by toLabor and the International Center for Traditional Childbearing, she recently cofounded the Doula Collective to support adolescent mothers in Rhode Island. Her plays have been produced at Brown University (*Ariel,* 2008), the Drama Bookshop (*Ariel,* 2008), and the University of Massachusetts, Dartmouth (*Free at Last?,* 2013). She holds a bachelor's degree in Africana studies from Brown University.

Griselda Rodriguez is a doula and mother. She is interim director of the International Studies Program at the City College of New York. She was raised in Brooklyn by an immigrant mother from the Dominican Republic. Her PhD in sociology from Syracuse University is a collective accomplishment in the face of institutionalized impediments. She is committed to reclaiming the power that is systemically ripped from the wombs, hearts, and minds of women of African descent.

Loretta J. Ross is former coordinator of SisterSong, a reproductive justice network of women of color founded in 1997. After leading Women of Color Programs for the National Organization for Women and working at the National Black Women's Health Project, she helped originate the Reproductive Justice framework in 1994. She was codirector of the 2004 March for Women's Lives in Washington, DC, worked against white supremacist groups, and founded the National Center for Human Rights Education in the 1990s.

Viviane Saleh-Hanna, associate professor of crime and justice studies at the University of Massachusetts, Dartmouth, wrote *Colonial Systems of Control: Criminal Justice in Nigeria*. She is a black feminist addressing hauntology, historic memory, and black musicianship; tracing the European transatlantic slave route through lyrics, she highlights black ideological contributions made through Afrobeat, Reggae, and hip-hop. She serves on the board of editors for the *Journal of Prisoners on Prisons* and the *African Journal of Criminology and Justice Studies*.

Jacinda Townsend is author of *Saint Monkey*, portions of which have been published in *Mythium Journal, PMS poemmemoirstory*, and *Women Arts Quarterly*. A former Fulbright fellow and fiction fellow at the University of Wisconsin, she has published short fiction in numerous literary magazines. A former Hurston-Wright Award finalist and a graduate of Harvard University, Duke Law School, and the Iowa Writers Workshop, she is working on a novel about transnational adoption set partially in Marrakech, Morocco.

Darline Turner, BS, MHS, PA-C, is owner of Mamas on Bedrest & Beyond, an online support and education website for high-risk pregnant women on prescribed bed rest. Following her two high-risk pregnancies, she produced *Bedrest Fitness*, a modified exercise DVD for women on bed rest. In May 2014 she published *From Mamas to Mamas: The Essential Guide to Surviving Bedrest*. She is currently developing a community-based perinatal education and support program for black women in Austin, Texas.

Syrus Marcus Ware, a visual artist, activist, and educator pursuing his PhD in the Faculty of Environmental Studies at York University, cocreated TransFathers 2B, the first course for trans men considering parenting in North America, and *Primed: A Back Pocket Guide for Trans Guys and the Guys Who Dig 'Em*, the first comprehensive sexual-health resource for gay and bisexual transgender men. Ware works with Blackness Yes! to produce Blockorama, the black queer and trans stage at Toronto's Pride Festival.